I0808140

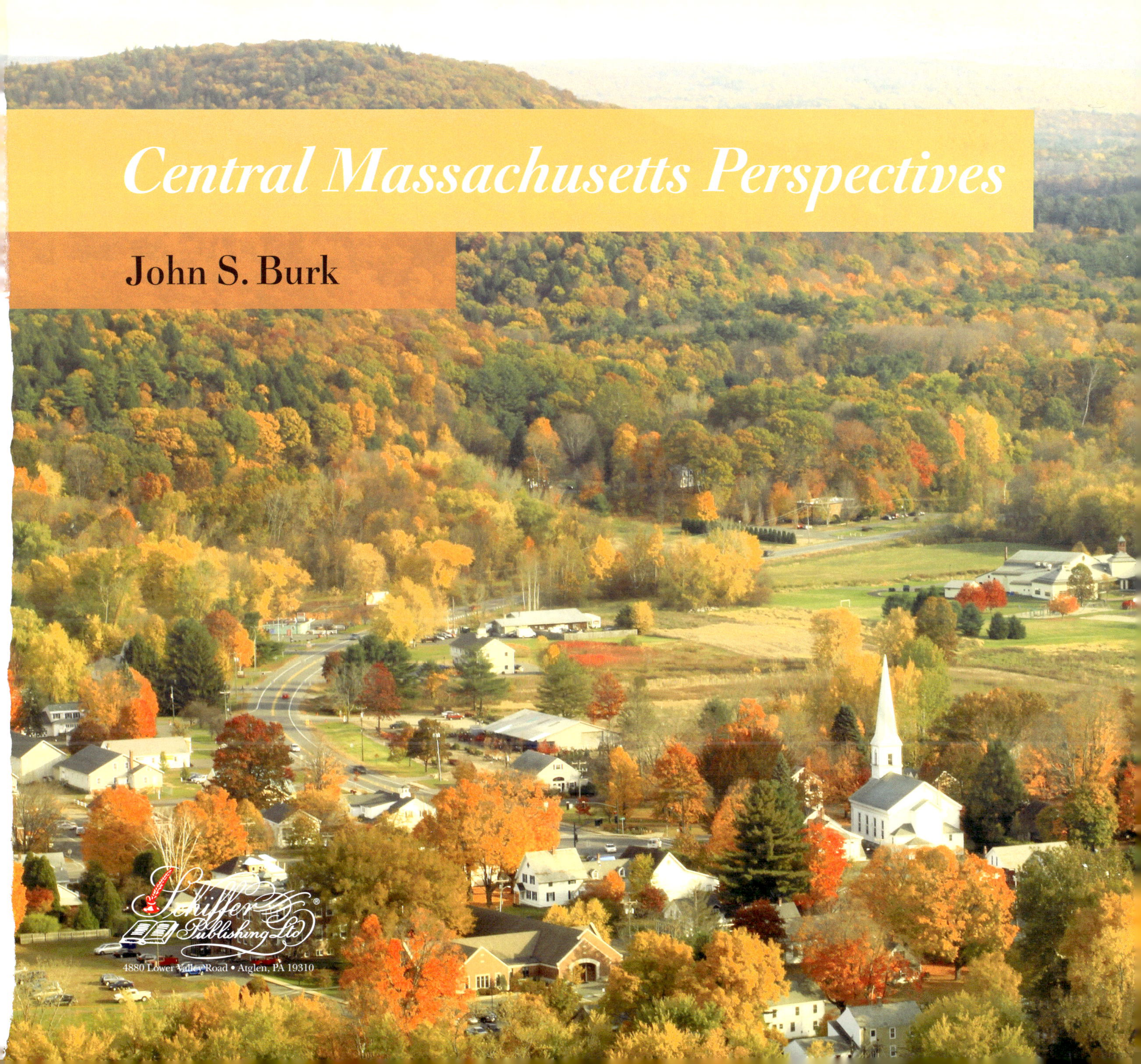

Central Massachusetts Perspectives

John S. Burk

Schiffer Publishing Ltd
4880 Lower Valley Road • Atglen, PA 19310

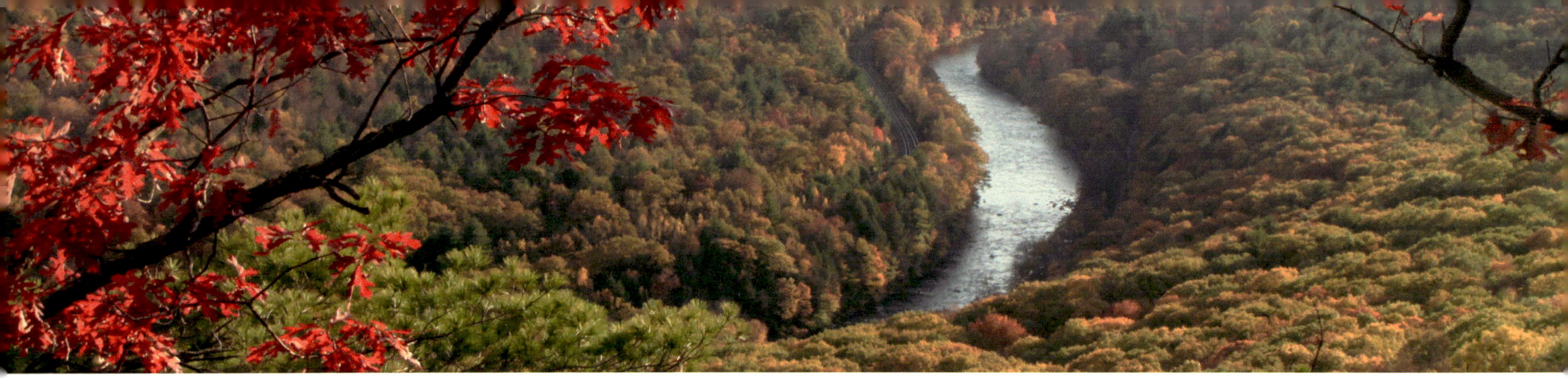

COPYRIGHT © 2014 BY JOHN S. BURK

Library of Congress Control Number: 2014949128

All rights reserved. No part of this work may be reproduced or used in any form or by any means—graphic, electronic, or mechanical, including photocopying or information storage and retrieval systems—without written permission from the publisher.

The scanning, uploading, and distribution of this book or any part thereof via the Internet or via any other means without the permission of the publisher is illegal and punishable by law. Please purchase only authorized editions and do not participate in or encourage the electronic piracy of copyrighted materials.
"Schiffer," "Schiffer Publishing, Ltd. & Design," and the "Design of pen and inkwell" are registered trademarks of Schiffer Publishing, Ltd.

Designed by Danielle D. Farmer
Cover Design by Molly Shields
Type set in Acanthus/Verlag

ISBN: 978-0-7643-4704-7
Printed in China

Published by Schiffer Publishing, Ltd.
4880 Lower Valley Road
Atglen, PA 19310
Phone: (610) 593-1777; Fax: (610) 593-2002
E-mail: Info@schifferbooks.com

For our complete selection of fine books on this and related subjects, please visit our website at www.schifferbooks.com.
You may also write for a free catalog.

This book may be purchased from the publisher. Please try your bookstore first.

We are always looking for people to write books on new and related subjects. If you have an idea for a book, please contact us at proposals@schifferbooks.com.

Schiffer Publishing's titles are available at special discounts for bulk purchases for sales promotions or premiums. Special editions, including personalized covers, corporate imprints, and excerpts can be created in large quantities for special needs. For more information, contact the publisher.

Title page image: Rolling forested hills, valley farms, and classic New England villages such as Sunderland characterize the landscape of west-central Massachusetts.

Acknowledgments

Thanks to the conservation and tourism groups in the area that I have collaborated with, including Harvard Forest, Mount Grace Land Conservation Trust, Appalachian Mountain Club, Johnny Appleseed Trail Association, and North Quabbin Woods. Many additional useful resources were provided by the Athol Public Library, Erving Public Library, Massachusetts Audubon Society, Massachusetts Department of Conservation and Recreation, Newton Library in Royalston, Petersham Memorial Library, Quabbin Park Visitor Center, Sturgis Library in Hadley, Trustees of Reservations, Wheeler Library in Orange, and the Woods Memorial Library in Barre.

Special thanks to Bob Clarke, Tony D'Amato, Elizabeth Farnsworth, Dave Orwig, Allen Young, and Leigh Youngblood for passing along primary sources and/or providing quotes related to their excellent work in the region. For sharing their knowledge of the area via sources, field trips, sighting reports, and useful discussions, thanks to Earle Baldwin, Beth Bazler, Dan Bolton, Sue and Ron Cloutier, Bob Curley, Karen Davis and the Sweetwater Farm, Elaine Doughty, Molly Stevens Dubois and the Carter Stevens Farm, Cindy Dunn and Chris Eaton of the Wachusett Meadows Wildlife Sanctuary, Aaron Ellison, Chris Ellison, Don Flye, David Foster, John Foster, Paul Gryzbowski, Brian Hall, Anne Harding, Don Hoffes, Johnson's Farm in Orange, Dave Kotker, M and M Green Valley Farm, Glenn Motzkin, John McCarter, Kathy Morris, John O'Keefe, Perkins Farm, Polly Pillsbury, Tom Pirro, Nathan Rudolph, Dave Small, Ivan Ussach and the Millers River Watershed Council, Nick Wiznewski and Valorie Major of the Walnut Hill Tracking and Nature Center, and Tom Wansleben.

And of course, thanks to Pete Schiffer, my editor Doug Congdon-Martin, and the staff of Schiffer Publishing for the opportunity to pursue another project, and my family and friends for support and encouragement, and accompanying me on hikes and site visits.

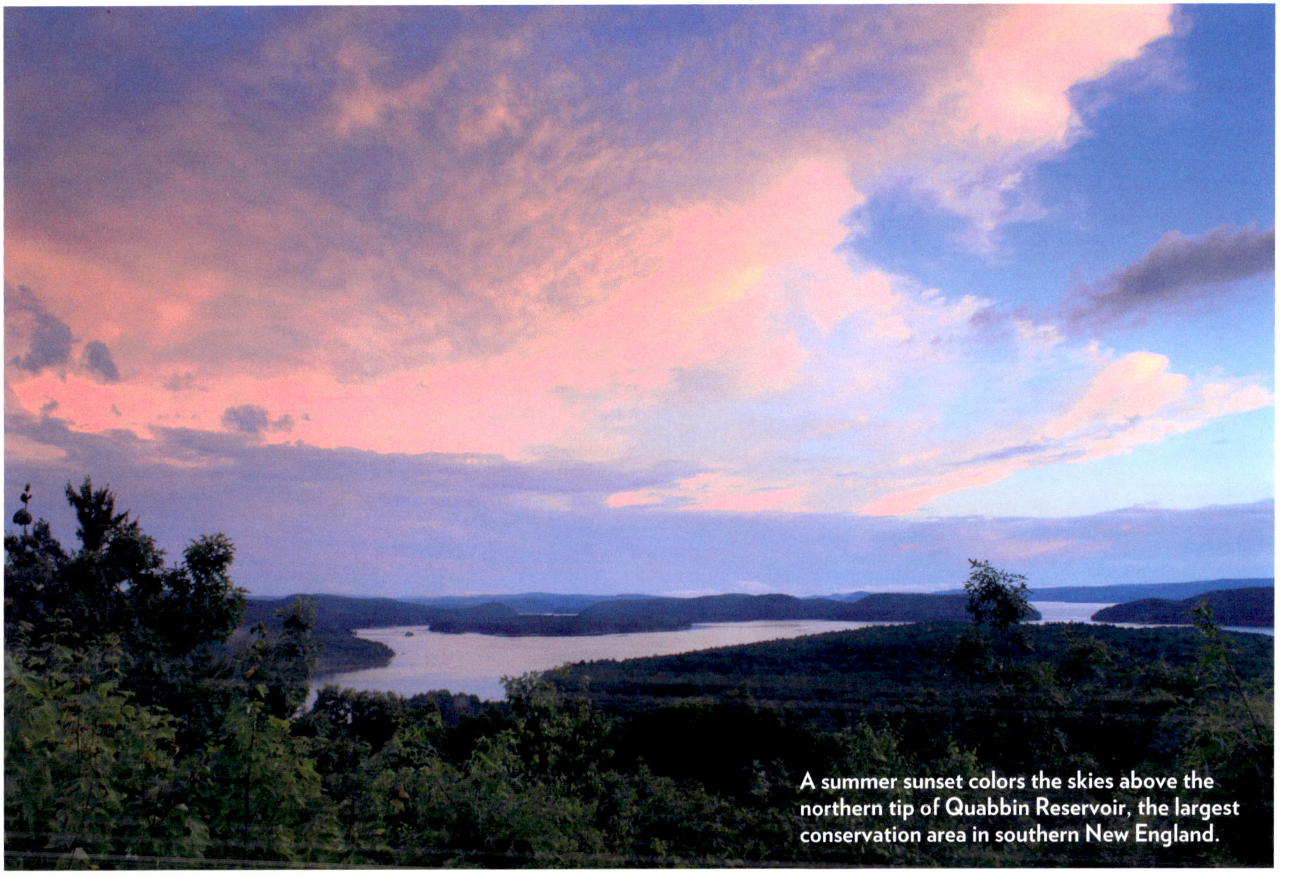

A summer sunset colors the skies above the northern tip of Quabbin Reservoir, the largest conservation area in southern New England.

On a recent summer evening, I hiked up to a favorite hilltop lookout above the northern tip of an expansive lake near my home. In the golden, late-day light, panoramic views across the water and islands unfolded to the south, while the distant profile of Mount Monadnock rose over unbroken forests to the north. The loud, laughing calls of common loons, a sound synonymous with the New England wilderness, echoed from several coves in the valley below, while a bald eagle drifted along the tops of the trees below the ridge. As I approached a large beaver pond on the way back, a final reward was a glimpse of a large bull moose as it crossed the trail before vanishing into the forest without a sound.

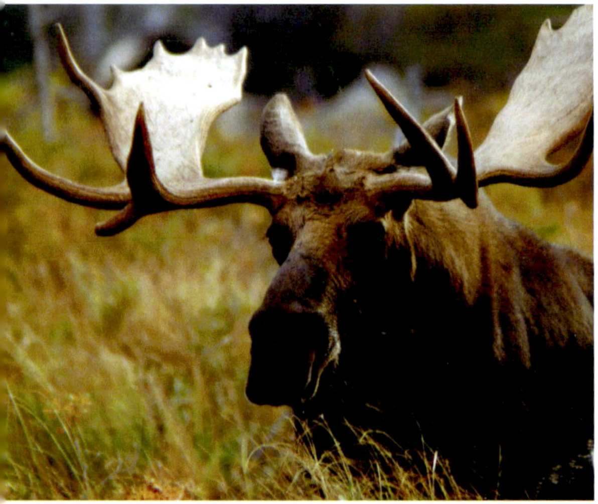

The above might well seem like an account of an expedition to northern New England, but in this instance the setting was Quabbin Reservoir in the heart of central Massachusetts, just 70 miles west of Boston and an hour's drive from the greater Worcester and Springfield areas. Indeed, while less-known than other regional destinations such as Cape Cod, the Berkshires, and the White and Green Mountains, within these hills and valleys are tens of thousands of acres of protected land with thriving wildlife populations and outstanding recreational opportunities. In a regional context, the land connects with additional conservation areas in adjacent southern New Hampshire and Vermont to form an extensive network of protected land in the heart of New England, including a corridor that stretches to Mount Cardigan in New Hampshire's lakes region.

Thanks to conservation efforts and the regrowth of mature forests, wildlife, such as this bull moose, is again common in New England.

At the heart of the Valley region is the watershed of the Connecticut River, New England's longest and most celebrated waterway. Along its 410-mile course, which begins at a chain of lakes in the mountains on the Quebec border, the Connecticut drains more than 11,000 square miles in four states. Its major tributaries in Massachusetts include the Millers and Chicopee (formed by the Swift, Ware, and Quaboag Rivers) in the central uplands, and the Deerfield and Westfield, which drain the rugged, scenic Appalachian slopes of the eastern Berkshire Hills; the latter was the state's first designated National Wild and Scenic River. The early 20th century saw the creation of the massive Quabbin and Wachusett Reservoirs, the two largest freshwater lakes in southern New England, as part of the expansion of the Massachusetts water supply network; in the process, the Nashua River became connected to the watershed.

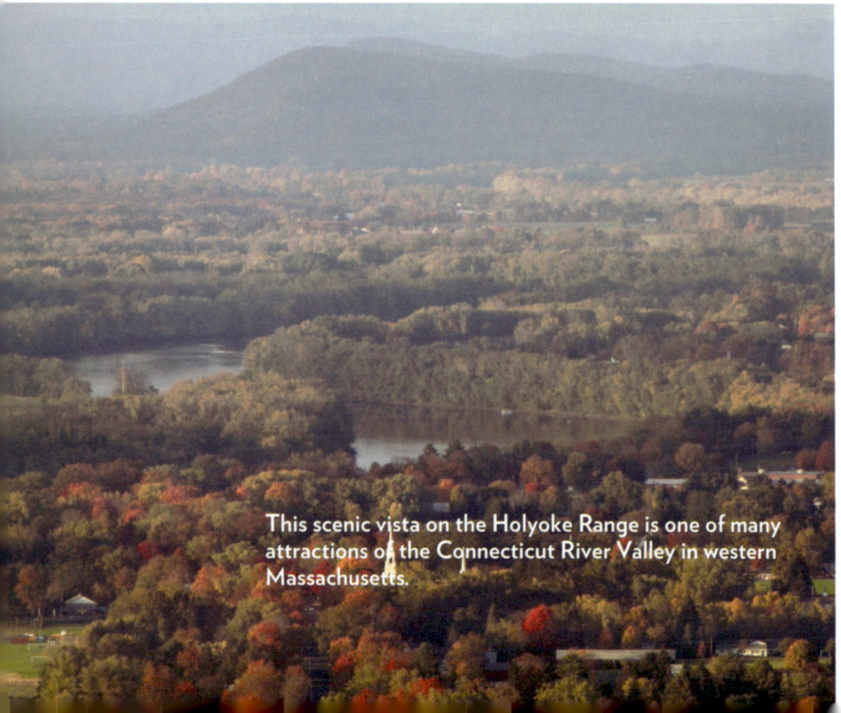

This scenic vista on the Holyoke Range is one of many attractions of the Connecticut River Valley in western Massachusetts.

Interspersed throughout these woodlands and wetlands are artifacts of the region's rich natural and human history:

dinosaur tracks preserved in ancient bedrock along the banks of the Connecticut River; historic Native American paths and camp sites; countless stone walls and old mill remains; engineering landmarks, such as railroad bridges and tunnels, and abandoned roads; and stone foundations from the lost towns of the Quabbin and Wachusett Reservoirs. Many of the small towns and villages retain a timeless character with well-preserved commons and historic districts.

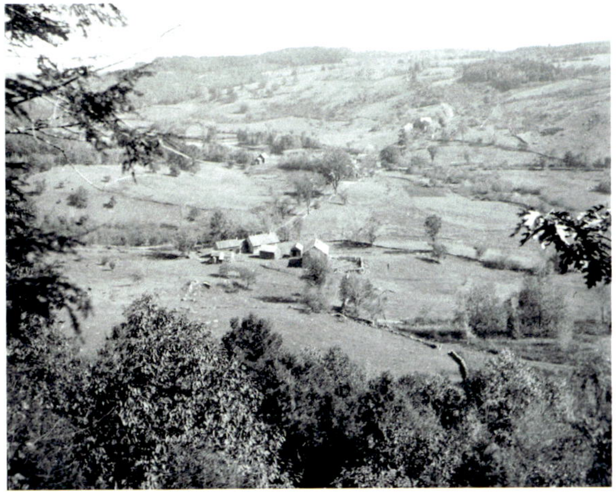

These artifacts reflect the remarkable cycle of change that this landscape, like the rest of New England, has undergone over the past 400 years. Indeed, a visitor to the aforementioned overlook 100 to 150 years ago would have taken in an entirely different scene. The reservoir would not have existed, as it was built during the early 20th century as a water supply for eastern Massachusetts, and many of the region's other ponds and lakes are products of old industrial or flood control dams. As the black and white photo of the Swift River Valley clearly shows, the land was considerably more open, with many active or recently abandoned farms in the place of today's woodlands. And our visitor would have little to no chance of encountering many of the creatures we take for granted now, including moose, deer, bears, beavers, fishers, great blue herons, and wild turkeys, as these and other species were entirely or nearly eliminated by land clearing and hunting.

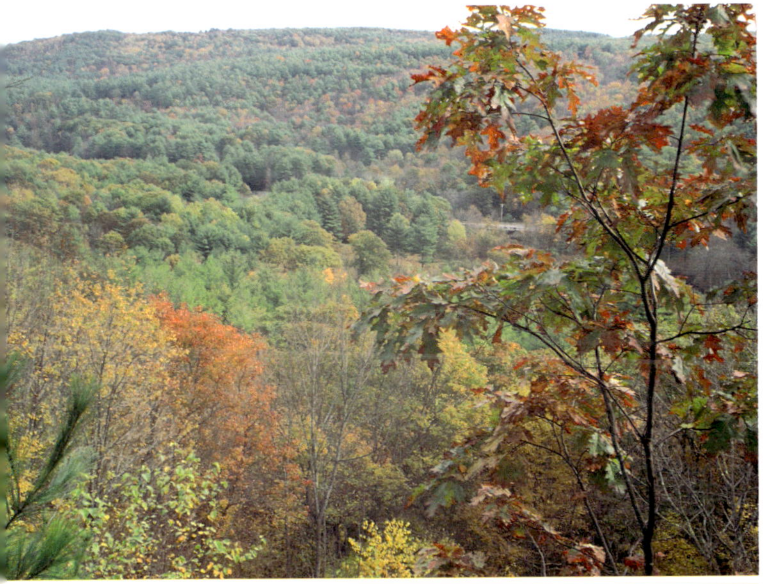

These two images, taken from the same viewpoint in the Swift River Valley in Petersham in 1910 and 2003, illustrate the dramatic changes in New England's landscape over the past 100 years.

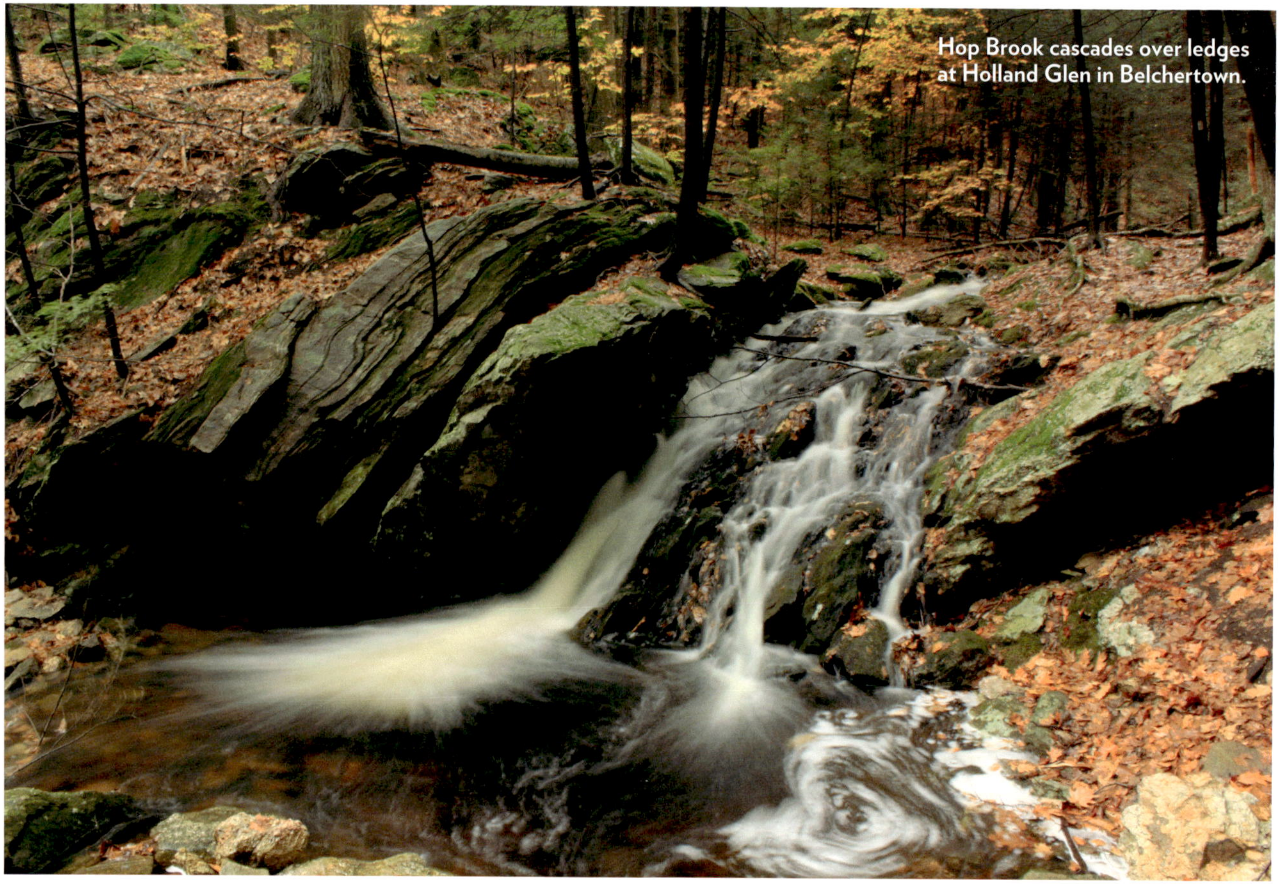

Thanks to the regrowth of the forests over the past 150 years and the efforts of many conservation groups, the area again has a largely natural, wild character, as evidenced by the extensive groves of maturing forests. Many wildlife populations are thriving, though some species have only returned in recent years and top predators remain extirpated from the Northeast. Recreational opportunities abound, with countless miles of trails and old woods roads that wind through the forests, over hilltops, and along wetlands. These include several long-distance routes, such as the Midstate Trail across central Massachusetts, the Tully Trail in the North Quabbin Bioreserve, and the recently dedicated New England National Scenic Trail, a federally designated route that offers hikers and backpackers a 230-mile walk from Connecticut to southern New Hampshire.

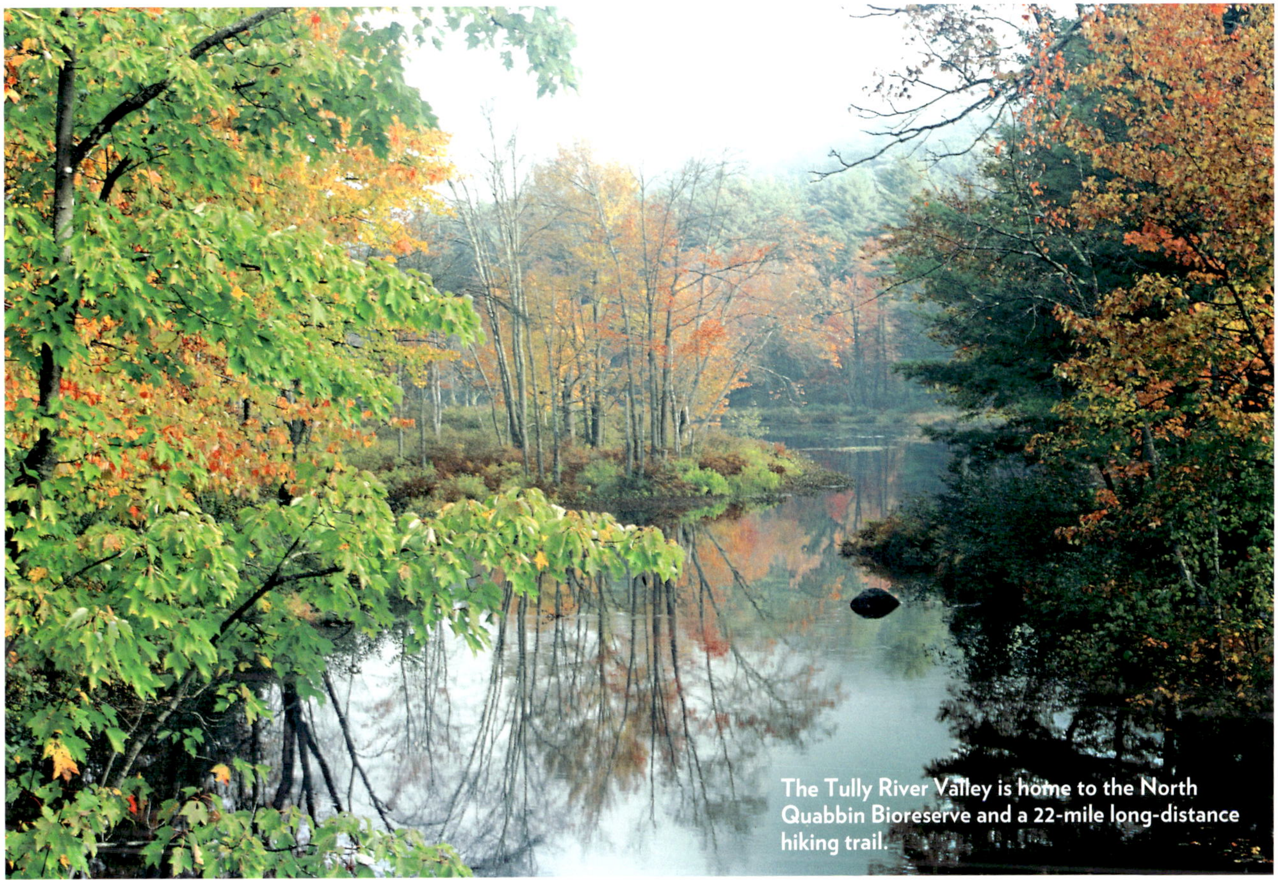

The Tully River Valley is home to the North Quabbin Bioreserve and a 22-mile long-distance hiking trail.

Our much less strenuous journey across the Valley region in these pages begins in the Appalachian foothills and the watersheds of the Deerfield and Westfield Valleys. These and other major west–east flowing tributaries such as the Farmington River actually predated the Connecticut River–in fact, they helped create it. Over thousands of years, their flow gradually eroded channels and south-flowing streams, known as "pirate tributaries," that ultimately became connected to form the Connecticut Valley. With deep mountain and hill valleys scoured by glaciers and abundant natural and cultural features, these rivers rank among the Northeast's most scenic waterways.

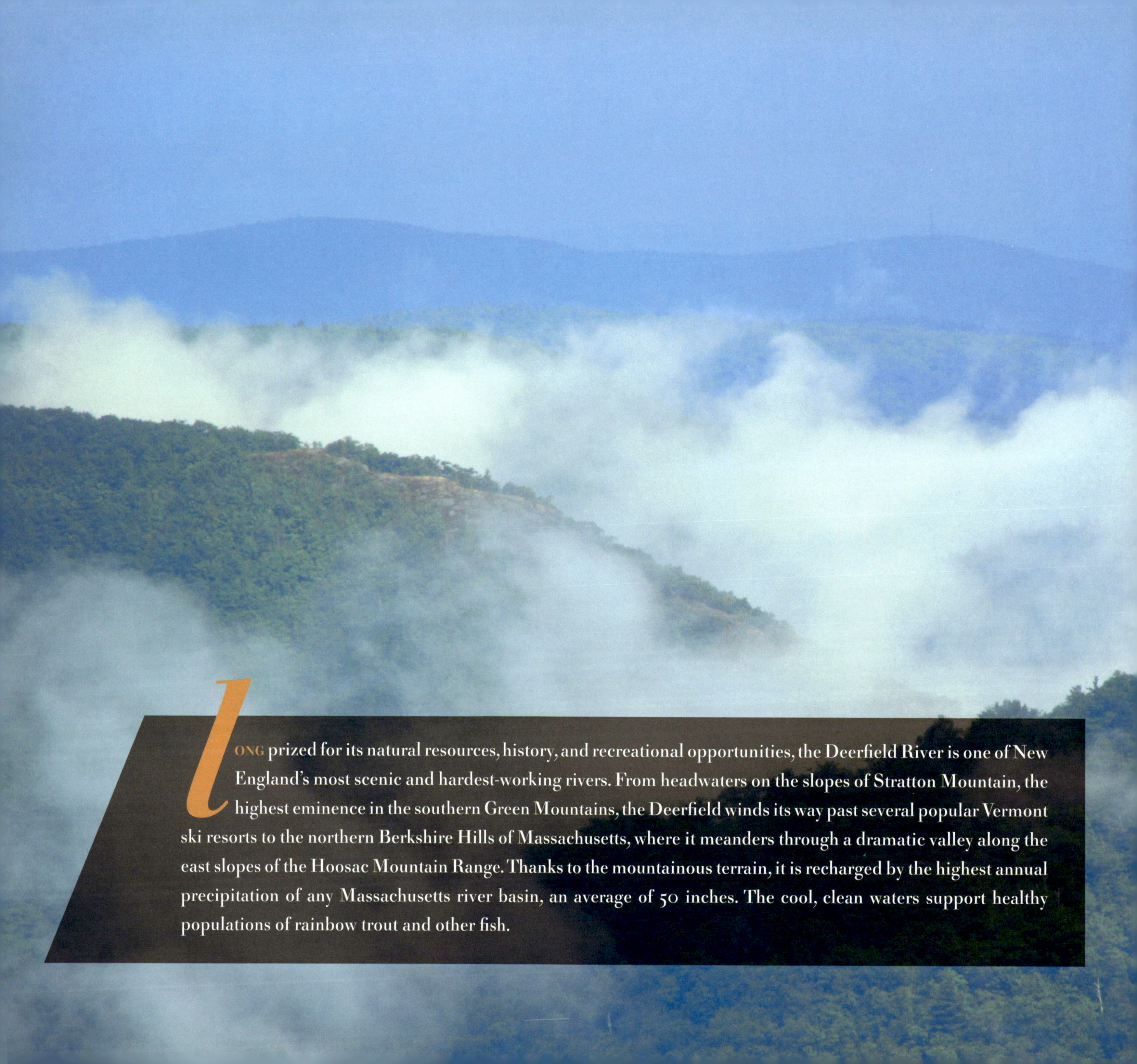

LONG prized for its natural resources, history, and recreational opportunities, the Deerfield River is one of New England's most scenic and hardest-working rivers. From headwaters on the slopes of Stratton Mountain, the highest eminence in the southern Green Mountains, the Deerfield winds its way past several popular Vermont ski resorts to the northern Berkshire Hills of Massachusetts, where it meanders through a dramatic valley along the east slopes of the Hoosac Mountain Range. Thanks to the mountainous terrain, it is recharged by the highest annual precipitation of any Massachusetts river basin, an average of 50 inches. The cool, clean waters support healthy populations of rainbow trout and other fish.

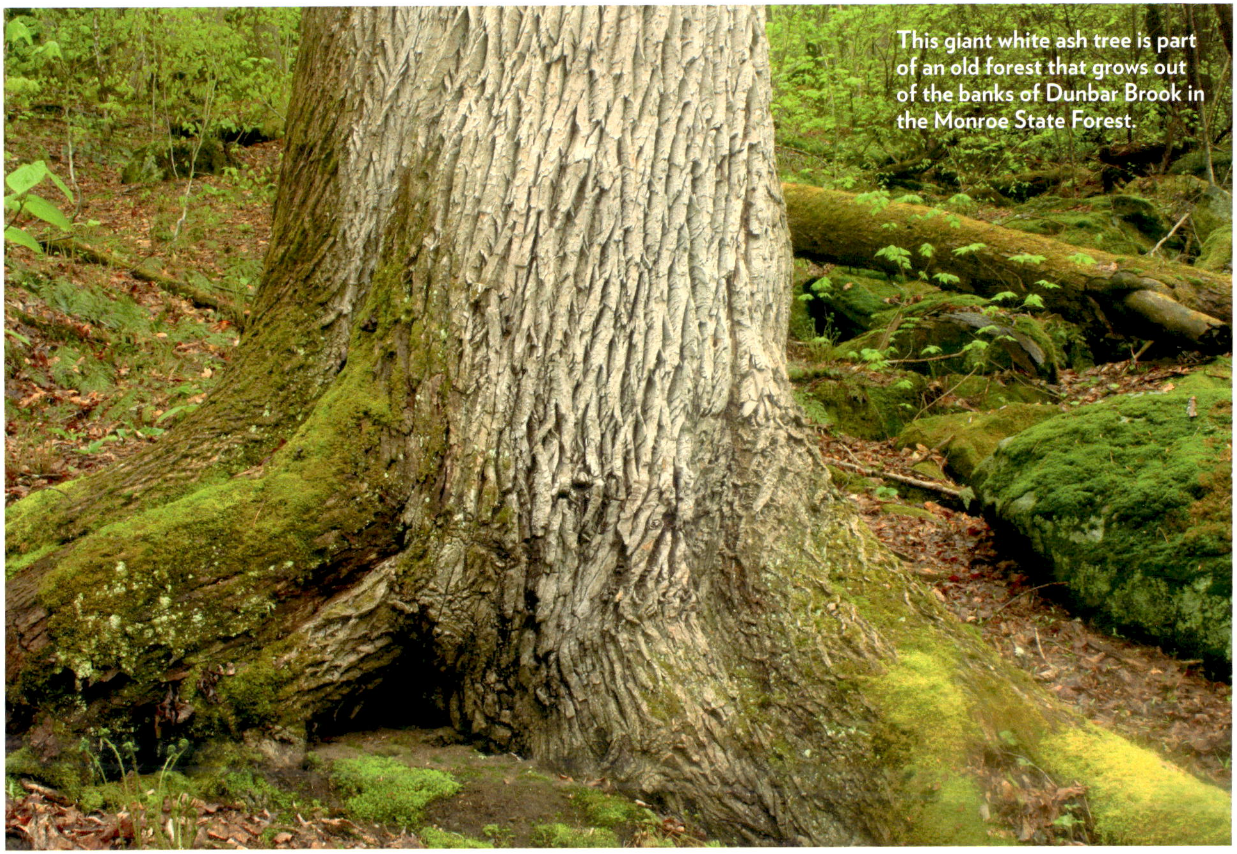

This giant white ash tree is part of an old forest that grows out of the banks of Dunbar Brook in the Monroe State Forest.

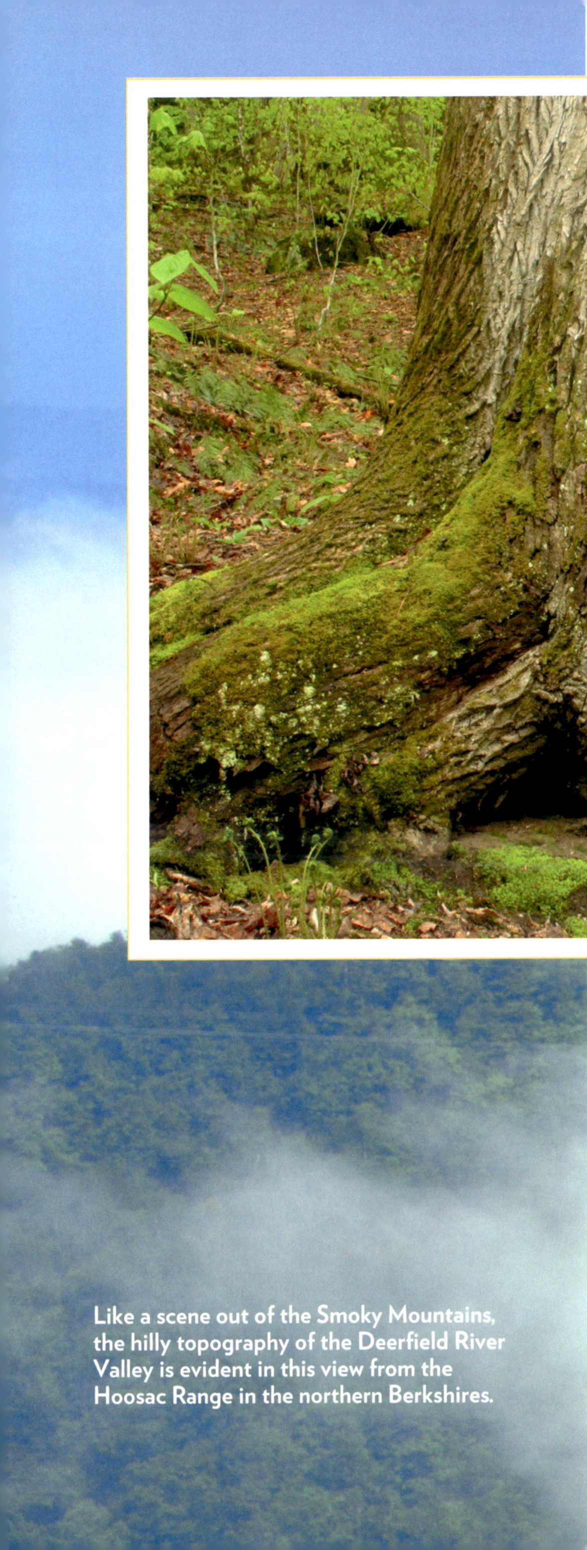

Like a scene out of the Smoky Mountains, the hilly topography of the Deerfield River Valley is evident in this view from the Hoosac Range in the northern Berkshires.

Scattered throughout this rugged terrain, where steep hills and ridges rise more than 1,000 feet above the riverbed, are roughly two dozen small groves of old-growth forest, a rare and ecologically significant commodity in the Northeast. While the bulk of the region's woodlands were cleared by settlers in colonial times, the steep topography of the upper valley made logging impractical in these sheltered pockets. As a result, visitors here enjoy unique glimpses of a landscape essentially unchanged since pre-colonial times, capped by giant hemlocks, pines, ashes, and other examples of some of New England's largest and oldest trees.

With their old forests, wildflowers, gorges, and remote back-country terrain, few places in New England can match the primeval feel of the Monroe, Mohawk Trail, and Savoy Mountain State Forests, which combine to protect nearly 20,000 acres of the upper valley. Rocky Dunbar Brook flows across the heart of the former, cascading beneath groves of ancient trees, including a giant white ash and the "Thoreau White Pine," which rises more than 160 feet above the banks. Downstream is the Mohawk Trail State Forest, which encompasses the high, rugged ridges at the junction of the Deerfield and Cold Rivers. More old hardwoods and giant pines grow out of the rocky slopes, while moose, bobcats, and a healthy population of black bears roam the forests (the bears, as rangers and visitors attest, periodically prowl the campgrounds as well). Hikers enjoy miles of trails, some of which follow footpaths once trod by Native Americans.

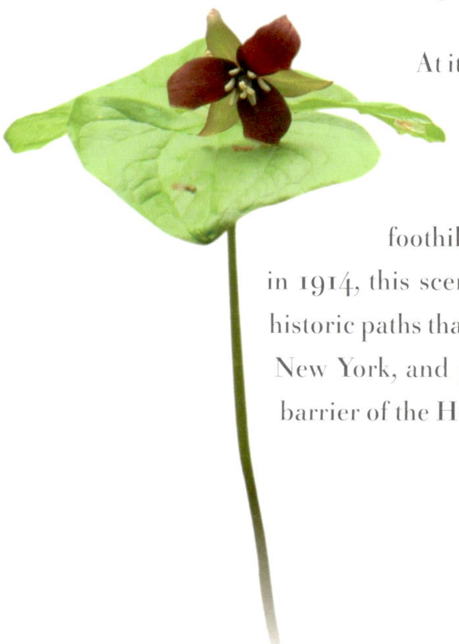

At its confluence with the Cold River, the Deerfield River bends sharply to the east and meets the fabled Mohawk Trail Highway (Route 2), which it generally parallels from the Berkshire foothills to the Connecticut Valley. When it opened in 1914, this scenic roadway became the latest in a series of historic paths that afforded a passage to the Berkshires, upstate New York, and points beyond by traversing the formidable barrier of the Hoosac Range.

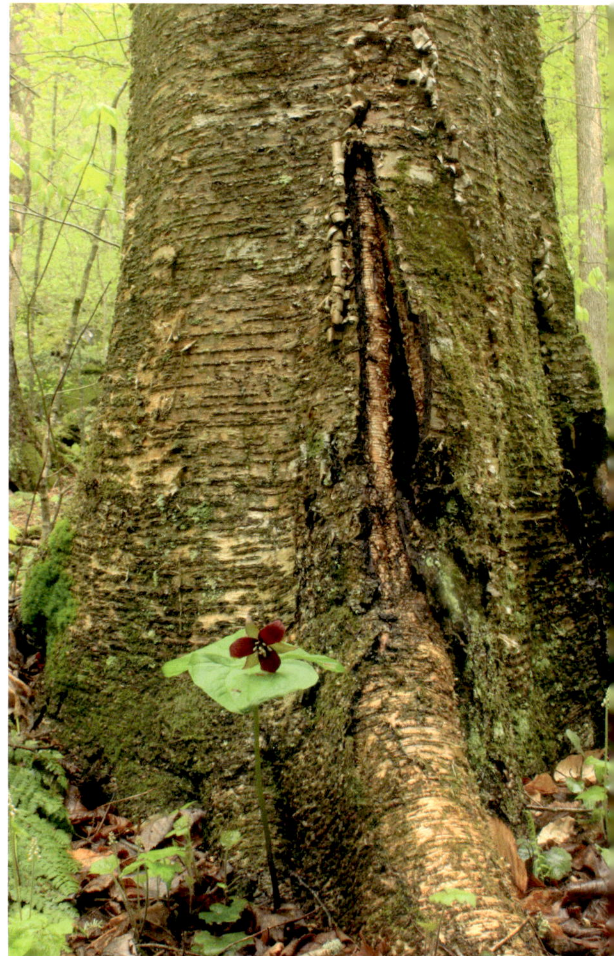

The rugged, nutrient-rich ridges of the upper Deerfield Valley sustain some of New England's largest and oldest trees and abundant wildflowers such as red trilliums.

The original footpaths that crossed this sliver of the Appalachian Mountains were used by Native American hunters, scouts, and messengers during their travels to upstate New York and Canada. Although the route is named for the Mohawks of New York, who used it as a passage to meetings and battles with other tribes, the actual inhabitants of the region were the Pocumtuc along the eastern portion of the path, and the Mahicans on the west side of Hoosac Mountain. The late 17th and early 18th centuries were a time of constant conflict and danger, as the Natives and the newly arrived English and French settlers fought for control of the region and its resources in a series of conflicts, beginning with King William's War in 1689 and ending at the close of the Seven Years War in 1763.

At the onset of King George's War in 1744, the English established Fort Massachusetts near present-day North Adams to mark the western boundary of Massachusetts Bay colony. Motivated by the need for a reliable route to get supplies to the new outpost, colonists built a rough horse and cart path that opened in 1753 and generally followed the course of the original Native footpaths. It was followed in 1764 by a second road, commissioned by local resident Samuel Rice, which merged with the original at the summit of Hoosac Mountain; Benedict Arnold and other soldiers used it during the American Revolution a decade later. 1786 saw the opening of a turnpike that paralleled the Deerfield River to the present-day Hoosac Tunnel area, and then snaked up the steep valley slopes to Whitcomb Summit. Rice's road became appropriately known as the "Shunpike," as it was used by those who wished to avoid paying the turnpike toll.

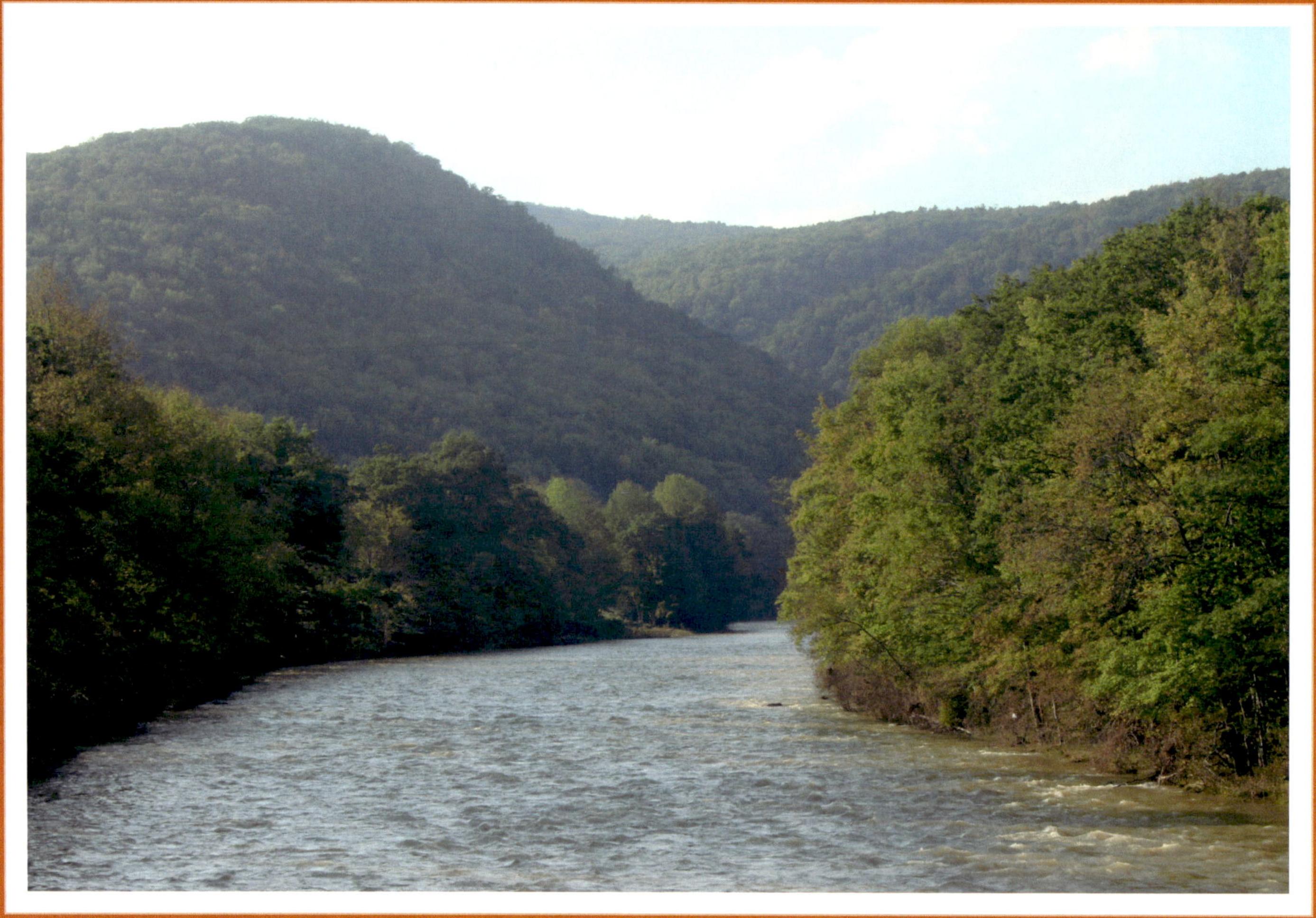

As it winds across the east slopes of the Berkshire Hills, the Deerfield River passes beneath hills and ridges that rise 1,000 feet above the riverbed. High water levels after Hurricane Irene are evident on the bottom right of this image.

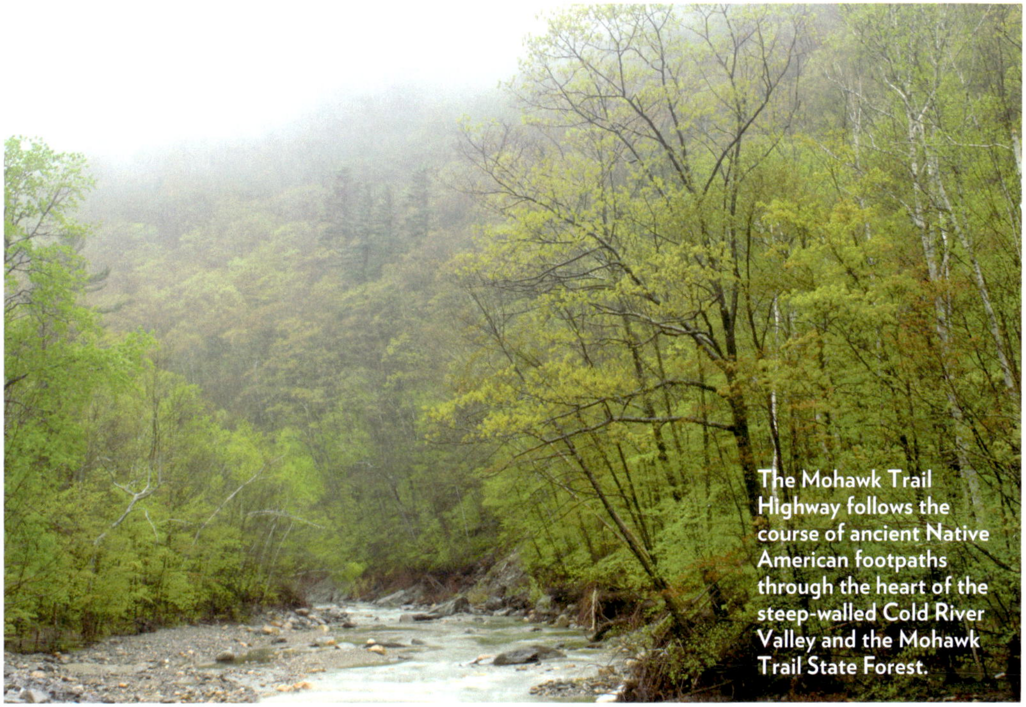

The Mohawk Trail Highway follows the course of ancient Native American footpaths through the heart of the steep-walled Cold River Valley and the Mohawk Trail State Forest.

The dawn of the American automotive era during the early 20th century necessitated the refurbishment of the nation's roadways, and improvements to the Greenfield-North Adams route began in 1912. After two years of construction, the revitalized Mohawk Trail was dedicated as a scenic highway and appropriately opened during the heart of the foliage season in October 1914. For the past century, it has been one of New England's best-known auto touring routes, and is an especially popular destination during the summer recreation season and in autumn, when tourists from across the globe arrive to view the colorful displays of the diverse forests.

While these roads afforded humans, horses, oxen, and, ultimately, automobiles a relatively safe passage over the Hoosac Range, the rugged, steep grades remained an insurmountable barrier to railroads and a direct line to the crucial markets of Albany and points west. During the mid-19th century, Alvah Crocker, who was the founder of the Fitchburg Railroad Company and an early pioneer in tunnel design and construction, was the chief proponent for a tunnel through the heart of the range, a project that posed immense engineering challenges given the technology of the time. The subsequent construction of the Hoosac Tunnel, a landmark of American railroad history, proved to be a lengthy and often tragic undertaking.

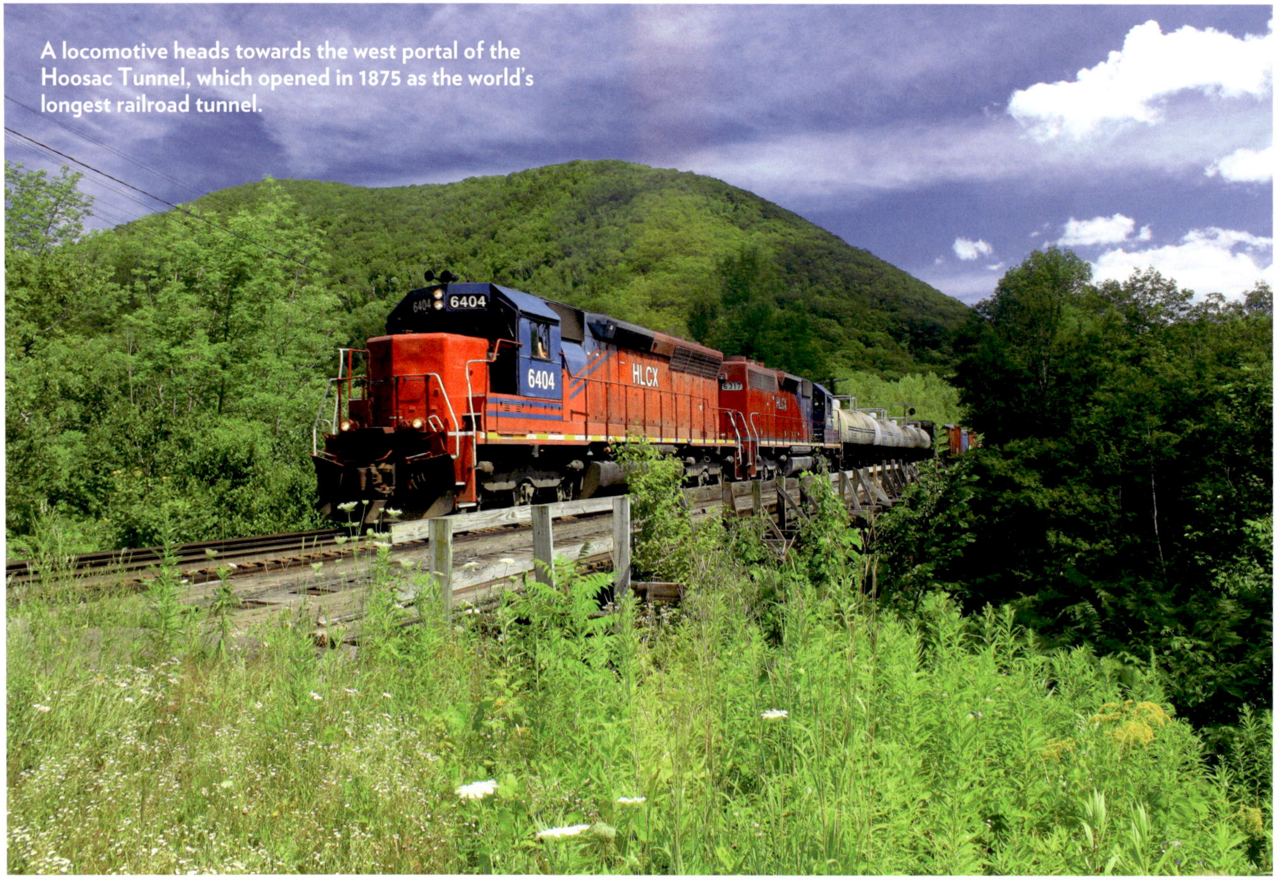

A locomotive heads towards the west portal of the Hoosac Tunnel, which opened in 1875 as the world's longest railroad tunnel.

After an aborted first attempt in 1852, when the drilling machine expected to chisel nearly five miles through the mountain lasted all of twelve feet before breaking down, construction resumed in 1856, but continued to be plagued and interrupted by political opposition, engineering complications, and accidents. Over the next twenty years, nearly 200 people were killed during the construction of the tunnel, mostly due to blasting accidents involving black powder and nitroglycerin. Nevertheless, it opened in 1875 as the world's longest railroad tunnel, and it remains the longest such structure east of the Rockies. Though passenger use ceased in 1958, the line continues to be regularly used by freight trains.

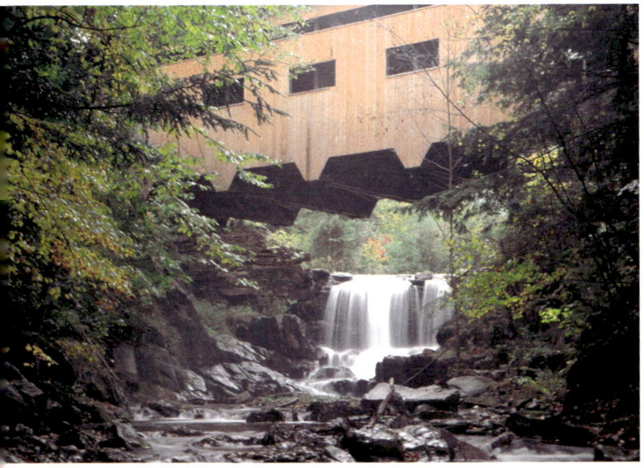

First erected in 1882 and rebuilt in 1950 and 2009, the Bissell Bridge is one of a handful of remaining covered bridges out of the 275 that once spanned the rivers of Massachusetts.

Another historic site associated with transportation is the much more diminutive Bissell Covered Bridge, which spans the narrow valley of Mill Brook a short distance upstream from its confluence with the Deerfield River at Charlemont. During the 19th and early 20th centuries, covered bridges were a familiar sight in Massachusetts, as roughly 275 were built across the state's waterways, including 100 railroad bridges. Most of these were located in the western hills, including 70 in Franklin County alone. Because of the inevitable ravishes of storms, floods, long winters, and wear and tear from automobiles and trucks, only a handful remain today, all of which have been renovated or entirely rebuilt in recent decades. At one time, towns looked forward to replacing the old wooden spans with hardier modern structures, but today covered bridges are highly valued as historic sites and tourist attractions.

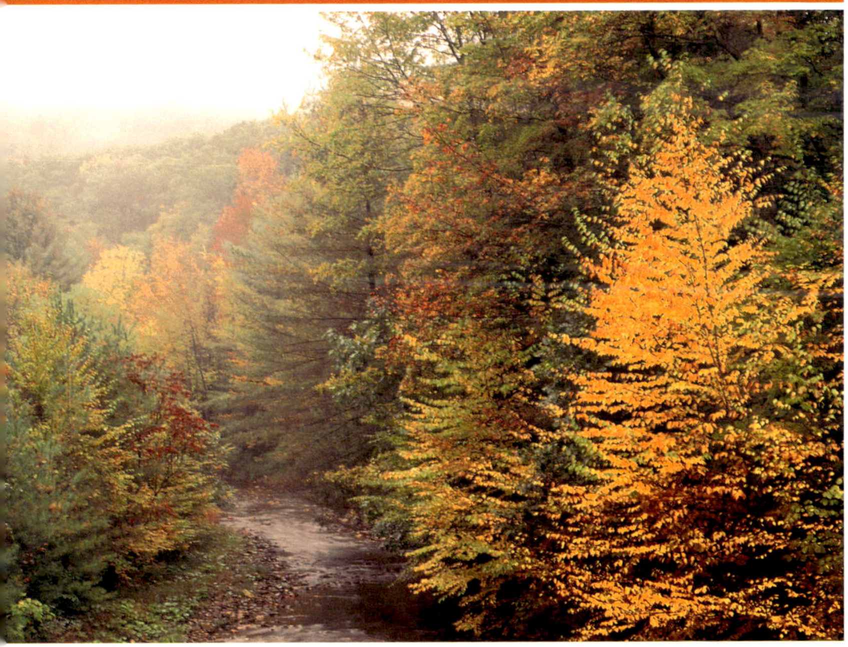

Mill Brook winds through a narrow, scenic valley in the Berkshire foothills as it flows towards its confluence with the Deerfield River in Charlemont.

Nestled in an 1800-foot high glacial depression in the valley hills south of Charlemont is the Hawley Bog, where hardy and wonderfully unique plants such as carnivorous sundews and northern pitcher plants, rootless bladderworts, cotton grass, and rose pogonias grow out of layers of "peat" (decomposed plant matter) well-preserved by the cool temperatures. Ringing the bog mat are spruce, red maple, and tamarack trees, all of which are also well-adapted to the stagnant, acidic waters. The bog is owned by the Five Colleges (a consortium of Amherst, Smith, Mount Holyoke, Hampshire Colleges, and the University of Massachusetts) and managed by the Nature Conservancy, a partnership that, in the words of noted ecologist Aaron Ellison, "has provided several generations of students and faculty with a unique opportunity to carry out long-term research in a high-elevation streamside setting." Adjacent to the trailhead is a historic site marking the old Hawley Common, which was once ringed by taverns, a church, an inn, and a post office before being abandoned around the mid-19th century.

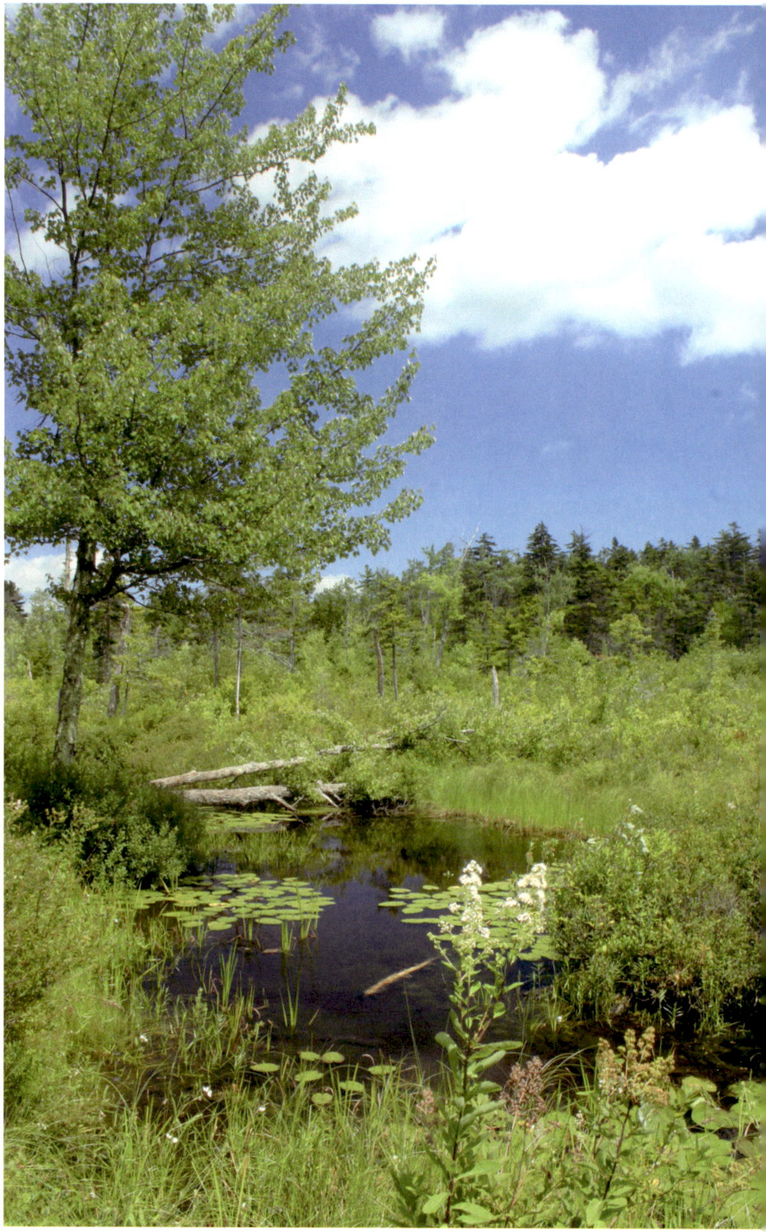

Home to a variety of unique flora, Hawley Bog is a rare example of a high-elevation bog in southern New England.

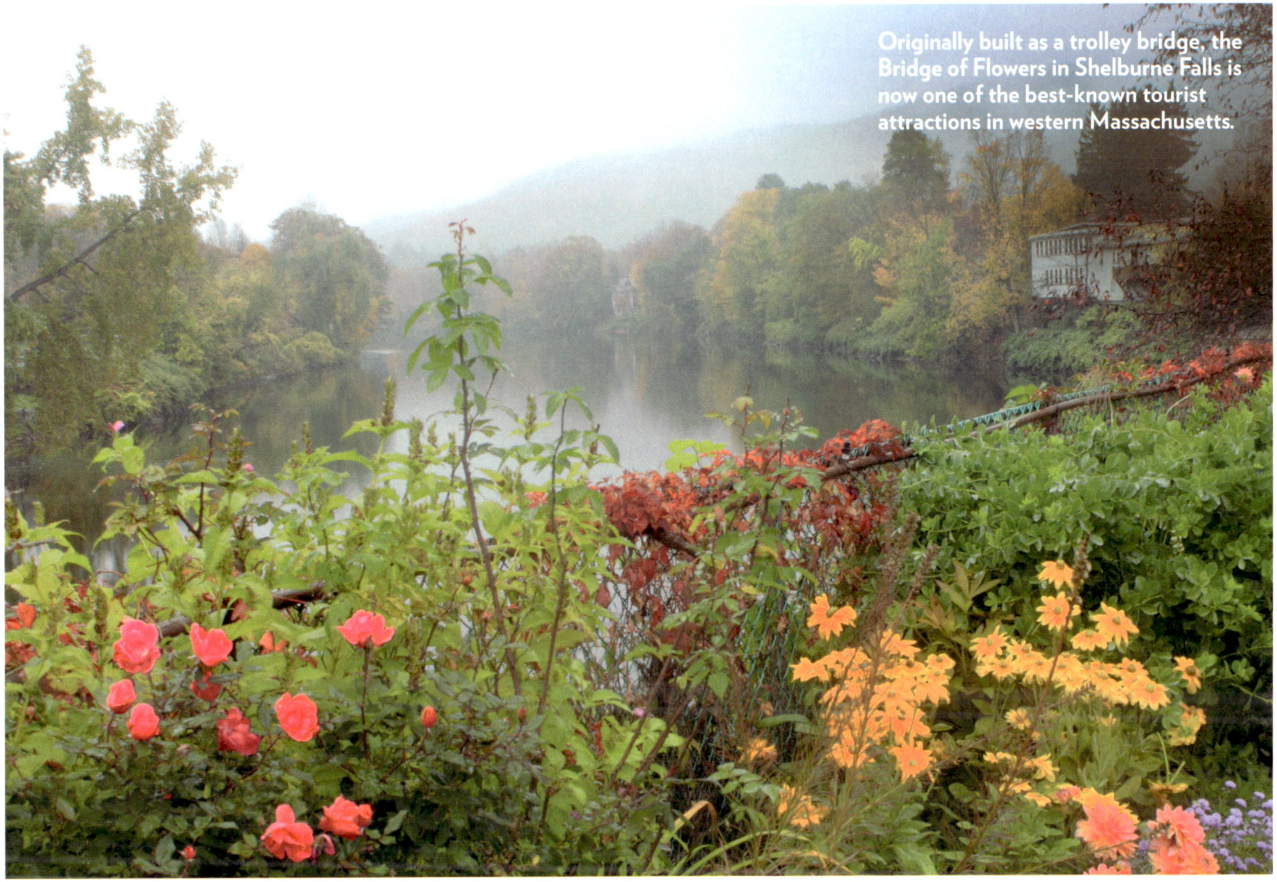

Originally built as a trolley bridge, the Bridge of Flowers in Shelburne Falls is now one of the best-known tourist attractions in western Massachusetts.

Beneath the steep valley hills at the confluence of the Deerfield and North Rivers is the picturesque artisans' village of Shelburne Falls, which was once appropriately known as "Salmon Falls" because of its rich fisheries that were prized by Native Americans and early colonial settlers. Thanks to its natural resources and accessibility via railroad, agriculture, mills, and manufacturing have all been significant components of the town's economy over the years. The opening of the Mohawk Trail Highway in 1915 prompted a shift towards tourism and artisan businesses during the 20th century, and the village is now a popular destination for visitors to western Massachusetts.

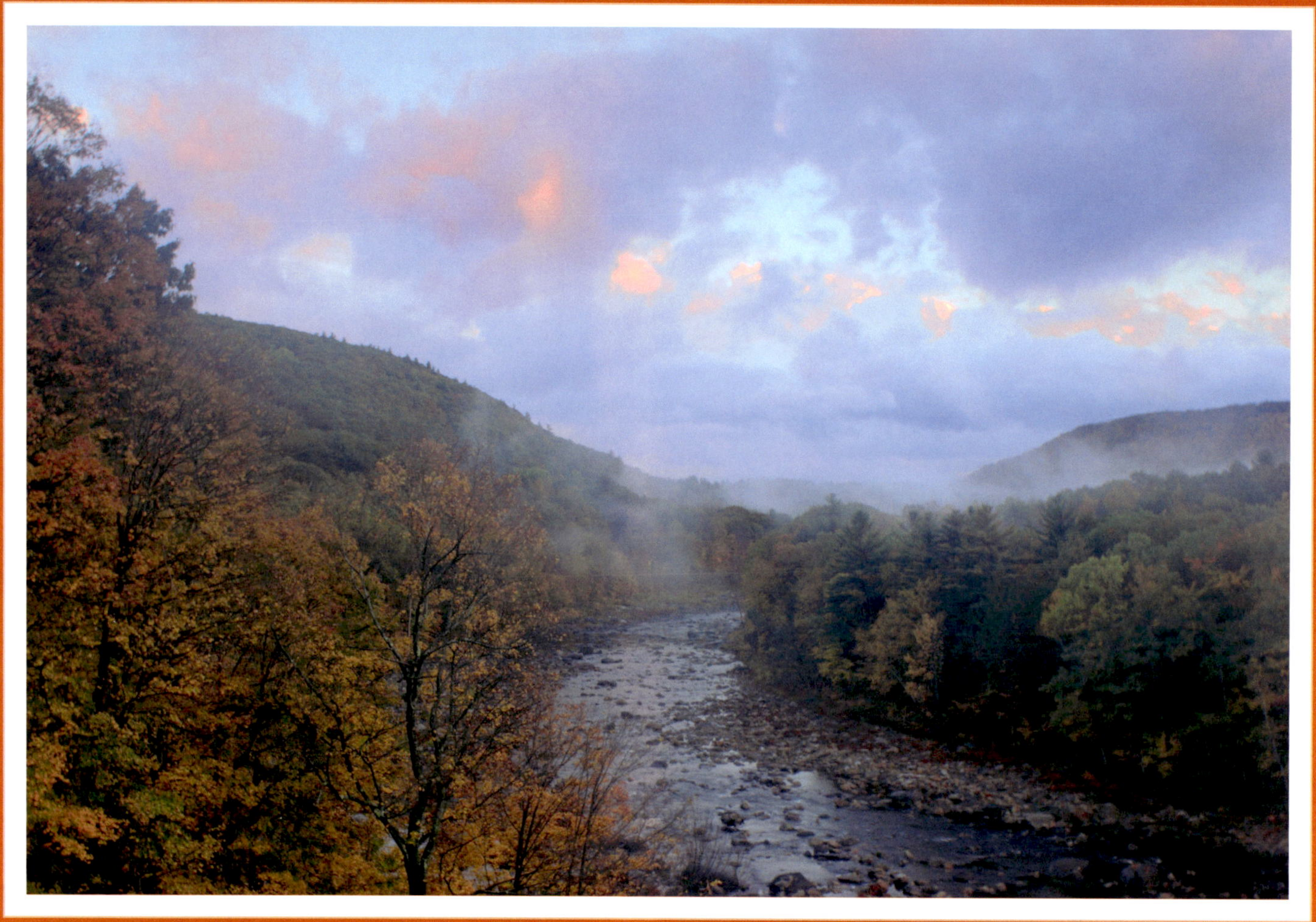

The Mohawk Trail is especially scenic in autumn when colorful foliage adorns the steep slopes of the Deerfield River Valley, seen here at Shelburne Falls.

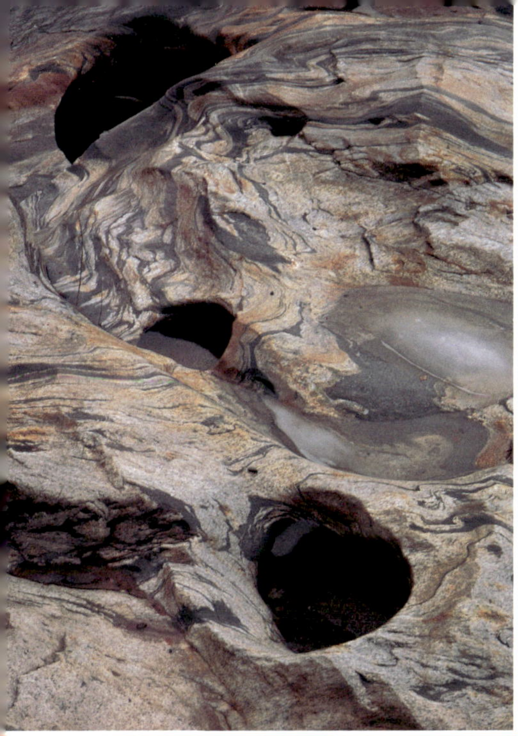

Shaped by glaciers and the Deerfield River, the Glacial Potholes of Shelburne Falls are a colorful artifact of the last ice age.

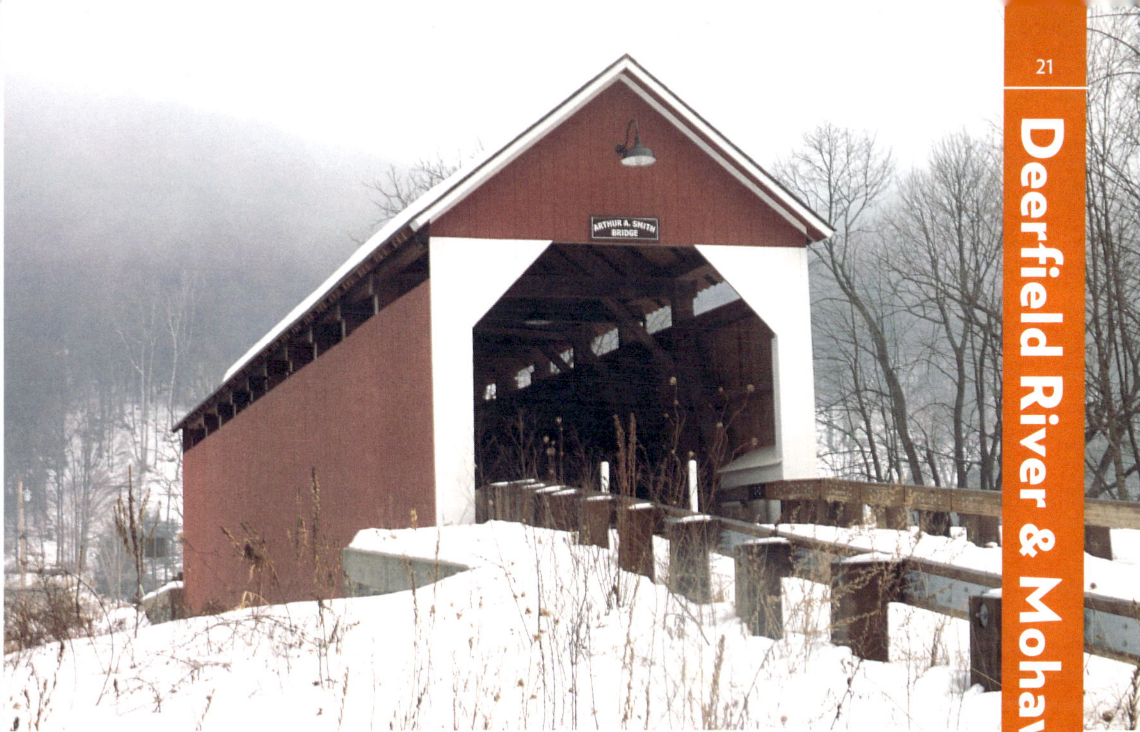

After sitting in disrepair in a farm field for fifteen years, the Arthur Smith Bridge was refurbished in 2006 and once again spans the North River near Colrain's village of Lyonsville.

Shelburne Fall's best-known attraction is the Bridge of Flowers, which was originally built in 1908 as a trolley bridge that was used to transport people and goods to the neighboring town of Colrain. After the line ceased operations in the late 1920s and the structure became overgrown with weeds, town resident Antoinette Burnham proposed that it be maintained as a pedestrian walkway with an elaborate flower garden. With the support of the Shelburne Falls Women's Club, some 500 varieties of colorful flora have been carefully planted and maintained over the past 80 years. The bridge was rehabilitated in 1983, celebrated its centennial in 2008, and survived Hurricane Irene in 2011 after being briefly inundated with floodwaters during the height of the storm. A short distance downstream are the colorful Glacial Potholes, a cluster of small pools scoured by receding glaciers and smoothed and polished by the river's active, swirling waters.

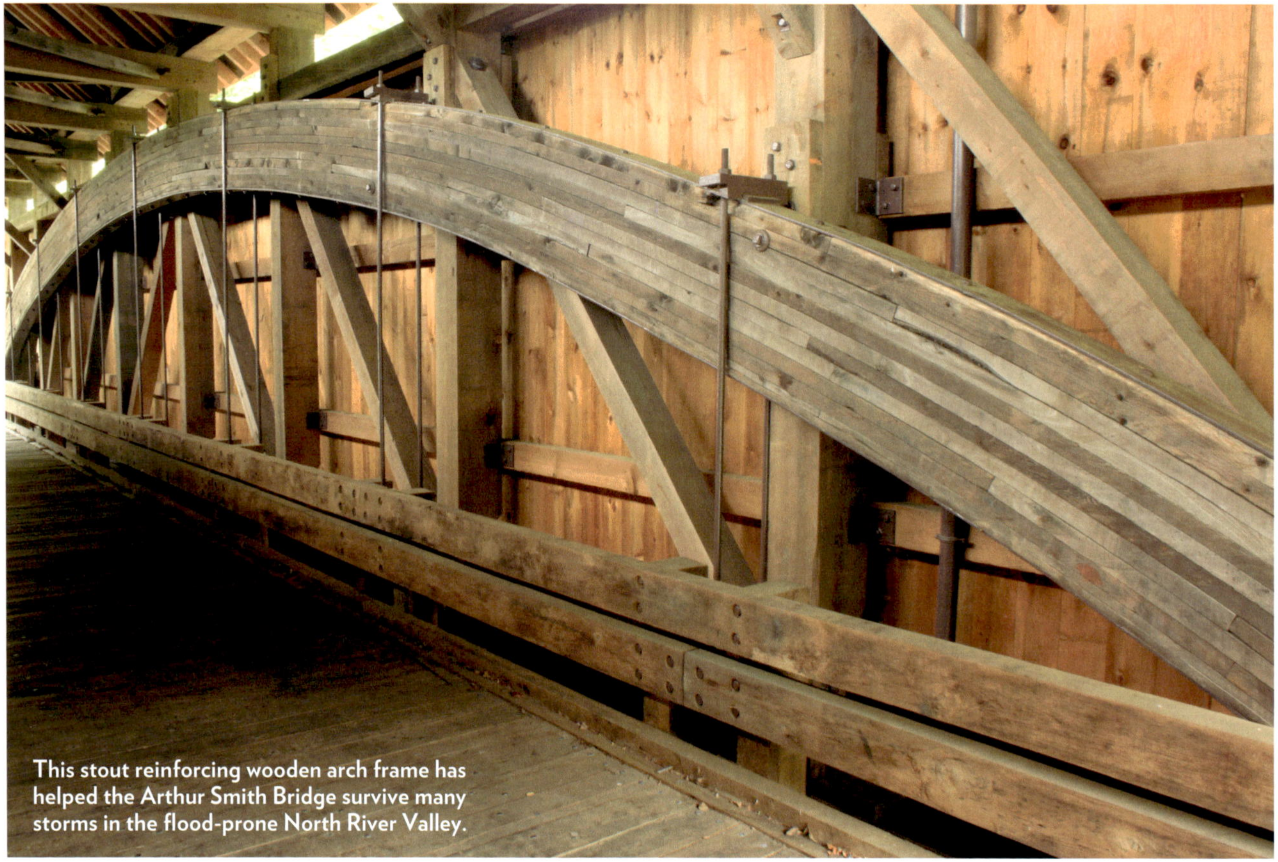

This stout reinforcing wooden arch frame has helped the Arthur Smith Bridge survive many storms in the flood-prone North River Valley.

The North River is a short but highly scenic tributary of the Deerfield, formed by two branches and a short main stem in the rolling hills of Colrain. Spanning the river near the village of Lyonsville is the Arthur Smith Covered Bridge, which has an unusually active history by the standards of covered bridges. It was originally built as a crossing between Griswoldville and Shattucksville villages in 1870, before being moved upstream to its present location in 1896. After surviving the series of devastating floods during the 1920s and 1930s that destroyed the town's numerous other covered bridges, it fell into considerable disrepair due to a lack of maintenance in the late 20th century, and the battered structure sat rather ignominiously in an adjacent farm field while the town sought funds for its repair. It was finally refurbished in 2006 and recently survived yet another storm, the floods of Hurricane Irene, in good order.

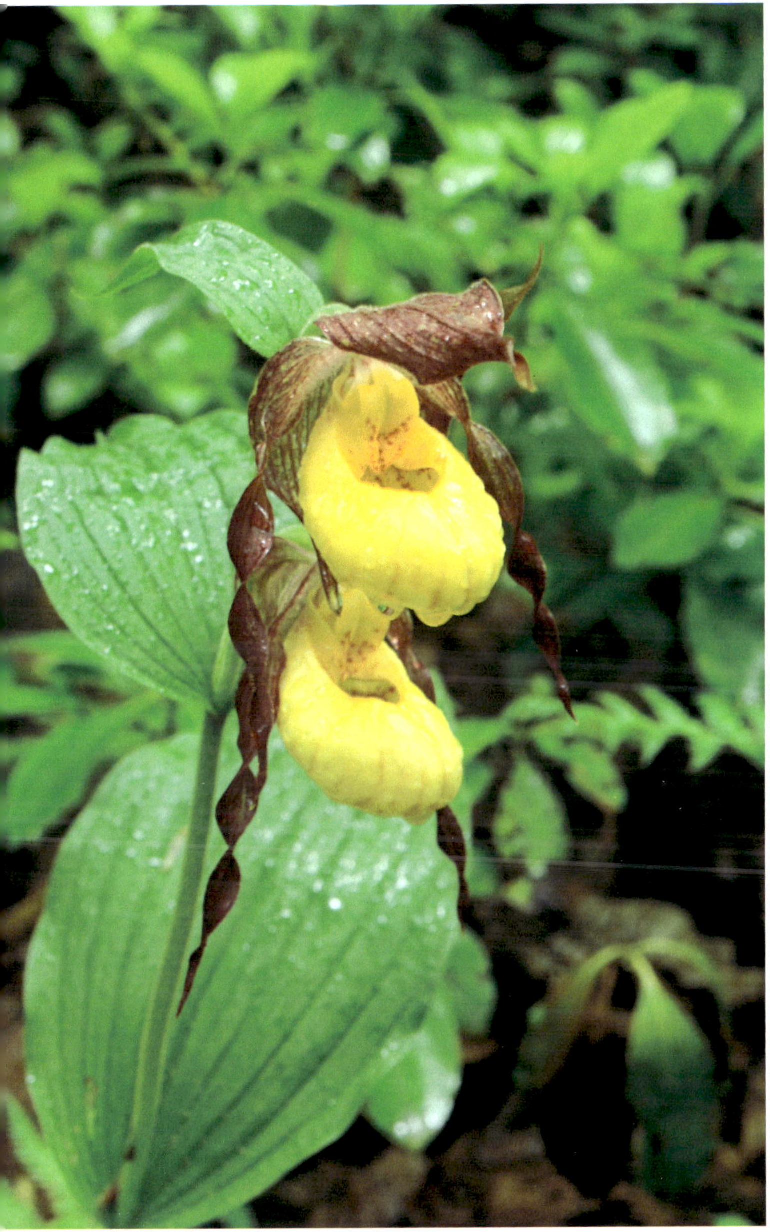

Atop the valley, high above Shelburne Falls, is a natural garden that thrives in the diverse habitats of the Massachusetts Audubon Society's aptly named High Ledges Sanctuary. During the spring, these forests, rocky outcroppings, and wetlands are alive with the colorful blooms of bloodroot, trilliums, columbine, lady's slippers, violets, pitcher plants, and many other woodland wildflowers. Fed by abundant limestone nutrients, the rich soils are characteristic of the mountains and hills of western New England in their great diversity of plant life. Indeed, more than 800 species have been recorded at several modest-sized nature preserves in western Massachusetts. A lookout atop the ledges offers panoramic views across the Deerfield Valley to Mount Greylock, whose distinctive profile rises out of the western horizon.

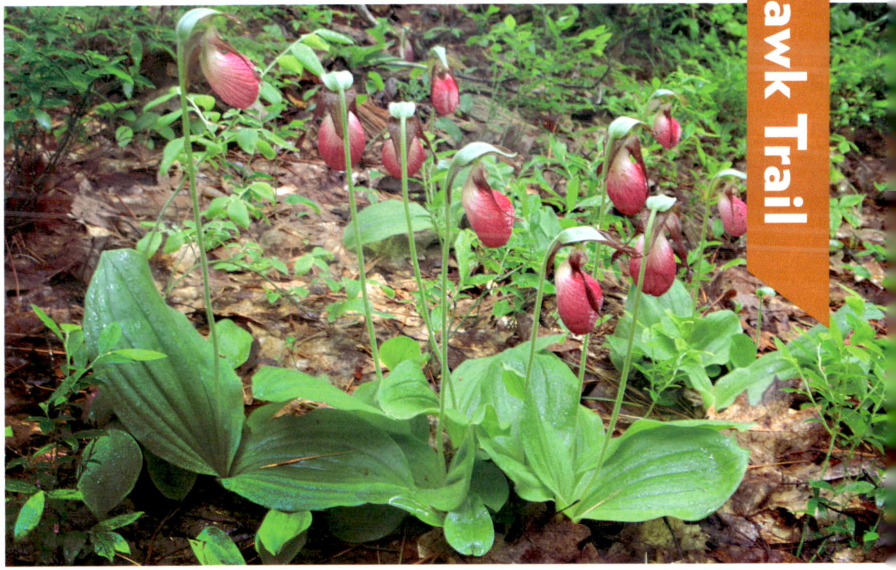

Colorful orchids, such as pink and yellow lady's slippers, are among the diverse wildflowers that flourish in the rich soils of the High Ledges Wildlife Sanctuary in Shelburne.

Another of the valley's botanical hot spots is the Bear Swamp Reservation, a mosaic of rocky outcroppings and wetlands nearly hidden amidst apple orchards in the hills of Ashfield. Hard as it may be to imagine today, these ridges were also once cleared for agriculture, a vivid example of the extent of agriculture in New England's past. Today, profuse blooms of spring ephemerals and summer ferns carpet the rocks. A short stroll out of the dark forest leads to a glimpse of the region's past from the "Apple Valley" hilltop lookout, where there are views across pastoral farm fields to the hills of the Deerfield Valley.

A herd of some 8,000 sheep once grazed the land around nearby Pony Mountain, which is distinguished by a 100-foot long open granite cliff that is favored by rock climbers. At its base, Chapel Brook makes three distinct drops, totaling 45 feet, as it assumes its brief four-mile course towards Poland Brook and the South River, one of the Deerfield's tributaries. Two grist mills were established along its waters during the mid-1800s. Now protected by the Trustees of Reservations, a private

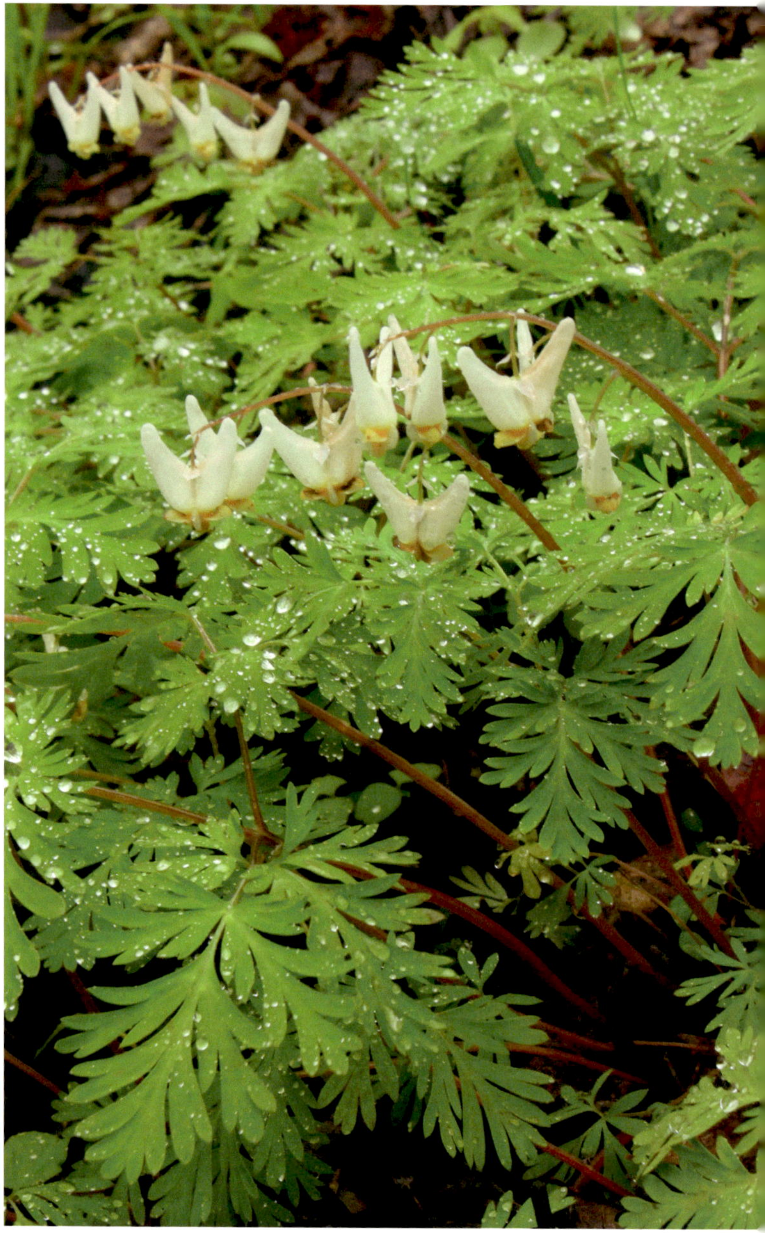

The rocky ridges of Bear Swamp Reservation in Ashfield are home to more spring ephemerals such as unmistakable and logically named Dutchman's breeches.

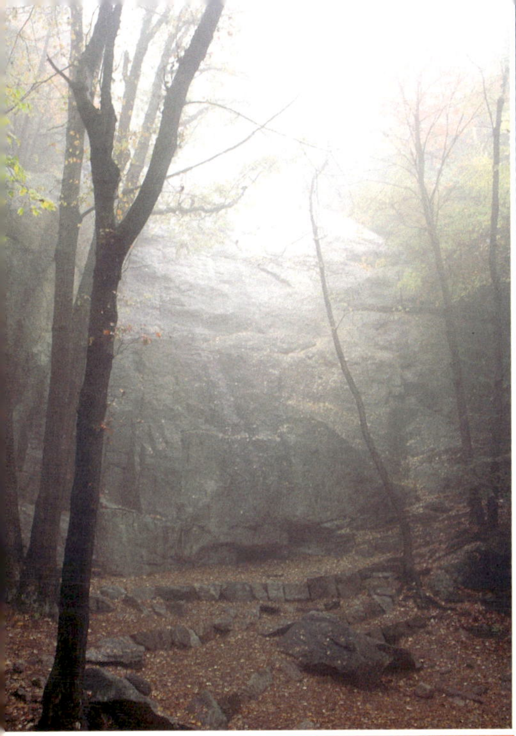

Popular with rock climbers, the 100-foot sheer granite face of Pony Mountain rises above the cascades of Chapel Brook in Ashfield.

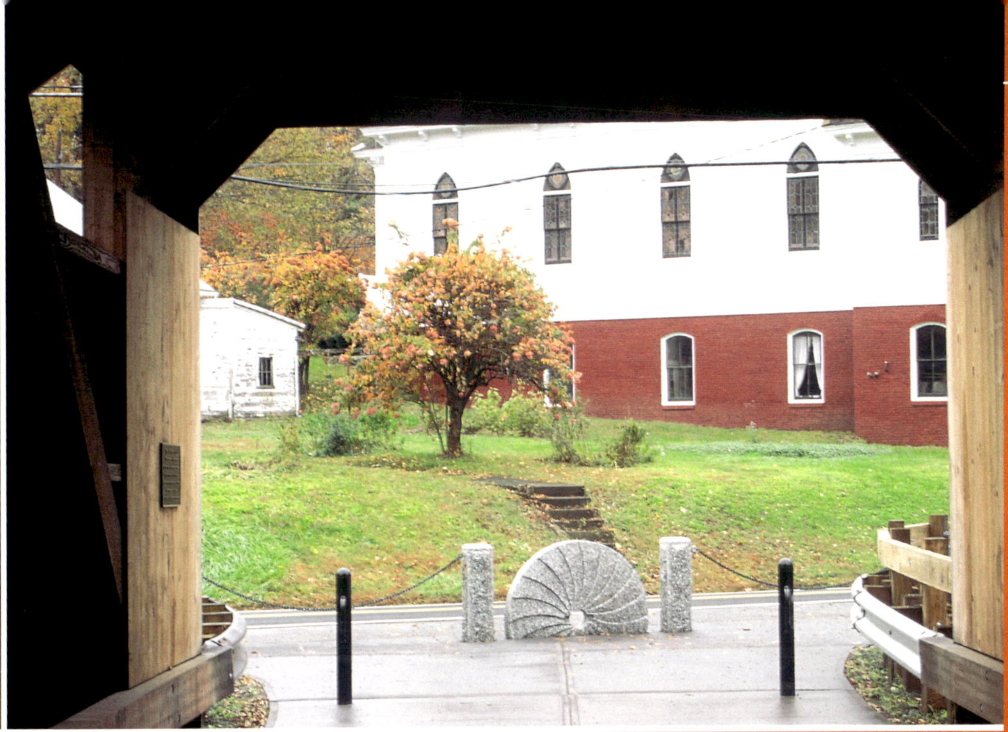

Built in 1870 and renovated in 2005, the covered bridge at Conway's village of Burkeville spans the South River next to a historic church.

conservation organization with more than 100 reservations across Massachusetts, the mountain and brook are home to walking trails that allow visitors to explore the brook, ridge, and an old sheep pasture site.

The South River is home to the southernmost of Franklin County's four remaining covered bridges, a 106-foot span located in and named for Conway's village of Burkeville. Its wooden frame is a variation of a "Howe" truss, a design that is named after an engineer named Nicholas Howe who hailed from the central Massachusetts town of Warren. The Howe truss, which was first used in a railroad bridge in his hometown, became widely used throughout North America, Europe, and Russia during the late 19th century. The Burkeville Bridge was erected in 1870 and renovated in 2005, and reopened to traffic in 2013. Situated adjacent to the village's historic Catholic church on scenic Route 116, it makes for a classic New England scene and photo opportunity.

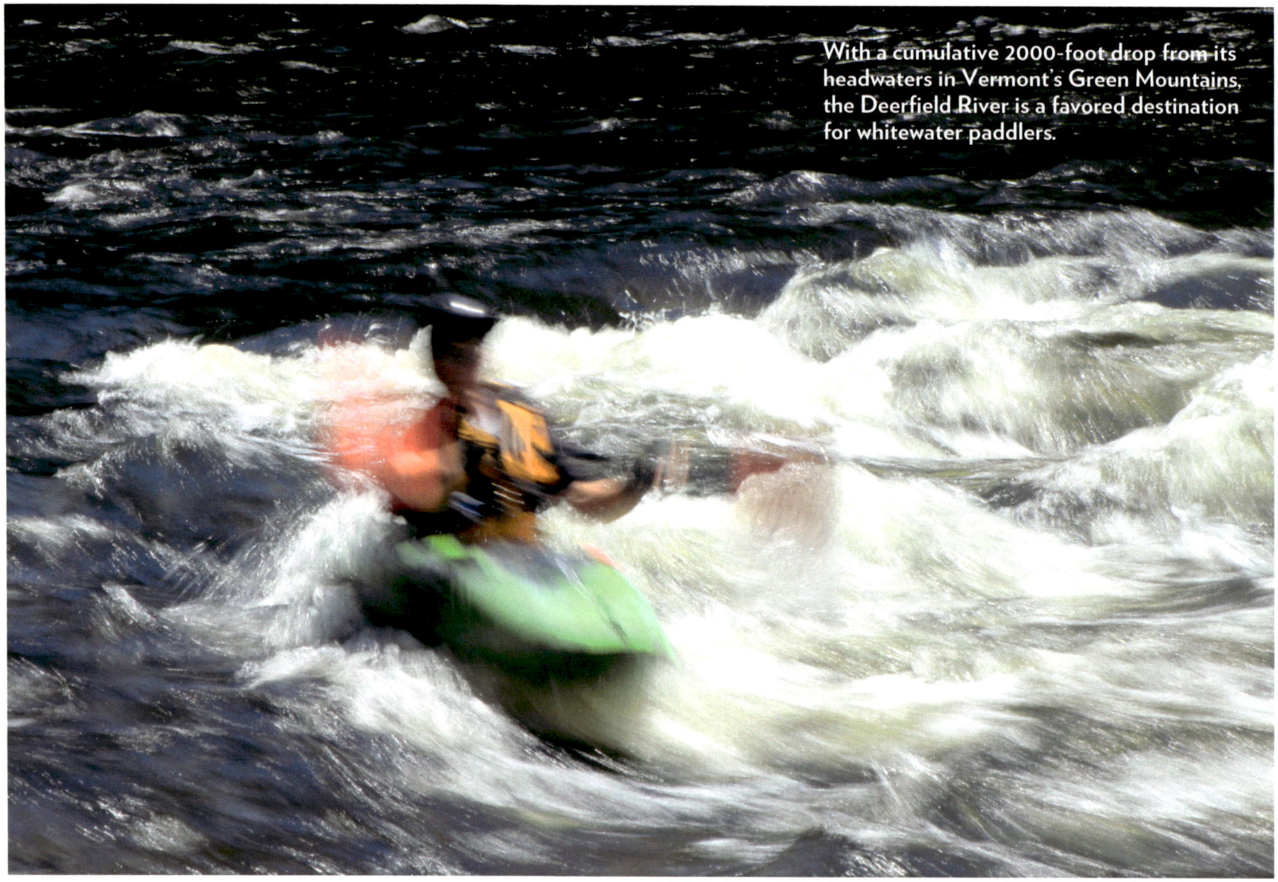

With a cumulative 2000-foot drop from its headwaters in Vermont's Green Mountains, the Deerfield River is a favored destination for whitewater paddlers.

After dropping 2,000 feet over 70 miles, which is nearly as much as the Connecticut River falls along its entire 410-mile course, the Deerfield River bends abruptly to the north and reaches its confluence with the Connecticut in a floodplain near Greenfield. Though its watershed is lightly populated—less than 50,000 people per the 2000 census—with no major cities, the river is one of New England's hardest working waterways, thanks to its considerable energy. Over the past century, ten hydroelectric power facilities have been built along its course, an average of one every seven miles. Whitewater sections and scenery make the river a very popular summer recreation destination, as evidenced by a number of thriving guide and rental establishments along the Mohawk Trail. Indeed, prospective Olympians use a section of the river in Charlemont to train for whitewater kayak races.

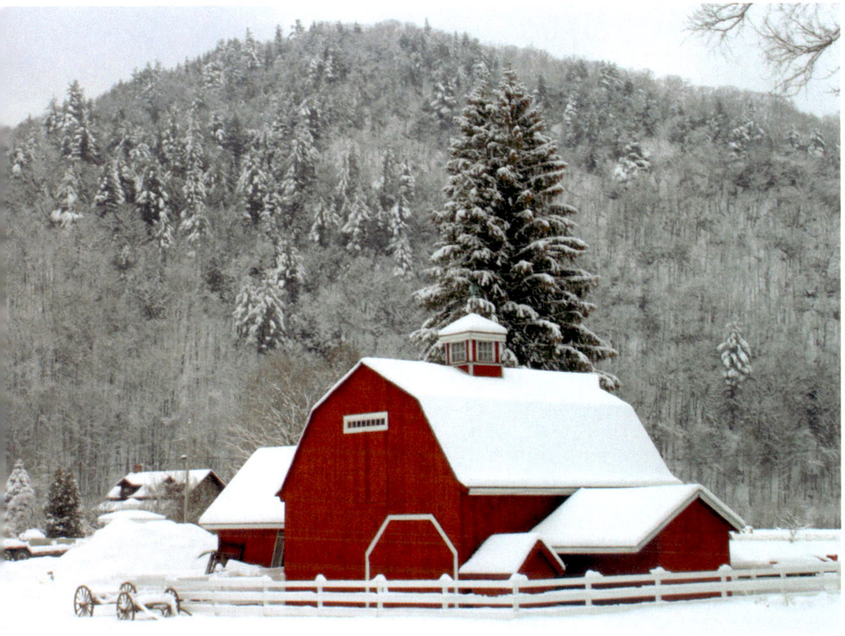

The diverse habitats of the Deerfield River Valley include fertile bottomlands and high rolling hills.

Like most watersheds in western New England's mountains, the Deerfield Valley suffered considerably from Hurricane Irene in late August 2011. The west side of the storm, which is where the heaviest precipitation falls in tropical storms, passed directly over the region, adding torrential rainfall to ground that was already saturated after unusually heavy precipitation during the previous months. Funneled through the narrow valleys, floodwaters washed out or heavily damaged many roads and bridges, temporarily stranding some communities. Landslides in the Cold River Valley caused extensive damage to the Mohawk Trail Highway, which was closed for several months. In Greenfield, the swollen Green River breached a dam and carved a new channel around the town's historic "Pumping Station" covered bridge, which barely survived the storm.

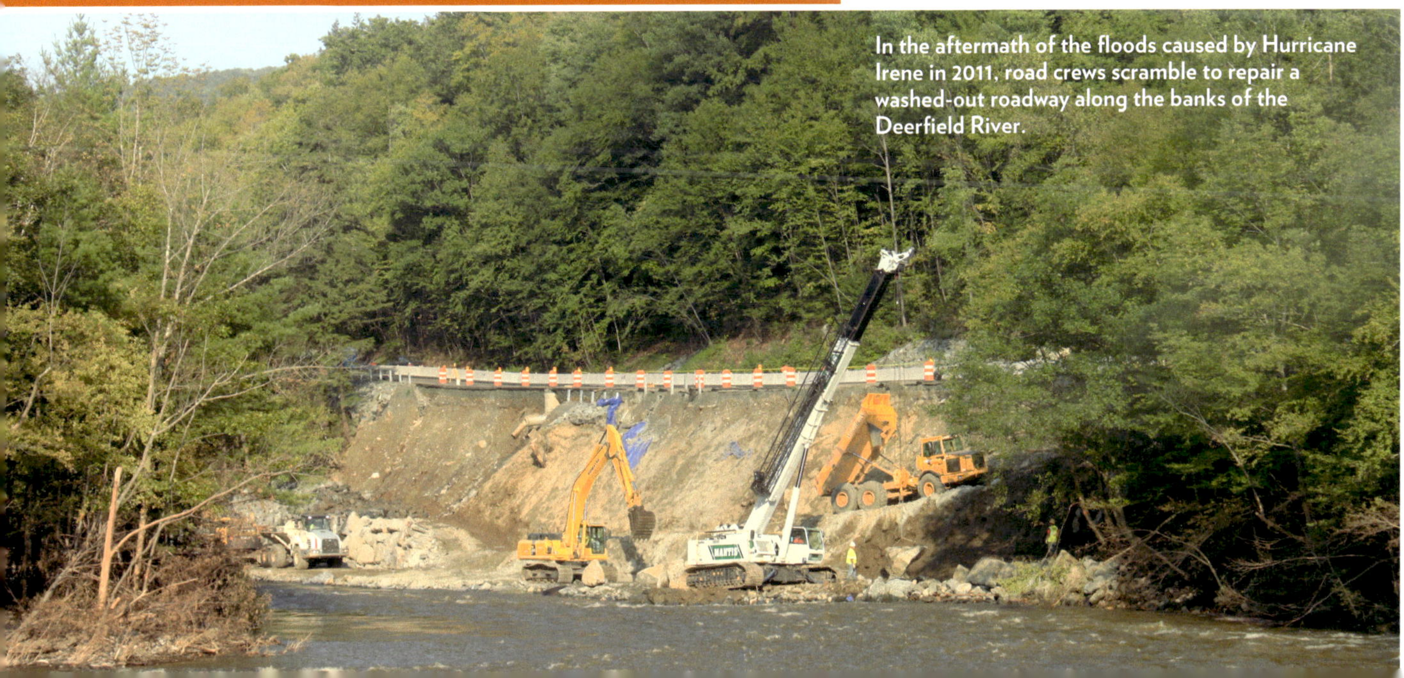

In the aftermath of the floods caused by Hurricane Irene in 2011, road crews scramble to repair a washed-out roadway along the banks of the Deerfield River.

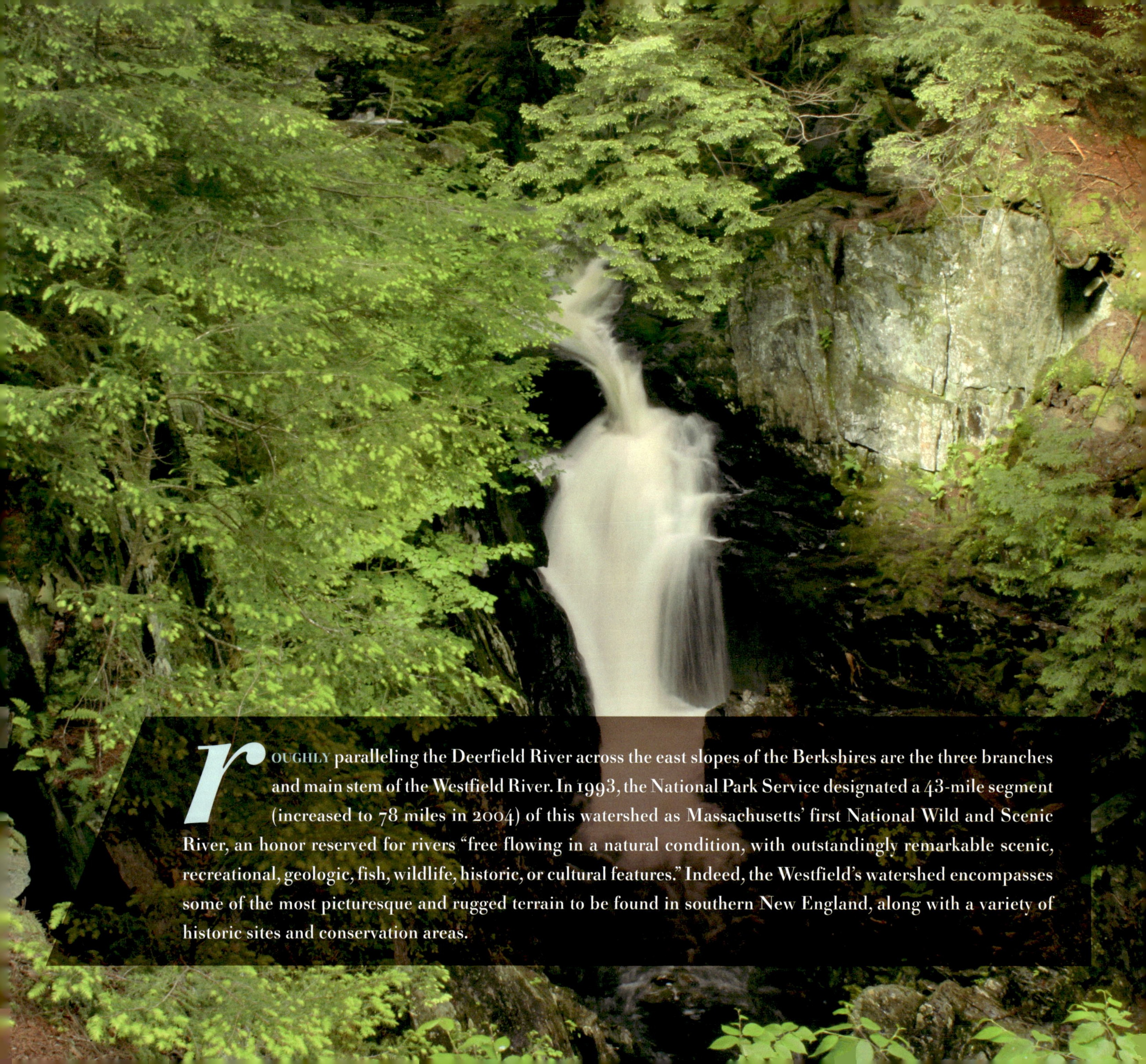

ROUGHLY paralleling the Deerfield River across the east slopes of the Berkshires are the three branches and main stem of the Westfield River. In 1993, the National Park Service designated a 43-mile segment (increased to 78 miles in 2004) of this watershed as Massachusetts' first National Wild and Scenic River, an honor reserved for rivers "free flowing in a natural condition, with outstandingly remarkable scenic, recreational, geologic, fish, wildlife, historic, or cultural features." Indeed, the Westfield's watershed encompasses some of the most picturesque and rugged terrain to be found in southern New England, along with a variety of historic sites and conservation areas.

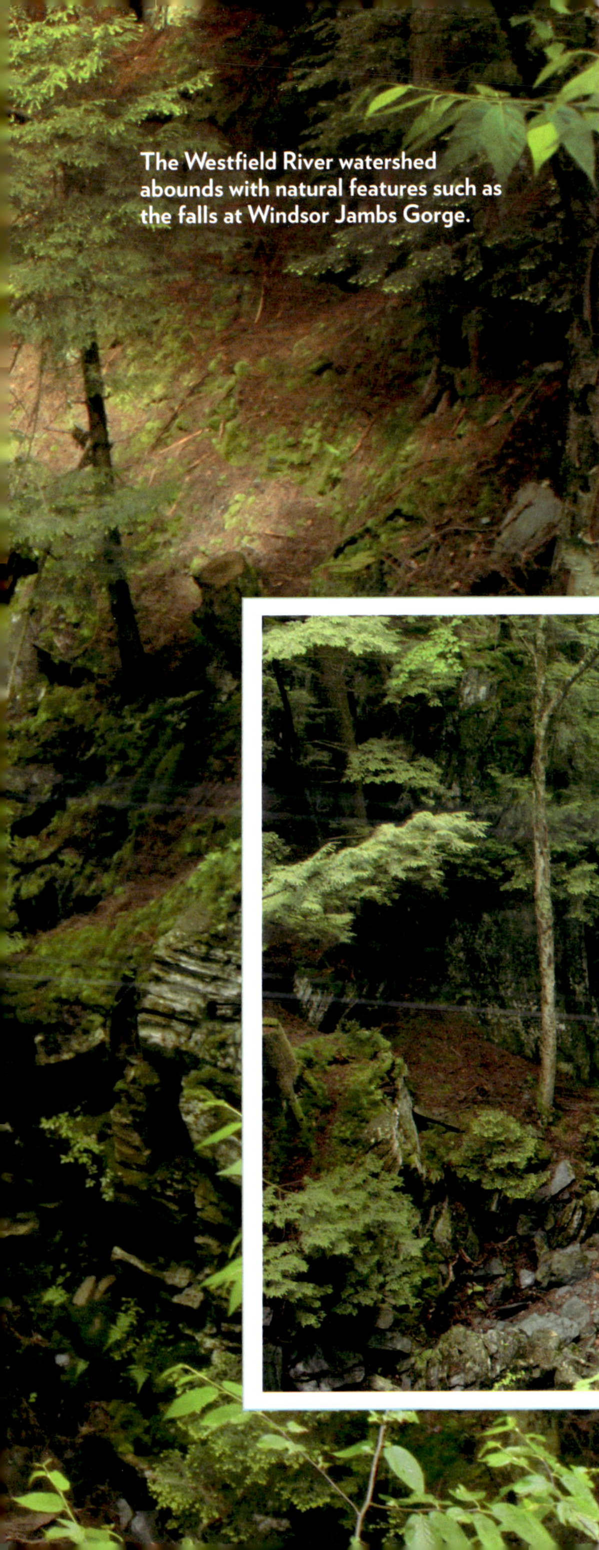

The Westfield River watershed abounds with natural features such as the falls at Windsor Jambs Gorge.

Within these 330,000 acres are 630 miles worth of rivers, woodland streams, and brooks, 80 lakes and ponds, and extensive forests that cover 80 percent of the land; a mere five percent of the watershed is developed. The basin owes its largely wild, remote character to the rugged, rocky terrain, where the summits of the Berkshire Hills transition to the foothills of the Connecticut River Valley. Indeed, more than one-third of this landscape is comprised of steep hills and ridges with topography and soils that have proved impractical for sustained agriculture and other human development.

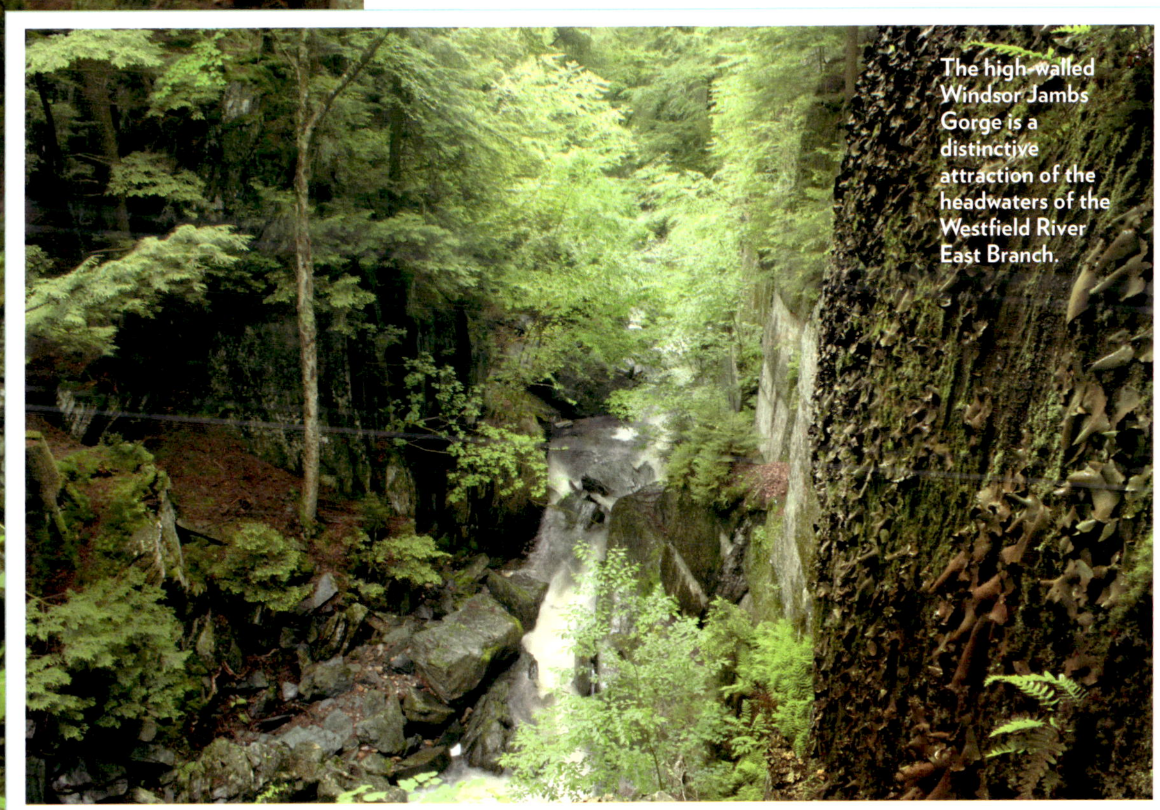

The high-walled Windsor Jambs Gorge is a distinctive attraction of the headwaters of the Westfield River East Branch.

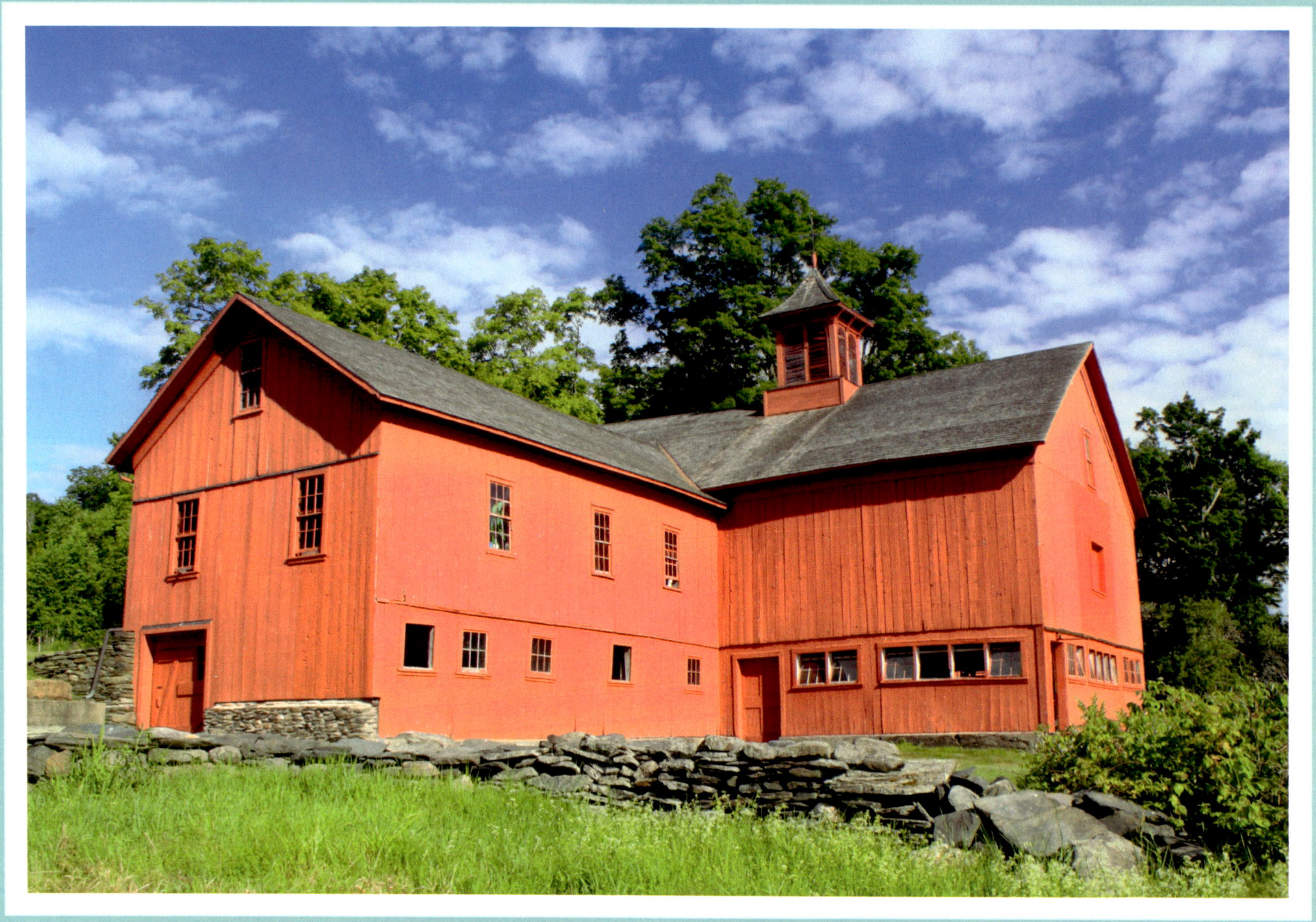

Acclaimed poet and editor William Cullen Bryant built this distinctive red barn as part of his summer retreat estate in Cummington.

From headwaters spread across the east slopes of the Berkshires, the three main branches converge in Huntington to form the main stem, which continues on a southeasterly course to its confluence with the Connecticut River at West Springfield. The longest of the trio is the East Branch, which originates from a series of tributary brooks just south of the Deerfield River drainage on the east slopes of the Hoosac Range and falls more than 1,000 feet over its first fourteen miles.

In the heart of this rugged terrain, one of these source waters carves a path through the Windsor Jambs Gorge as it nears its confluence with the East Branch in the Windsor State Forest. Some historical sources suggest that the name of this chasm, where lichen-covered granite walls rise as high as 80 feet above the churning waters, derives from "jams" in the narrow passage that made it unsuitable for timber drives. The surrounding quiet, remote groves of spruce, fir, and northern hardwood trees have a feel of the north woods of Maine or New Hampshire, especially for those fortunate enough to glimpse a moose or black bear.

After joining the Swift River (not to be confused with the Swift River that forms Quabbin Reservoir in central Massachusetts), the East Branch bends to the south as it flows through the foothills between the Berkshires and the Connecticut Valley. The quiet beauty of this rolling terrain held considerable appeal to William Cullen Bryant, the nationally acclaimed 19th-century poet and editor who was born in a log cabin in Cummington in 1794. After publishing his first poem at age 13, he composed his best-known work "Thanatopis" (or "Meditation on Death") around 1813, and by the 1830s he had achieved the status of the country's premiere poet.

Even after Bryant moved to New York City to become editor-in-chief of the *New York Evening Post*, a position he held for half a century, his connection to the Westfield Valley remained strong. In 1865, he purchased the site of his boyhood home and erected an elaborate Victorian house and large red barn on the grounds. He returned each summer until his death in 1878, leaving behind the city's heat and congestion. After inspecting his gardens and orchards and working at his home during the morning, he would often take long afternoon walks through the valley hills. The homestead is now preserved as a 200-acre historic site and natural area under the management of the Trustees of Reservations. The woods bordering the fields are home to some of New England's largest old trees, including giant hemlocks and pines that grow out of the banks along Rivulet Brook.

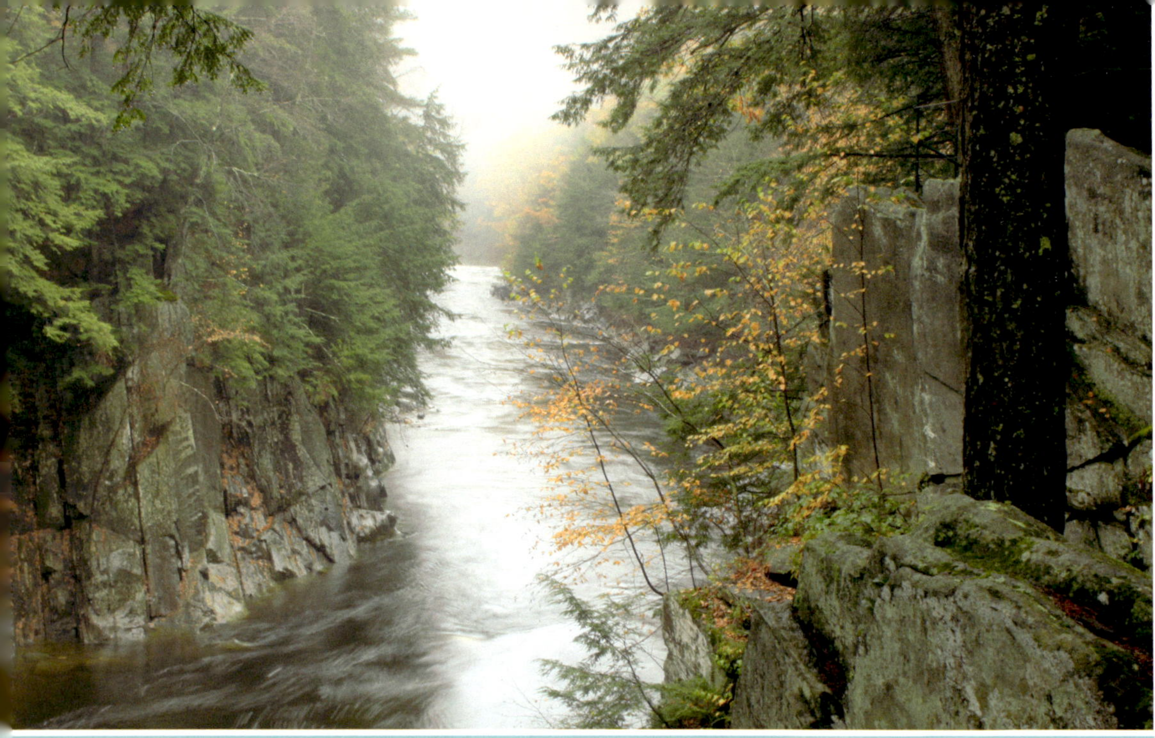

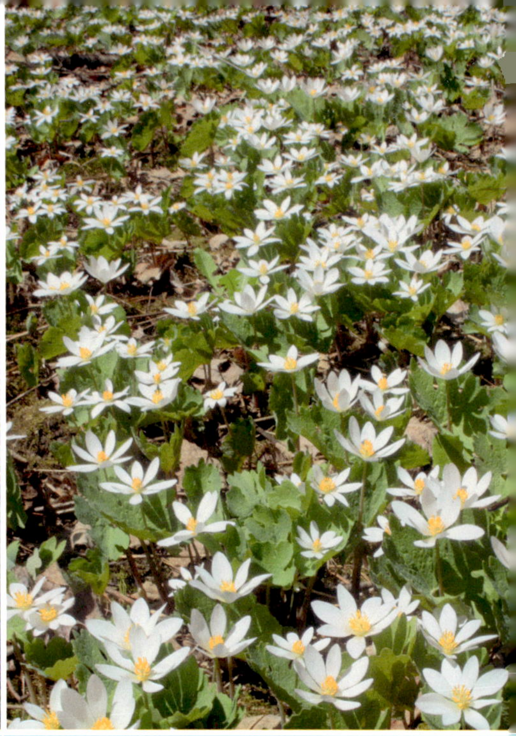

Carved by the waters of the East Branch, Chesterfield Gorge is one of the most dramatic natural features of the Westfield River watershed.

The Westfield River Valley's limestone-rich soils host colonies of wildflowers such as bloodroot.

A short distance downstream from the Bryant homestead is arguably the best-known natural feature of the Westfield River watershed, the dramatic Chesterfield Gorge. Here the East Branch carves its way between 70-foot high granite walls adorned with evergreen eastern hemlock trees. Such canyons are relatively uncommon in New England and the eastern United States, though ironically there is another Chesterfield Gorge on a tributary of the Connecticut River near Keene, New Hampshire.

At the head of the gorge are the neat, square abutments of the lost High Bridge, which was built across the river in 1762 as part of the old Boston-Albany Post Road. Following their defeat in the crucial American Revolution battle at Saratoga in 1777, British Redcoats crossed the river here during their retreat to Boston. Another visitor of note during this time was the Marquis de Lafayette, the French military officer who was an important ally of the Americans during the Revolution; he enjoyed the scenery from a stagecoach drawn by six white horses. The bridge was washed out in 1825 by a flood that also destroyed a number of area mills, and was never rebuilt.

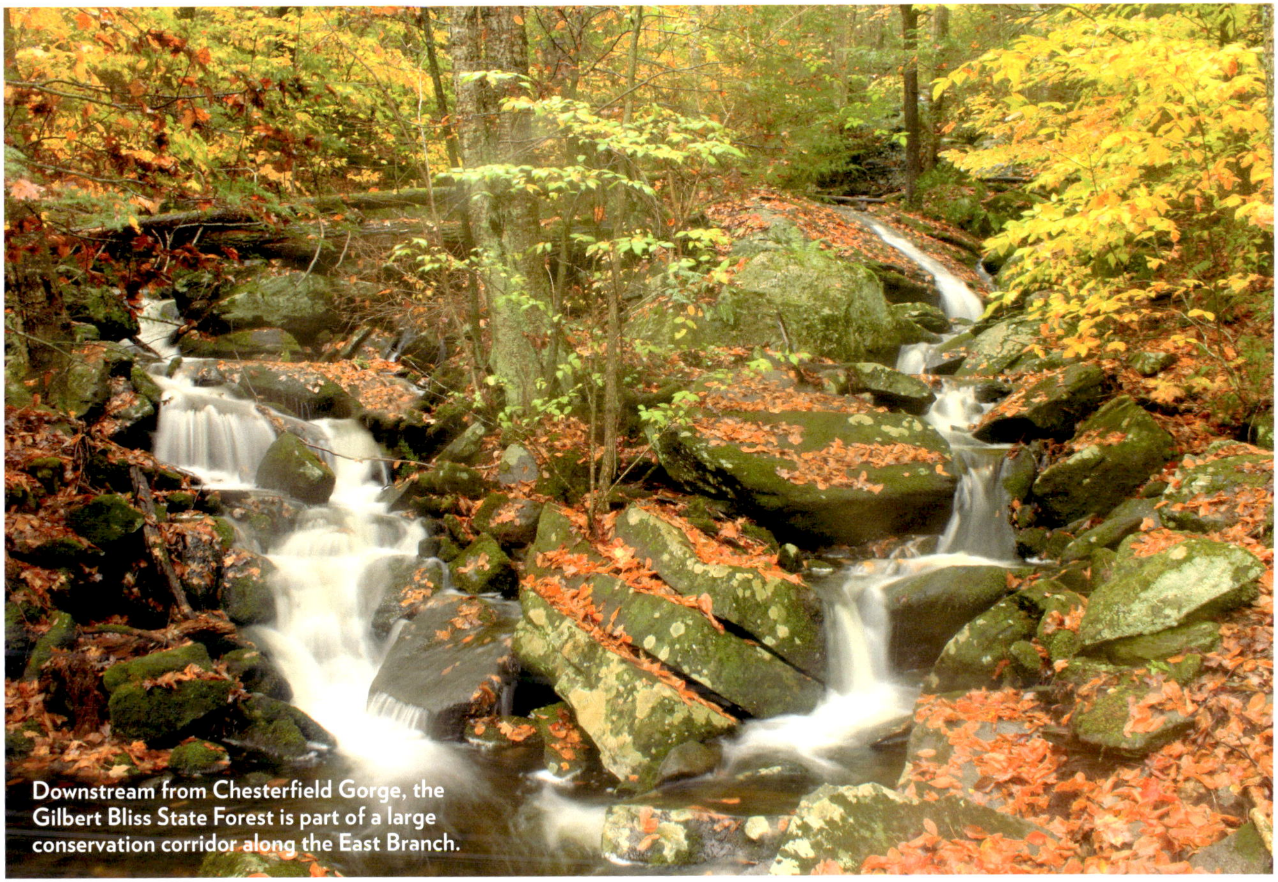

Downstream from Chesterfield Gorge, the Gilbert Bliss State Forest is part of a large conservation corridor along the East Branch.

Today the East Branch Recreational Trail follows an old cart road south from the gorge through an 8,000-acre corridor of protected land. A cascading seasonal stream, where twin waterfalls form when water levels are high, marks the boundary of the adjacent Gilbert Bliss State Forest, where black bears, moose, fishers, bobcats, songbirds, and other wildlife enjoy nearly 2,500 acres of prime forest habitat. It lies in the heart of the East Branch Forest Reserve, one of eight designated state preserves in Massachusetts where the forests are being allowed to fully mature with minimal, passive management. Anglers here enjoy one of the region's finest cold water fisheries, with abundant stores of brook and brown trout and other species.

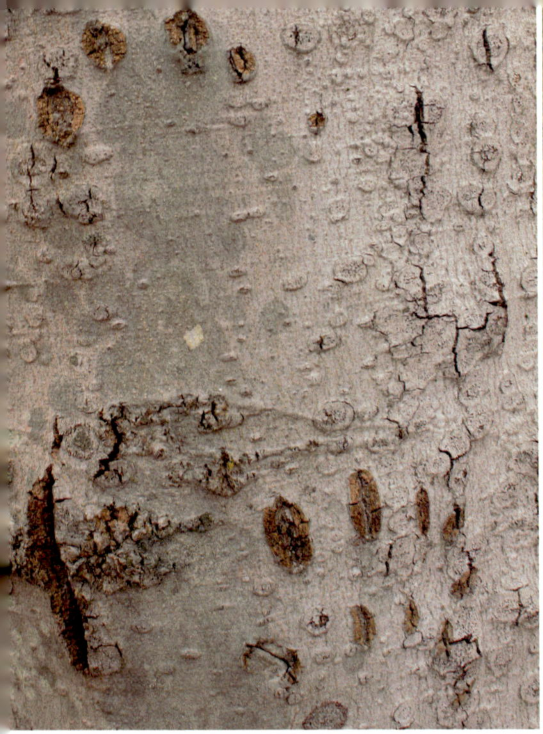

Claw marks on an old beech tree are evidence of a black bear's visit to Road's End, a Massachusetts Audubon sanctuary on an old farm in Worthington near Chesterfield Gorge.

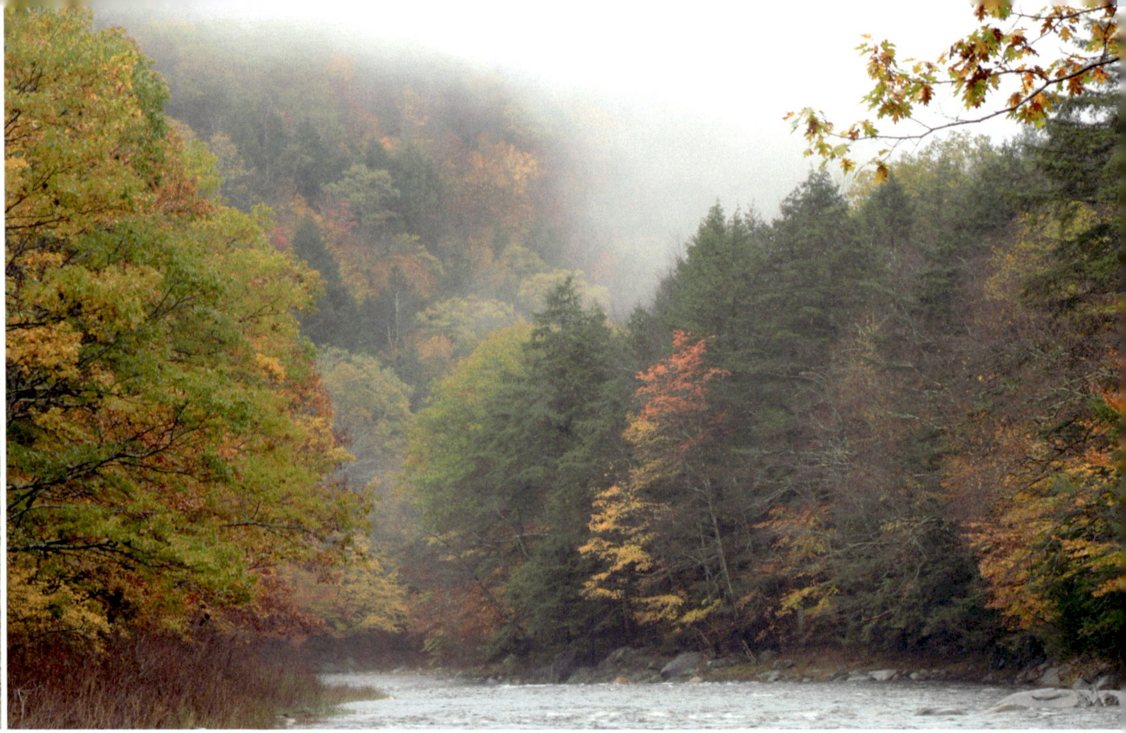

Steep hills and ridges comprise more than one-third of the Westfield River's watershed, and are largely the reason for the region's wild, undeveloped character.

Amidst the natural splendor are more artifacts of the river's history, including the remains of the Baker Dam, which was built by and named for Lemuel Baker in 1848 as part of a sawmill that operated for 21 years before being destroyed by another flood in 1869. Further downstream, in a broad area along the riverbanks known as Indian Hollow, is the stone abutment of an iron bridge that was removed during the 1930s.

Indian Hollow was a favored hunting and fishing site of Native Americans, whose presence in the valley dates at least as far back as far as 1500. The region was the domain of the Pochassic and Woronoco, both of which were part of the overall Algonquin Nation. The first European contact in the watershed was made by explorers John Cable and John Woodcock in 1635, and settlers arrived in the Westfield area during the late 1650s. Westfield was officially established in 1669 and held the distinction of the state's westernmost outpost until 1725, as the rugged, rocky Appalachian highlands to the west held little appeal to prospective settlers. Indeed, the hill towns of the upper valley weren't settled until the mid to late 18th century.

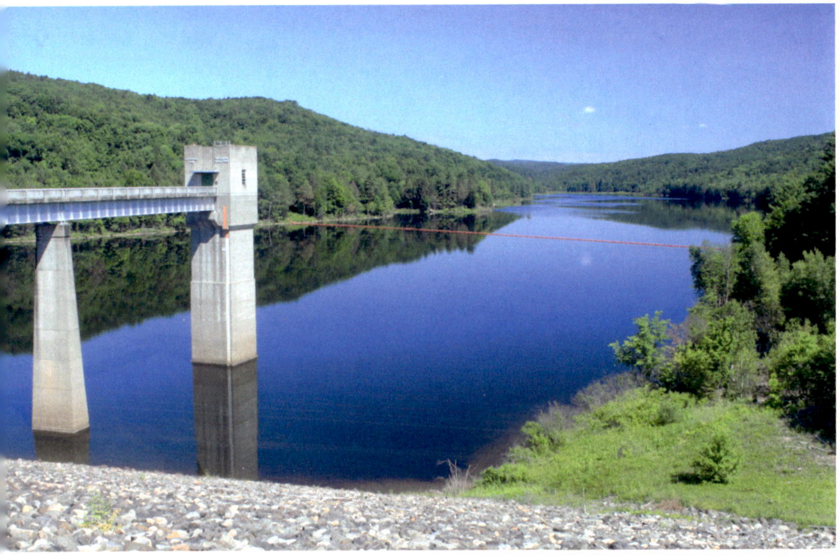

Scenic Littleville Lake stretches behind the Knightville Dam flood-control impoundment near the confluence of the three Westfield River branches in Huntington.

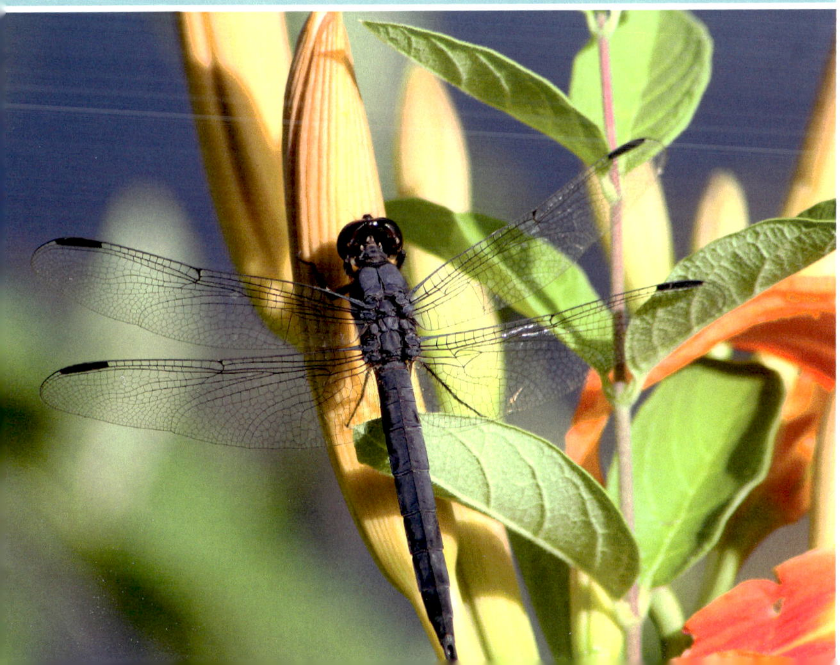

North of the center of Huntington, which was incorporated more than a century later than Westfield, the East and Middle Branches converge below the Knightville Dam, which was built in 1941 to mitigate damage in the flood-prone Westfield and Connecticut River Valleys. During the spring of 1987 alone, it saved residents and businesses an estimated $11 million dollars after heavy rains and melting snow caused a 50-foot rise behind the impoundment. Finger-like Littleville Lake stretches up the valley behind the dam and is the centerpiece of a popular 1,500-acre boating, swimming, and fishing area.

Somewhat lesser-known than the other two stems, the Middle Branch winds its way diagonally across the Berkshire foothills, slicing a course through remote rocky outcroppings, gorges, and cascades such as 50-foot West Worthington Falls. A number of uncommon species call these waters home, including eloquently named Harpoon Clubtail and Riffle Snaketail dragonflies and juvenile Atlantic salmon.

A slaty skimmer dragonfly perches on lilies while on hunting rounds at the edge of a wetland.

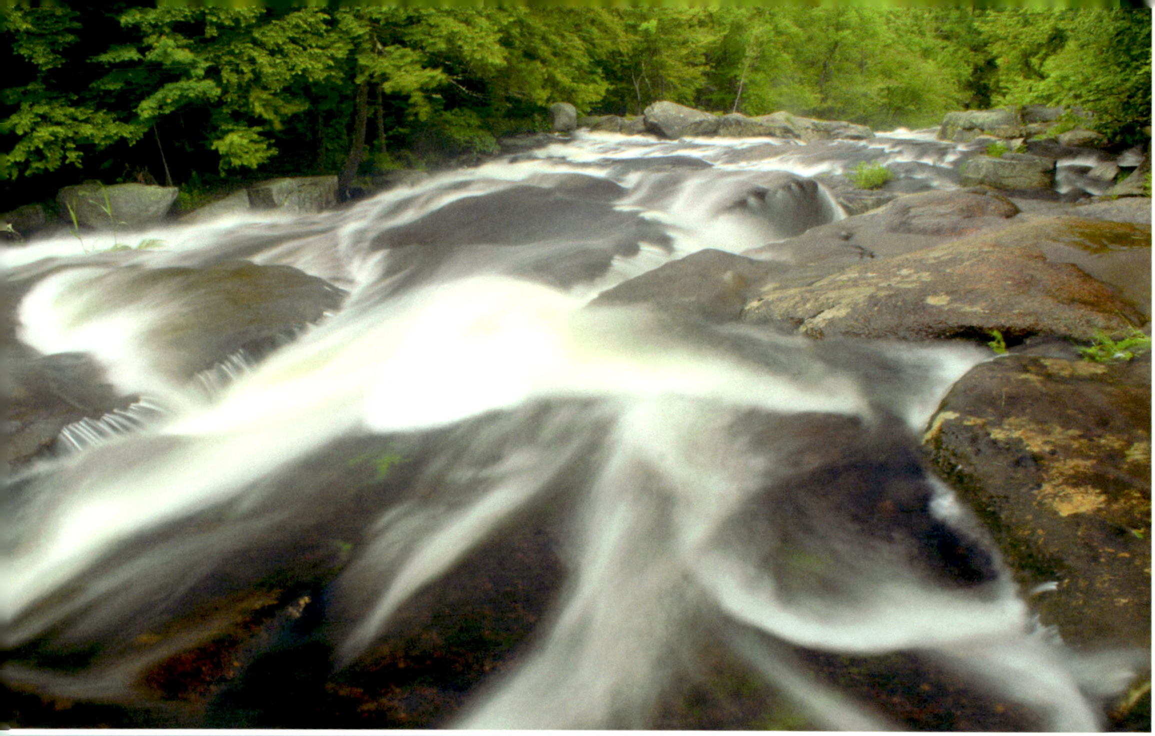

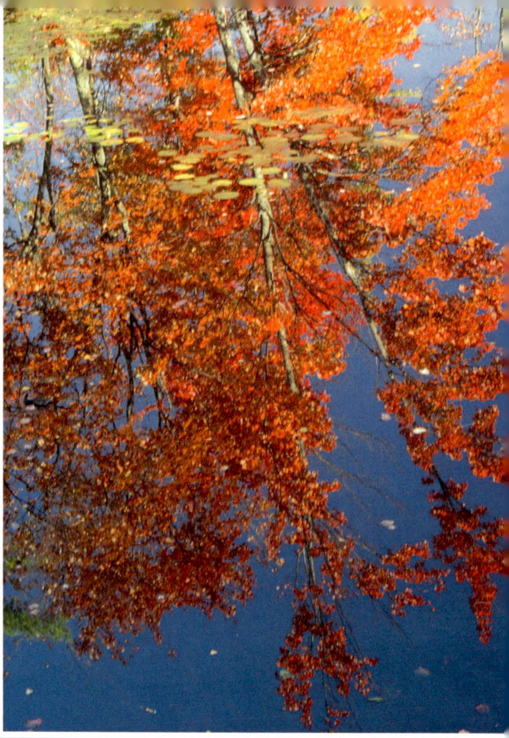

From the lip of Glendale Falls, one of the largest waterfalls in Massachusetts, the waters of Glendale Brook begin their long descent to the Middle Branch of the Westfield River.

Renowned for their brilliant foliage, red, or "swamp," maples are among the first trees to change color each autumn.

This valley's signature attraction is Glendale Falls, one of the largest waterfalls in Massachusetts. Here modest-sized Glendale Brook spreads into a long, wide chain of cascades framed by hemlocks, maples, birches, and colorful mountain laurel as it plunges more than 160 feet towards its confluence with the Middle Branch. From the 1060-foot high lip of the falls, there's a fine perspective of the hilly valley as the rushing waters begin their long descent over the granite rocks. When looking over this remote, densely forested area, it's hard to imagine that the rocky hillside adjacent to the falls was once cleared for pasture as part of the Glendale Farm.

Wetlands in the heart of the October Mountain State Forest, the largest state forest in Massachusetts, serve as the headwaters for the West Branch, which holds the significant distinction as the Commonwealth's longest unregulated waterway. As the river winds out of the central Berkshires through the towns of Middlefield and Chester, it churns beneath a series of giant stone arch railroad bridges known as the Keystone Arches. These distinctive spans were built as part of the Western Railroad, which, like the Hoosac Tunnel, was another engineering landmark that opened a crucial connection between markets in New England and New York State.

When the idea of a railroad through the heart of the Appalachian Mountains in western Massachusetts first came to light during the 1820s, one newspaper derided it as "useless as a railway to the moon" (a phrase also used when the Mount Washington Cog Railroad was proposed later in the century). Nevertheless, in the mid-1830s engineer Major George Washington Whistler was commissioned to design and build a line along the West Branch. Though the valley's rugged topography and the river's winding course presented a variety of engineering and logistical challenges, it also offered the lowest cumulative elevation gain of the potential routes.

After a painstaking surveying process that obliged engineers to coax frightened horses across the rocky slopes and use night signals from observation towers in the remote wilderness, the Western Railroad was completed in 1841. Nearly 30 bridges, including the ten stone arches, were built along its course through the narrow, winding valley. Among the many people impressed by the success of the new line was Czar Nicholas I of Russia, who subsequently commissioned Whistler to oversee the construction of the Trans-Siberian Railroad, the fabled 400-mile route that linked Moscow to Saint Petersburg.

In spite of their elaborate appearance, the bridges were actually cost-efficient, as the hardy stone structures required fewer maintenance expeditions to the remote hills by the railroad company. Several were abandoned when the line was rerouted to bypass some of the sharp curves, while others, including a distinctive double arch bridge, continue to be actively used by trains today. Three of the bridges were destroyed by the great flood of November 1927 after mill dams in Becket failed, sending torrents of water down the valley. The loss of these structures was a testament to the force of the flood, which also caused great damage throughout Vermont.

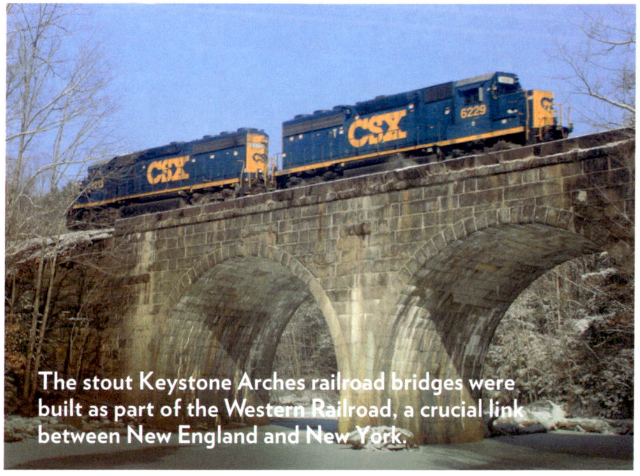

The stout Keystone Arches railroad bridges were built as part of the Western Railroad, a crucial link between New England and New York.

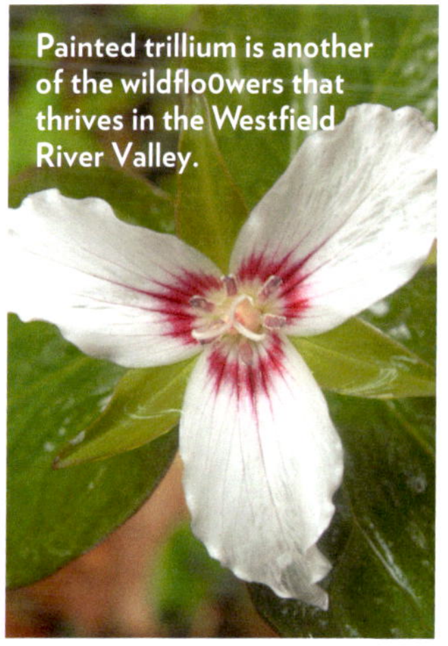
Painted trillium is another of the wildflo0wers that thrives in the Westfield River Valley.

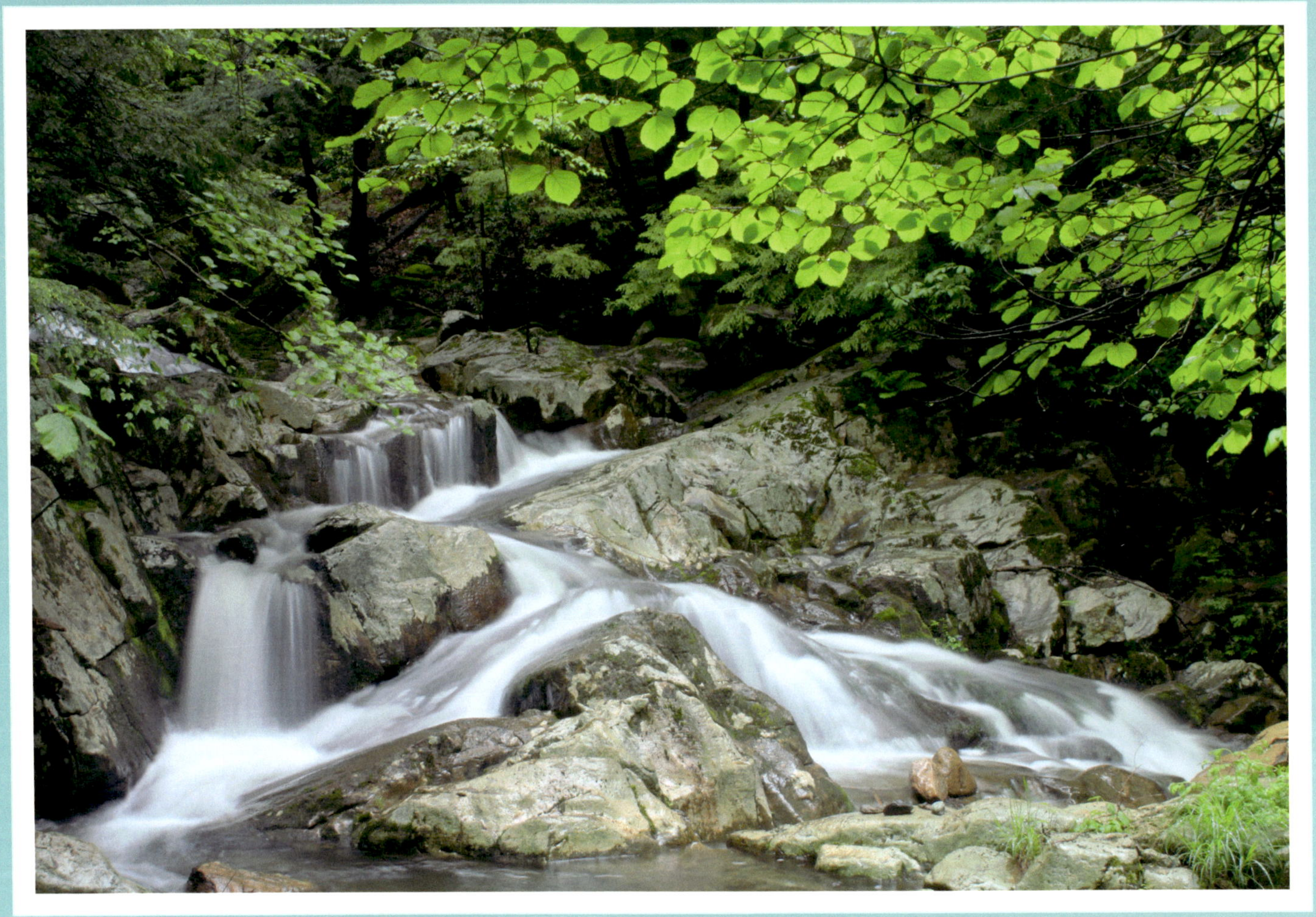

In addition to views of the historic bridges, the Keystone Arches Trail passes natural features such as this cascading stream.

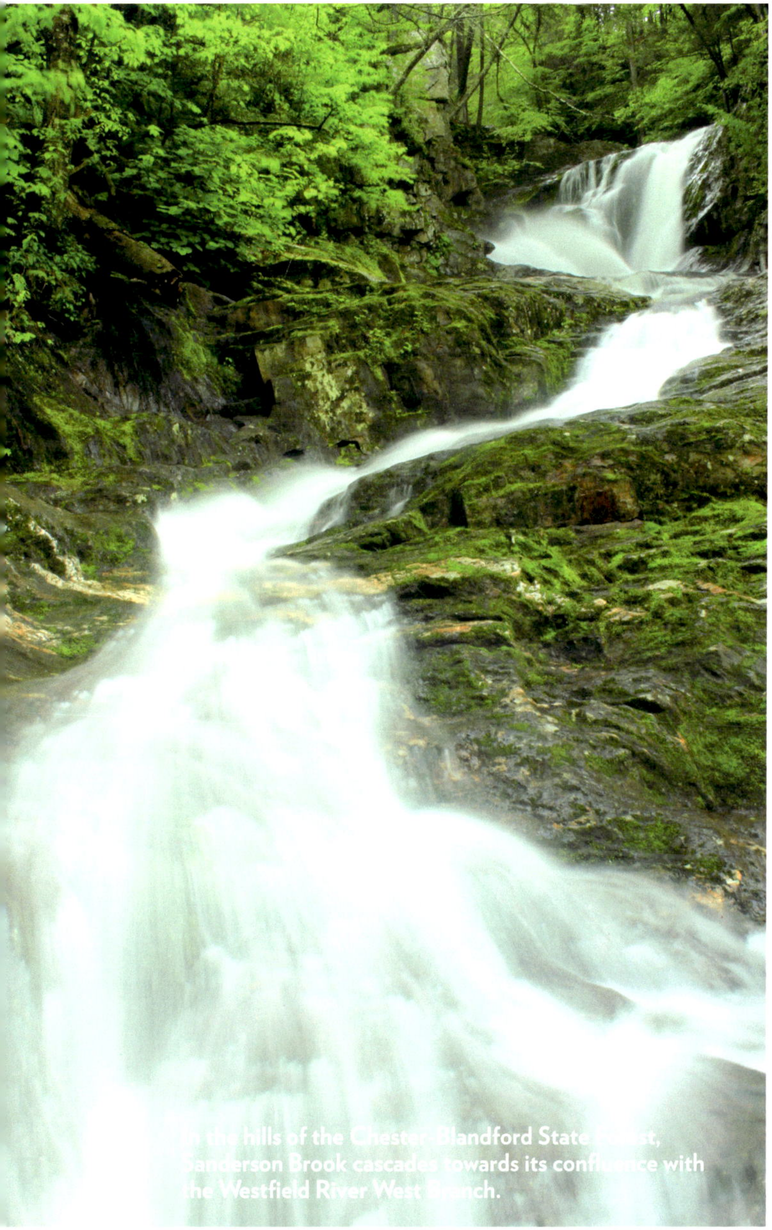

In the hills of the Chester-Blandford State Forest, Sanderson Brook cascades towards its confluence with the Westfield River West Branch.

Today, hikers enjoy a unique mix of history and backcountry scenery along the Keystone Arches Recreational Trail, which begins on Middlefield Road north of Chester and follows an old turnpike and rail line along and above the riverbank. A river-level view of the double arch bridge and a small waterfall is just a few hundred feet from the trailhead, while the abandoned bridges near the western end of the route offer fine perspectives of the valley hills and a deep river gorge. Freight and passenger trains regularly rumble along the opposite bank, linking the past and present and underscoring the legacy of the original Western Railroad.

Another hint of the valley's past are the names of some of the natural features and trails at the nearby Chester-Blandford State Forest, such as "Gold Mine Brook" and "Mica Mine Road." Indeed, these hillsides were once pocketed with small mines and quarries where minerals were extracted out of the steep slopes. Today the main attraction of the 2300-acre state forest is Sanderson Brook Falls, named for the tumbling waterway that drops 75 feet in a series of cascades and pools en route to its confluence with the West Branch. The Newman-Marsh Trail, which was created by the Civilian Conservation Corps during in the 1930s, offers a good sampling of the rugged terrain as it follows a steep slope to a high ridge with an overview of the valley.

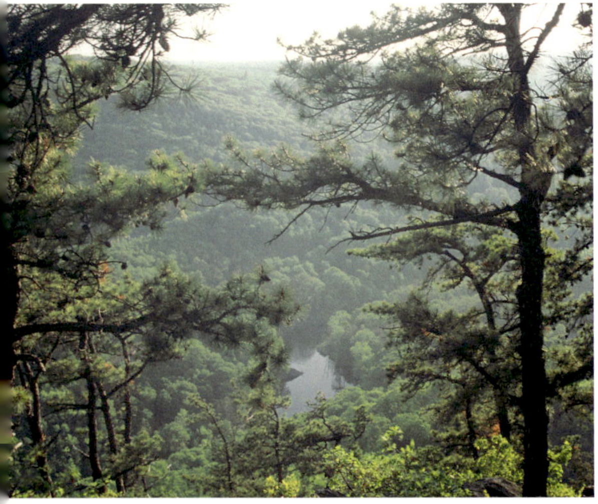

Regionally uncommon pitch pine trees frame this perspective of the Westfield River from the summit ridge of Tekoa Mountain.

A short distance downstream from the confluence of the Middle and East Branches in Huntington, the West Branch completes the main stem, which continues on a southeasterly course towards the gentler terrain of the Connecticut Valley. Rising above a long highway bridge on the Massachusetts Turnpike near Westfield is Tekoa Mountain, a low but rugged eminence easily distinguished by its partially barren slopes and ridge. These are the legacy of large fires caused by lightning in 1994, 1999, and other years; as related by Bruce Scofield in *Hiking the Pioneer Valley*, "during the fire in April of 1994, [a] small clearing did not burn and we found it filled with birds and wildlife that were escaping the flames." The 1,120-foot summit is capped by groves of regionally uncommon pitch pine trees, a hardy species that thrives in marginal growing conditions other species can't tolerate. Similar ridge top communities are a true rarity in the Northeast; others exist on Mount Everett in the Berkshires and Bear Mountain in northwestern Connecticut.

Tekoa Mountain's scenic views of the Westfield and Connecticut Valleys served a practical purpose for Patriot soldiers during the American Revolution, who used the lookouts to scan the countryside for British soldiers and spies. During the war years, the north slopes also sheltered a secret armory, where local resident and Bunker Hill veteran Richard Falley built muskets for the Continental Army.

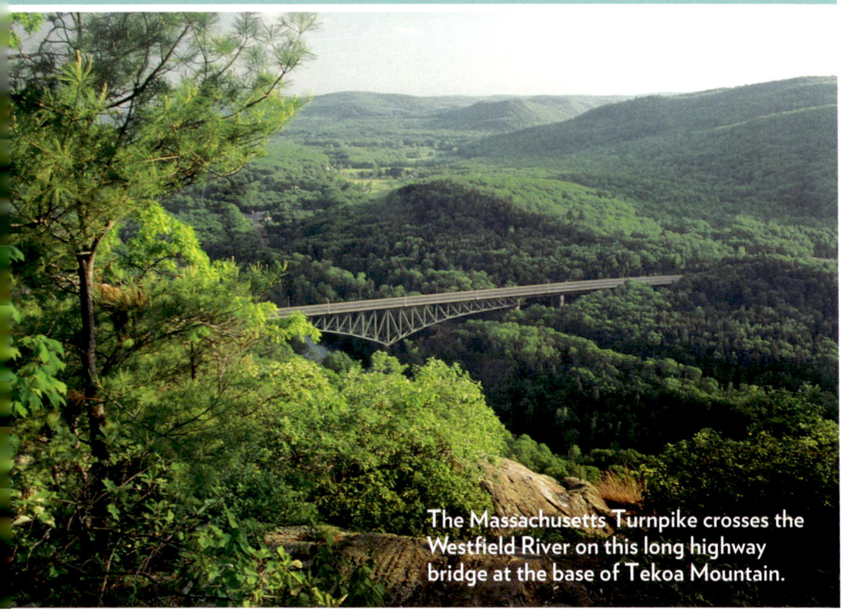

The Massachusetts Turnpike crosses the Westfield River on this long highway bridge at the base of Tekoa Mountain.

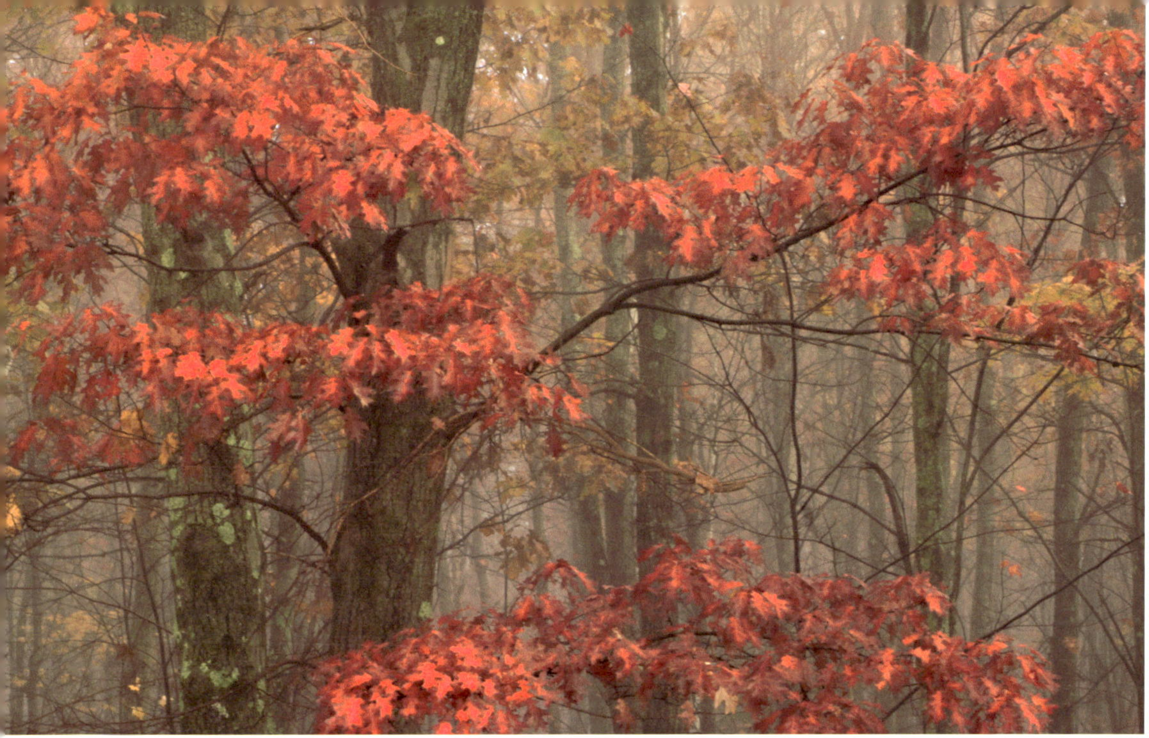

As the fall foliage season draws to a close, late-turning oaks and beeches add a final splash of color to the lowlands near the mouth of the Westfield River.

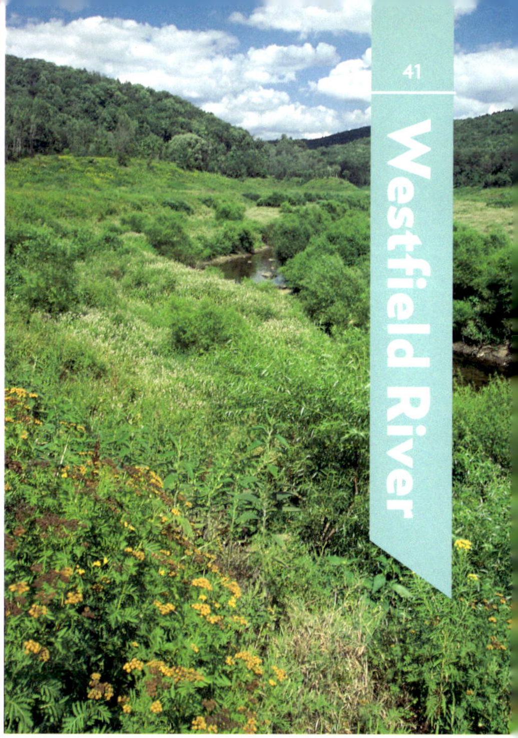

This wildlife area above the Knightville Dam offers diverse habitats that benefit a variety of flora and fauna.

The past century has seen significant changes in the use of the Westfield Valley's natural resources. Not surprisingly, as happened throughout most of New England, farmers largely abandoned the hills and their rocky soils by the close of the 19th century, allowing much of the watershed to gradually revert back to forest. Paper manufacturing became an important industry during the early 20th century, as evidenced by the establishment of several large mills from 1911 to 1928. Manufacturing tailed off as the century progressed, particularly during the Great Depression years, and few mills remain today. Today, the watershed supports a number of public water supply reservoirs, including the Cobble Mountain system, which is the largest in Massachusetts outside of the Quabbin/Wachusett network and serves a quarter-million residents in the Pioneer Valley.

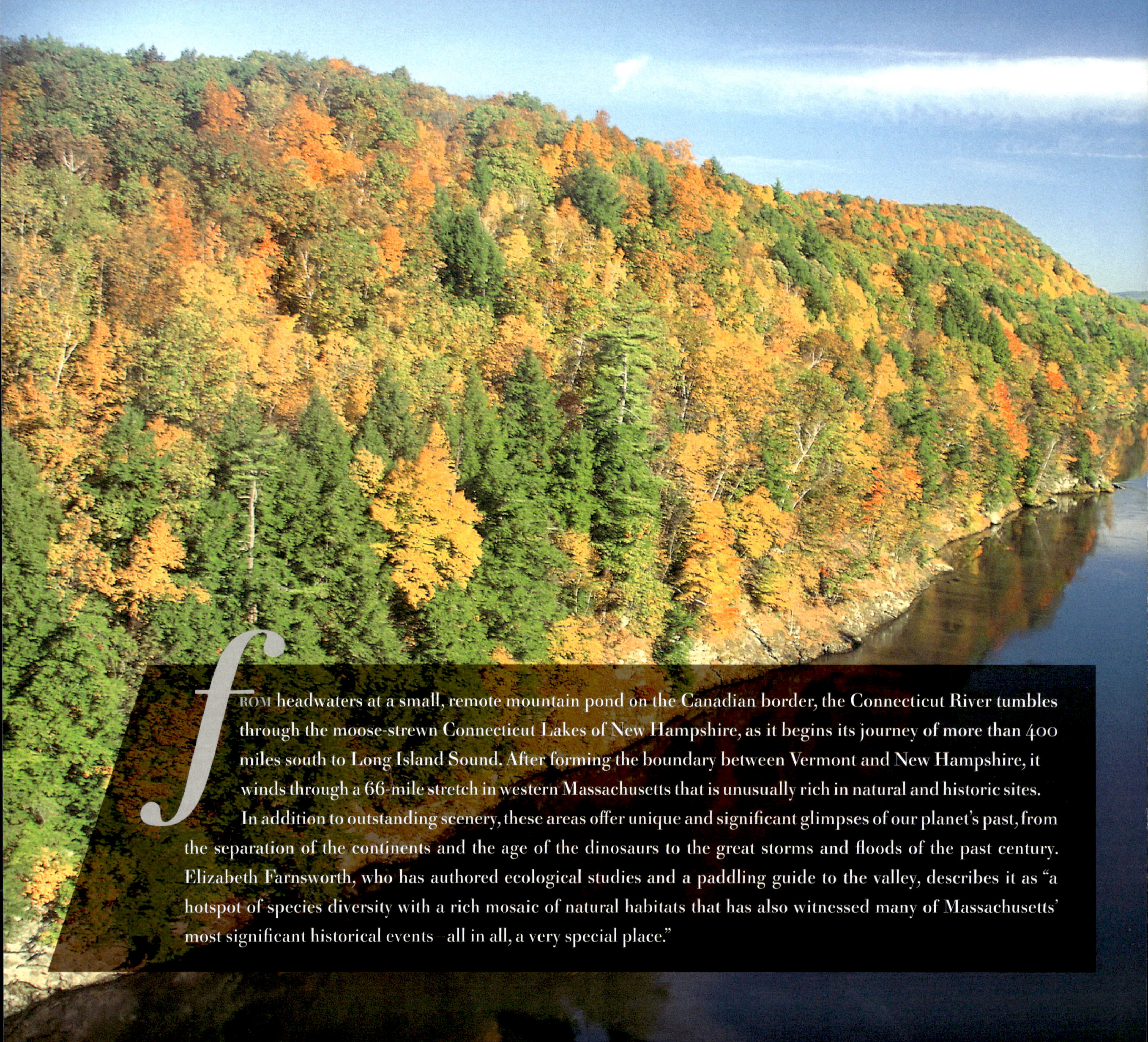

FROM headwaters at a small, remote mountain pond on the Canadian border, the Connecticut River tumbles through the moose-strewn Connecticut Lakes of New Hampshire, as it begins its journey of more than 400 miles south to Long Island Sound. After forming the boundary between Vermont and New Hampshire, it winds through a 66-mile stretch in western Massachusetts that is unusually rich in natural and historic sites.

In addition to outstanding scenery, these areas offer unique and significant glimpses of our planet's past, from the separation of the continents and the age of the dinosaurs to the great storms and floods of the past century. Elizabeth Farnsworth, who has authored ecological studies and a paddling guide to the valley, describes it as "a hotspot of species diversity with a rich mosaic of natural habitats that has also witnessed many of Massachusetts' most significant historical events—all in all, a very special place."

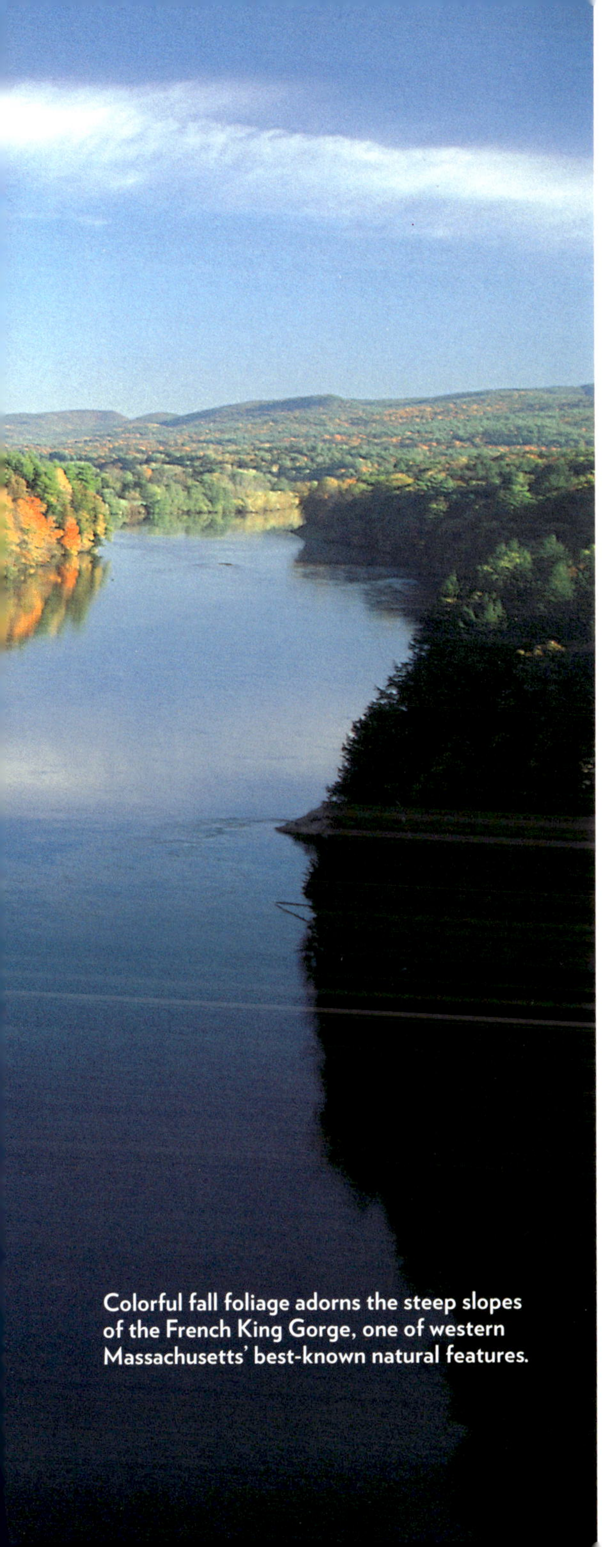

Colorful fall foliage adorns the steep slopes of the French King Gorge, one of western Massachusetts' best-known natural features.

The French King Gorge is an appropriate starting point for an overview of the Connecticut Valley, as not only is it one of western Massachusetts' most popular attractions, but it also offers a window into the origins of the valley more than 250 million years ago. As the earth's continents began to assume their present form, North America and Africa nearly diverged along the Eastern Border Fault, a 130-mile long fracture that stretched from New Haven, Connecticut to Keene, New Hampshire. Had this happened, present-day Springfield, Northampton, and Greenfield would have become coastal communities, and the Boston area would have drifted away as part of Africa (a concept that some western residents would undeniably warm to). The Border Fault's legacy was an ancient (or "rift") valley that ultimately evolved into the Connecticut River Valley as we know it today. Similar processes formed Death Valley in California and several historic valleys in Africa.

The Border Fault runs through the heart of the French King Gorge, and the steep walls offer geologists and rock hounds ample artifacts of the valley's history. On the east bank are older metamorphic rocks from the Paleozoic era, while those on the west bank are millions of years younger and sedimentary, formed by a series of volcanoes and lava spurts associated with the fault. Out of sight far below the waterline are the two deepest points along the Connecticut River's 410-mile long riverbed, a 130-foot abyss and a 100-foot underwater cliff.

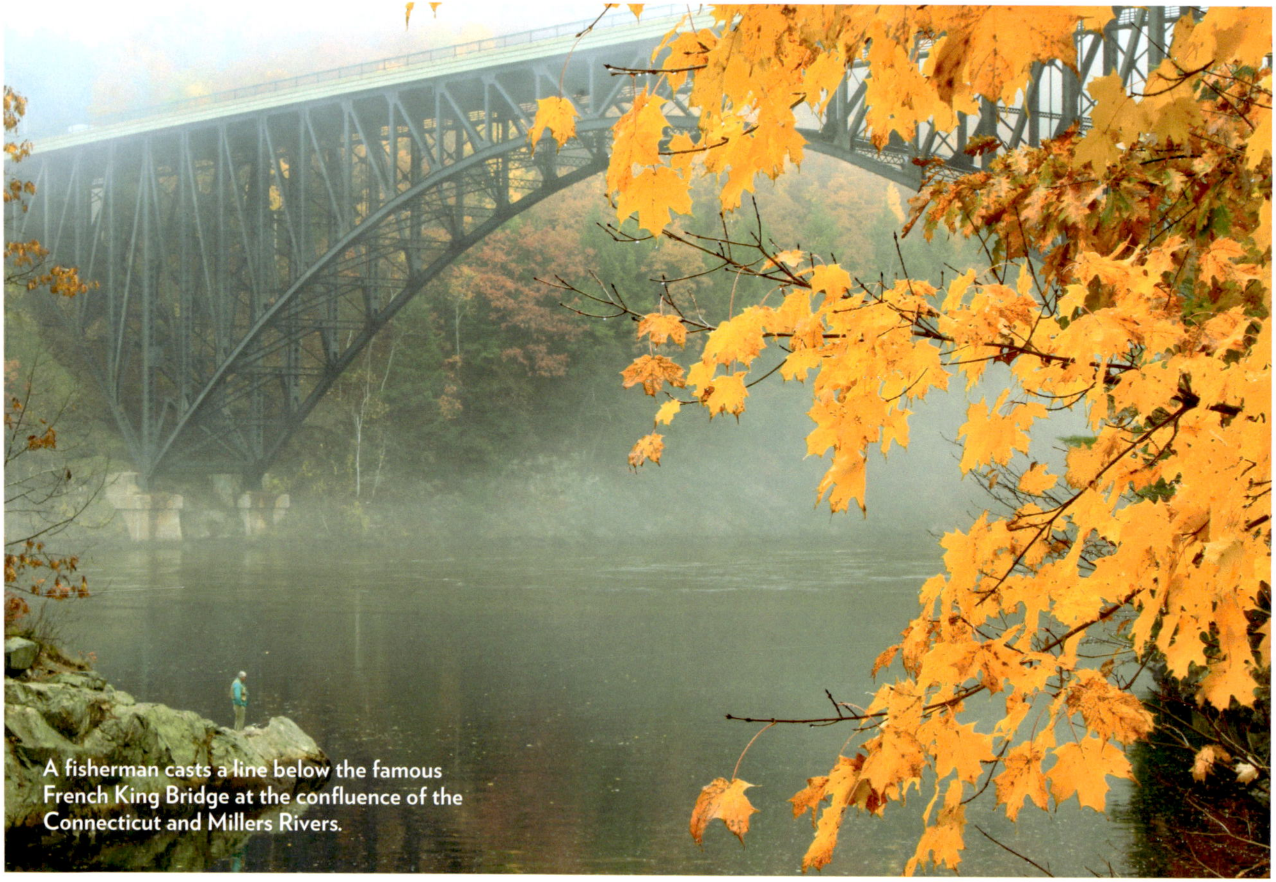

A fisherman casts a line below the famous French King Bridge at the confluence of the Connecticut and Millers Rivers.

The gorge has been a popular tourist destination since 1932, when the famous French King Bridge was built across its top. The new span and an adjacent six-mile highway offered a safer passage across the upper valley that the previous route, which obliged motorists to negotiate a winding, rather dangerous roadway between Turners Falls and Millers Falls. More than 15,000 people attended the opening ceremony for the bridge on September 10th, which included a parade that featured historic transportation along the Mohawk Trail, including oxen-drawn carts and horse carriages. The bridge, which has received many engineering awards, offers visitors striking views of the valley from 135 feet above the river, while boaters enjoy river-level perspectives of the steep walls.

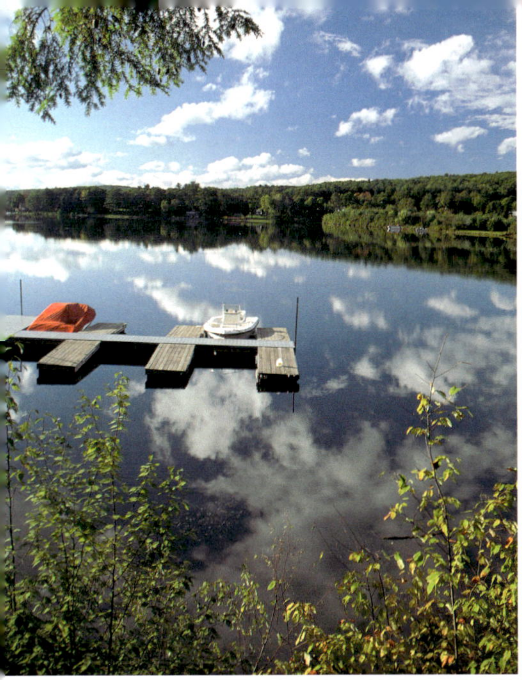

Adjacent to the French King Gorge is scenic Barton Cove, home to nesting bald eagles and a variety of waterfowl.

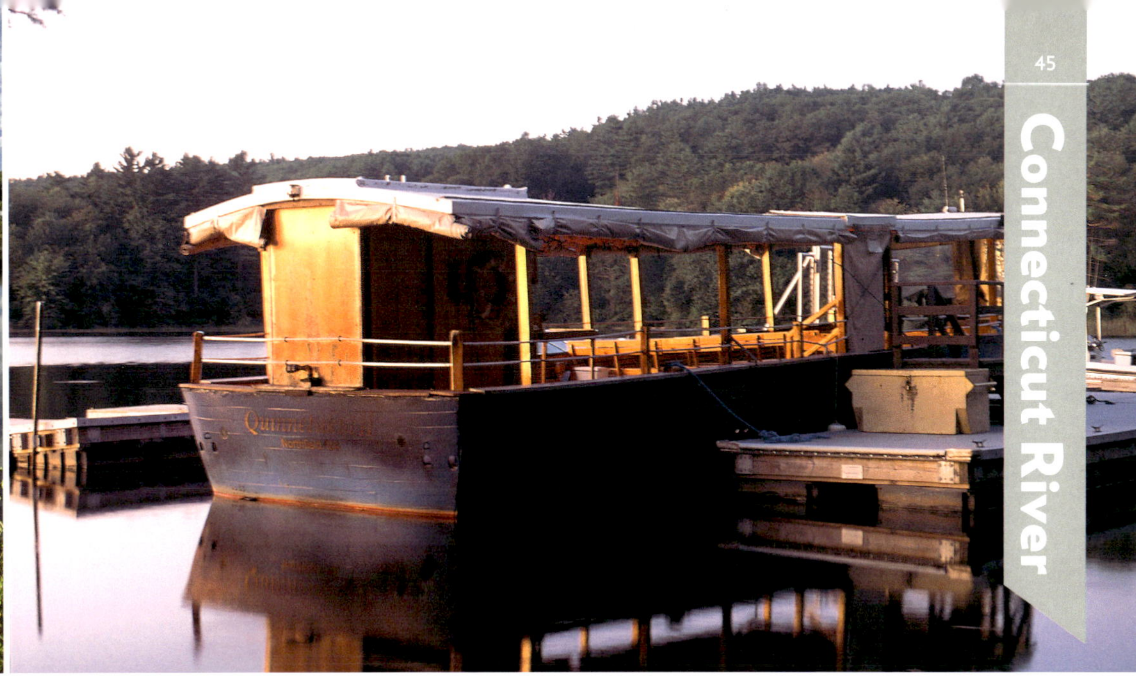

The Quinnetucket II tour boat has offered tourists a river-level perspective of the French King Gorge and Barton Cove for more than 30 years.

At a sharp bend in the Connecticut River near the southern end of the gorge is picturesque Barton Cove, which formed when the nearby Turners Falls Dam was built in the late 18th century. Historically, it was once the site of two giant glacial waterfalls, and, as will be detailed shortly, dinosaur tracks have been uncovered in its rocky outcroppings. The cove is now well-known as an excellent birding location that has hosted nesting bald eagles for many years. Indeed, a recent storm brought down a long-established nest that may have weighed a ton or more, but fortunately the eagles were satisfied enough with the fishing that they have made a new home in another nearby tree. Other birds that have visited the cove include locally rare cackling geese and red-headed woodpeckers, and large flocks of migratory waterfowl.

Another, more prominent legacy of the Border Fault volcanoes is the Metacomet Range, a 100-mile long chain of low mountains and ridges that extends from Greenfield to the Connecticut coast. Familiar Connecticut Valley landmarks such as Mount Tom, the Holyoke Range, Mount Sugarloaf, Mount Toby, and the Pocumtuck Ridge are all products of these ancient eruptions. With their distinctive basalt (or "traprock") formations comprised of hardened lava, the Metacomet mountains represent some of the world's best-preserved examples of historic volcanoes.

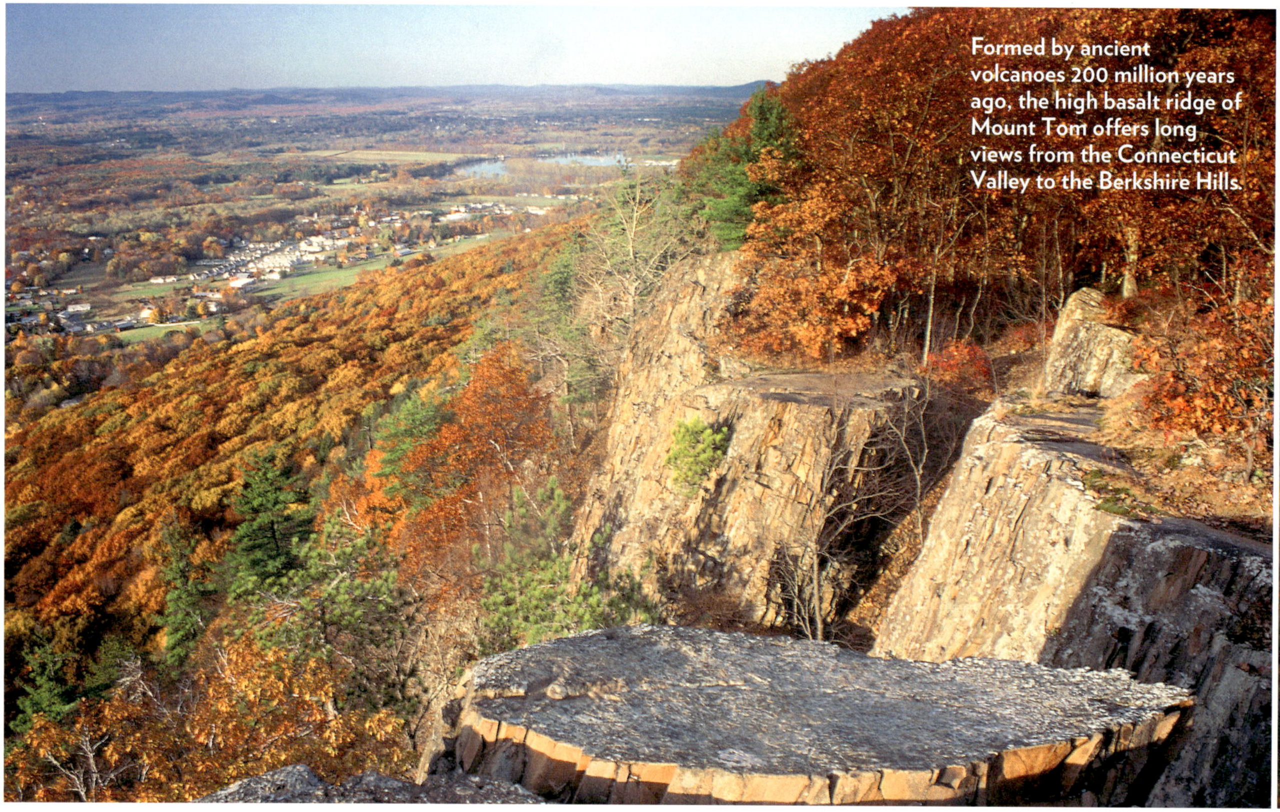

Formed by ancient volcanoes 200 million years ago, the high basalt ridge of Mount Tom offers long views from the Connecticut Valley to the Berkshire Hills.

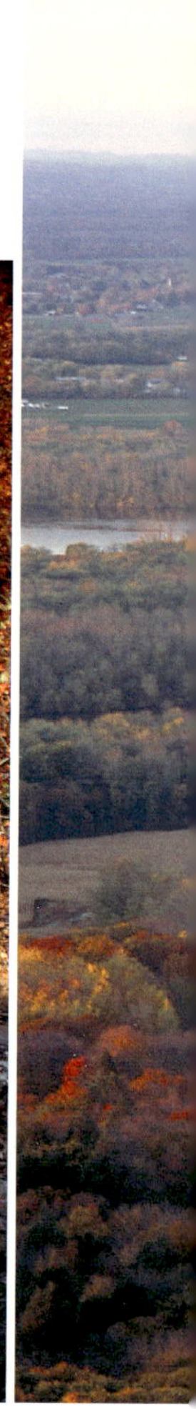

With its array of sheer cliffs, basalt columns, and exposed ledges, the spectacular long summit ridge of Mount Tom, which protrudes above the countryside of Easthampton and Holyoke, offers arguably the most dramatic views of the unique traprock geology. Large flocks of migrating hawks and songbirds pass along the ridge during their annual journeys to and from wintering grounds in central America. Human fliers also are drawn to these cliffs, as the ridge is a popular launching point for hang-gliders. The 1201-foot summit, easily identified from afar by its array of communications towers (it lies just outside of the state reservation boundary), was home to two elaborate but short-lived hotels that were lost to fires between 1897 and 1929. Other now-defunct developments included a large amusement park on the east slopes from 1897 to 1988, and the Mount Tom Ski Area, which closed in 1998 after nearly 40 years of operations.

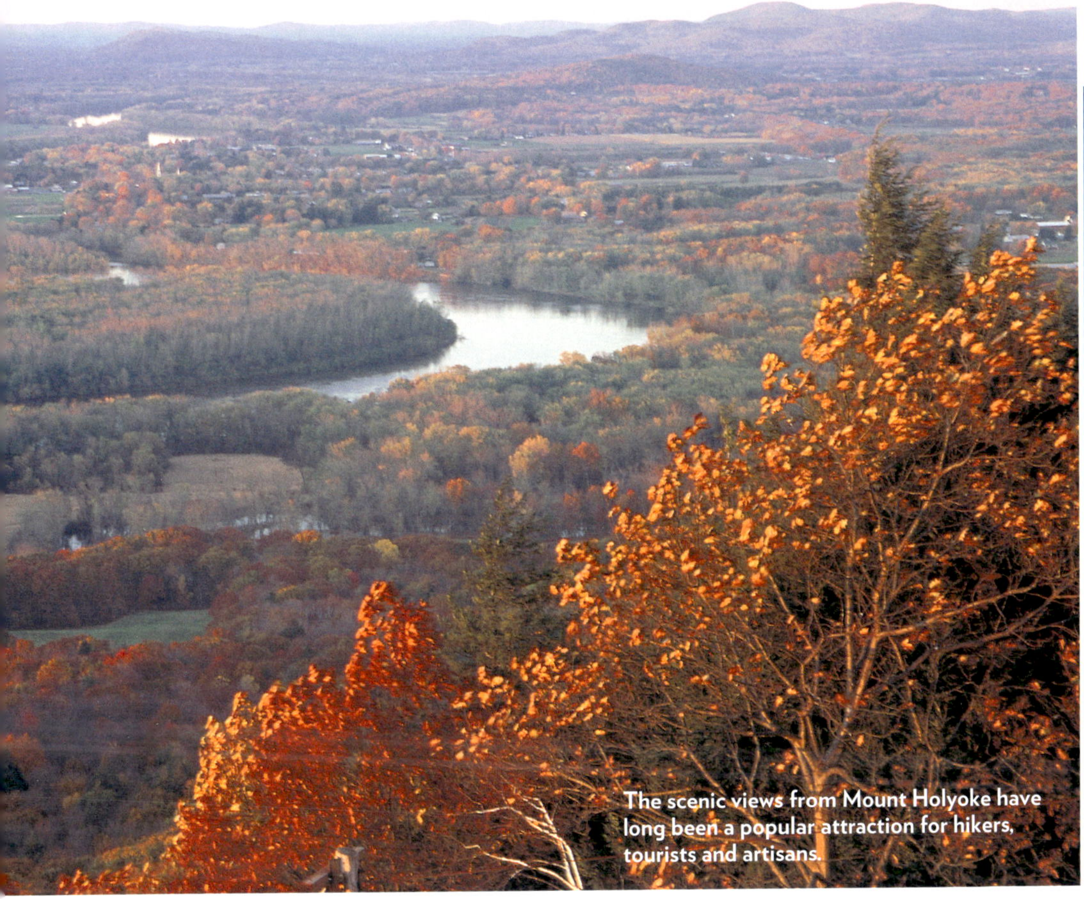

The scenic views from Mount Holyoke have long been a popular attraction for hikers, tourists and artisans.

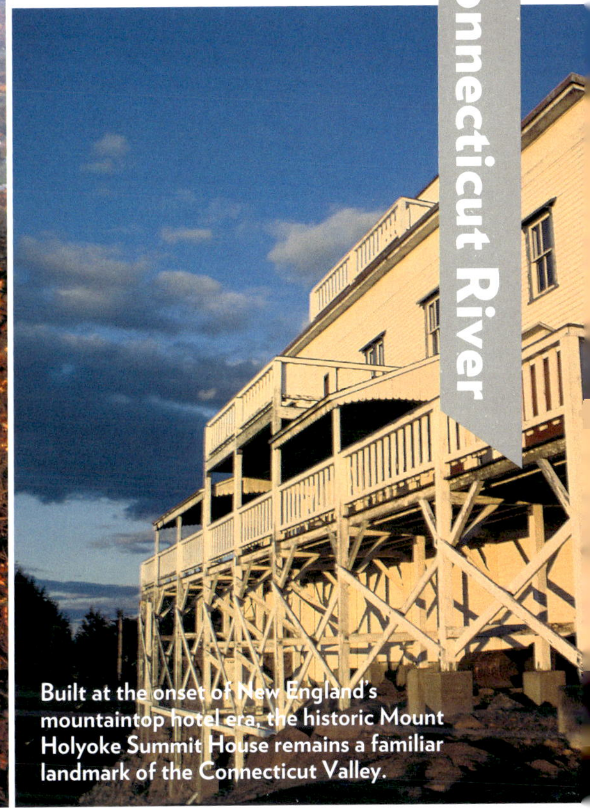

Built at the onset of New England's mountaintop hotel era, the historic Mount Holyoke Summit House remains a familiar landmark of the Connecticut Valley.

Arguably the most famous rendition of the Metacomet Range is acclaimed artist Thomas Cole's *The Oxbow*, a seminal American landscape painting (1836) that depicts a thunderstorm clearing a bend in the Connecticut River near Northampton. On the margins of the scene, dark, ominous clouds pass over groves of untamed forest, while golden sunlight illuminates pastoral fields in the valley below. The painting has long been a popular and much-discussed subject of for art scholars and landscape historians, who generally interpret it as representing America's transition from a savage wilderness to a civilized, well-managed land (nowadays, of course, natural settings and old forests are viewed in a favorable light).

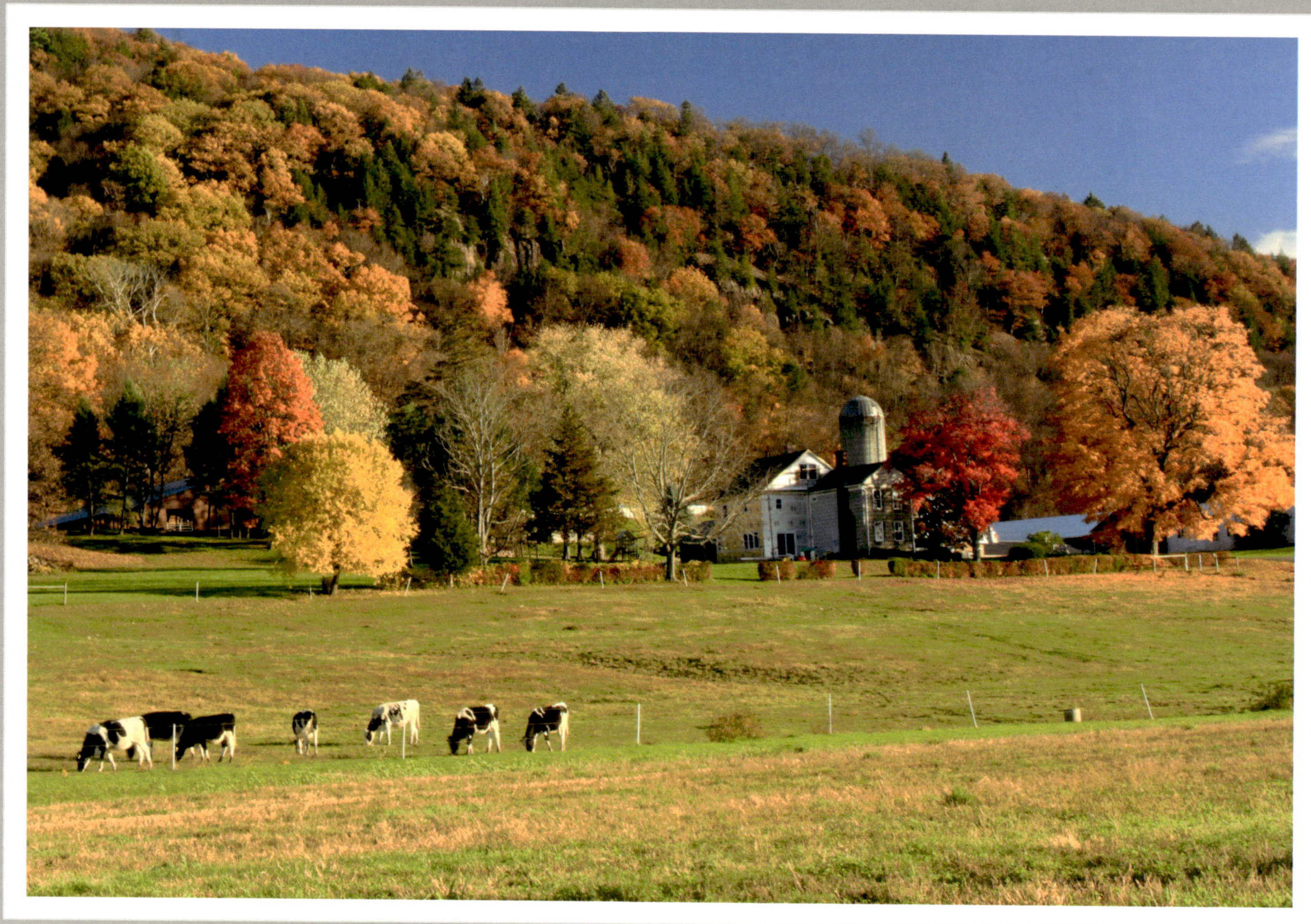

Mount Holyoke's summit ridge rises high above Barstow's Longview Farm near the east banks of the Connecticut River in South Hadley.

Cole's vantage was the summit of Mount Holyoke, the westernmost of a chain of low, bump-like peaks that rise out of the long ridge of the Holyoke Range across the valley from Mount Tom. Even before his painting, the mountain's increasing popularity in the early 19th century inspired several enterprising businessmen from Northampton to build a small cabin on the summit in 1821 that saw several thousand visitors annually. It was followed in mid-century by the Summit House, an elaborate mountaintop hotel erected at the onset of an era when similar structures were built atop many of New England's familiar peaks, including nearby Mounts Tom, Sugarloaf, and Toby, and even the windswept heights of New Hampshire's Mount Washington. Charles Dickens and singer Jenny Lind were among the many notable guests of the Summit House; Abraham Lincoln's name appears in the guestbook, but the signature was likely a well-crafted forgery. 1938 was a year of transition for the mountain, as damage from the great September 21st hurricane ended the hotel's commercial operations and prompted the establishment of the present state park.

Beneath the ridge of Bare Mountain, which offers additional fine views across the countryside of Amherst and Hadley, is the Notch, a narrow gap in the range, where Route 116 snakes past a popular state park visitor center. A short distance further east is the highest peak of the chain, 1,106-foot Mount Norwottuck, home to sweeping views that include Mount Greylock, the southern Green Mountains, Mount Monadnock, and the surrounding Pioneer Valley.

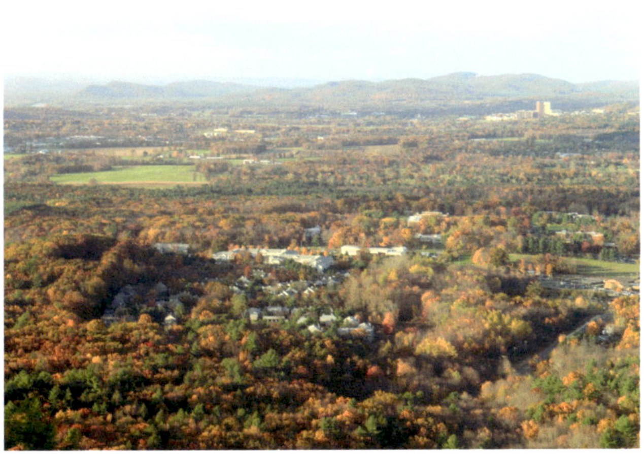

From the Notch of the Holyoke Range, the rocky ledges of Bare Mountain offer views across Amherst and the Connecticut Valley.

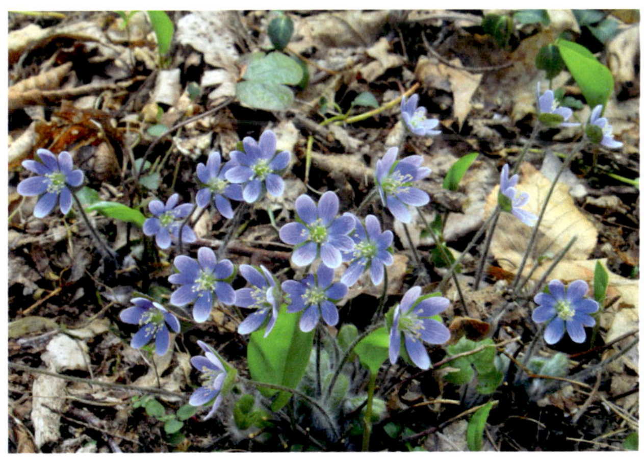

A welcome early sign of spring, a colony of round-lobed hepatica wildflowers emerges from the rocky ledges of Mount Norwottuck near the Horse Caves.

Below Mount Norwottuck's summit are the "Horse Caves," rock ledges that were reputedly used as a hideout by Daniel Shays and fellow western Massachusetts during the tax revolt known as Shays' Rebellion. This uprising stemmed from heavy taxes that were causing western residents to lose their farms and homes, many of which were earned through service during the American Revolution. In response, Shays, who had served with distinction as a captain during the war, and a band of fellow disgruntled farmers began their rebellion against the state in 1786.

After disrupting the courthouses at Springfield and Northampton, the militia made an ill-fated attempt to occupy the armory at Springfield, during which they were driven away by government soldiers. Most of the rebels were subsequently captured after they returned to the Swift River Valley, though Shays escaped to Vermont. Though the rebellion initially earned Shays a death sentence *in absentia*, he was pardoned in 1788 and lived the rest of his life in upstate New York. In a supreme bit of irony, Shays lived in and planned the rebellion at a tavern in a village that was subsequently incorporated as the town of Prescott, which was one of the four Swift River Valley towns taken over by the state and flooded during the creation of Quabbin Reservoir as a water supply for Boston and eastern Massachusetts during the 20th century. The portion of Route 202 along the western perimeter of the reservoir was named in Shays's honor; one can only imagine what his feelings might be on the matter.

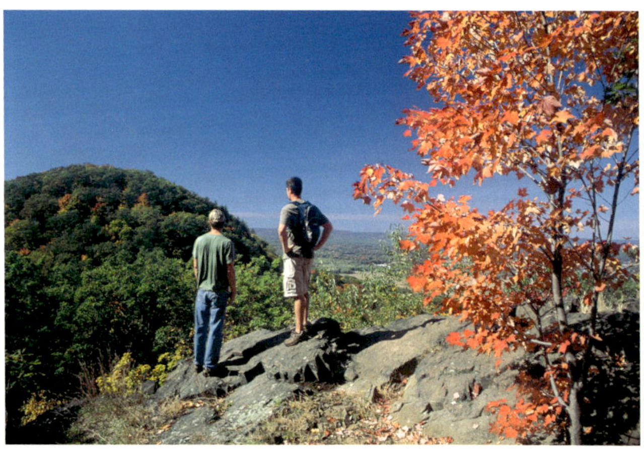

Hikers enjoy one of the numerous vistas of the Holyoke Range, which is a highlight of the long-distance New England National Scenic Trail.

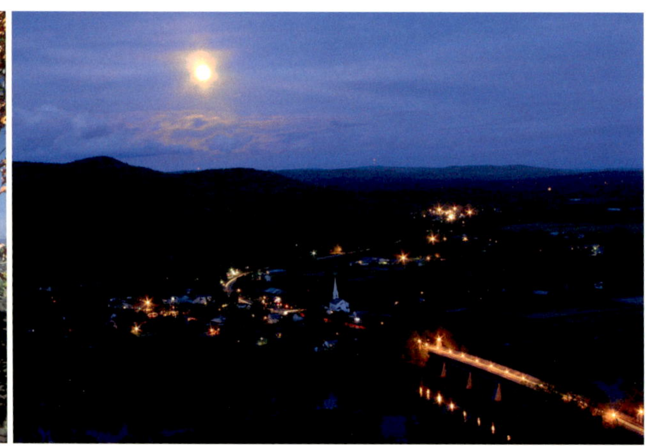

A full spring moon rises over the village of Sunderland and the Connecticut River, as seen from the summit of Mount Sugarloaf.

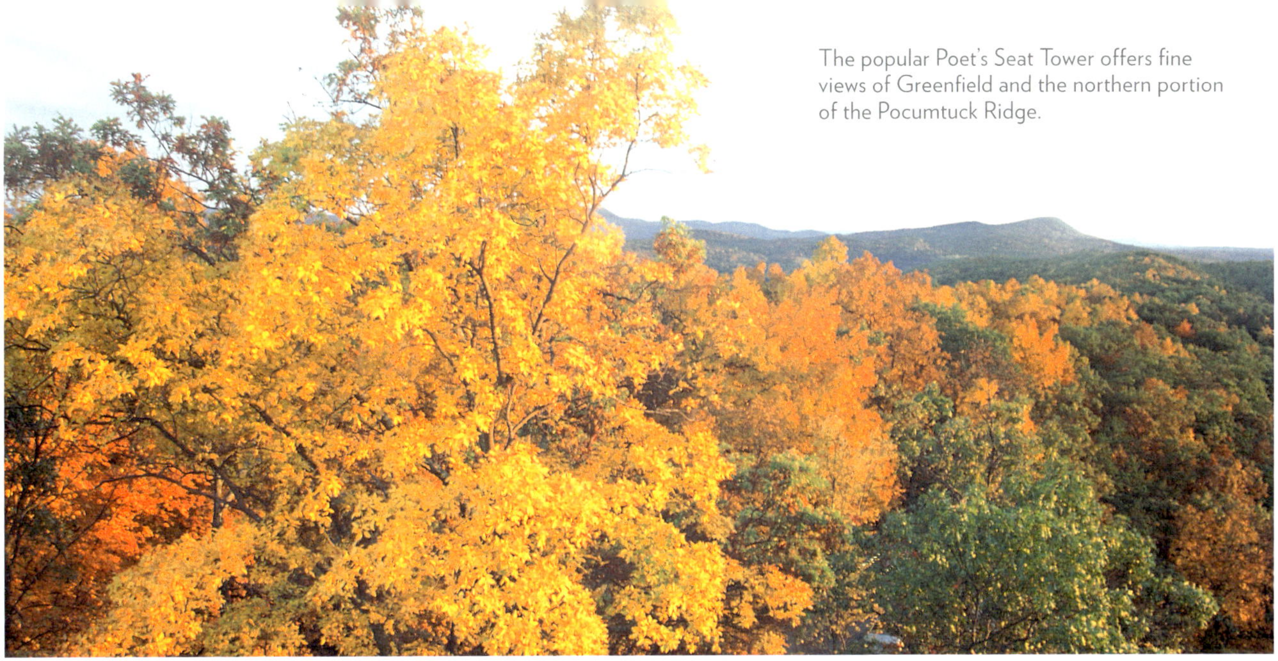

The popular Poet's Seat Tower offers fine views of Greenfield and the northern portion of the Pocumtuck Ridge.

Today, Mount Tom, the Holyoke Range, and many of the region's other natural attractions are linked as part of the New England National Scenic Trail corridor. This long-distance footpath, which extends 230 miles from the Connecticut coast to New Hampshire, received federal National Scenic Trail designation in 2009, putting it in the company of elite hiking routes such as the Appalachian, Pacific Crest, and Nez Perce Trails. The New England National Scenic Trail combines two historic paths, the Mattabesett Trail in Connecticut and the Metacomet-Monadnock Trail in western Massachusetts. The latter, which was first conceived by University of Massachusetts Professor Walter Banfield during the 1950s, connects the Metacomet hills and ridges of the valley to the central uplands and the popular summit of Mount Monadnock in southern New Hampshire (the New Hampshire portion of the trail presently does not have federal designation).

Another of the region's scenic footpaths is the 15-mile long Pocumtuck Ridge Trail, which connects the popular lookouts atop South Sugarloaf Mountain in South Deerfield and Rocky Mountain in Greenfield. Though roughly half the size of Mount Tom at a modest 652 feet, South Sugarloaf boasts one of the finest views of the Connecticut Valley, a classic New England scene of pastoral fields, forested hills, and the village of Sunderland, marked by a white church steeple that rises above the river. According to Native lore, the mountain is the remains of a giant, human-eating beaver that once roamed the waters of Lake Hitchcock, a massive glacial lake that once filled the valley (more on this shortly). In 2008, the south summit was used as a setting in the movie *Edge of Darkness*. The much quieter north summit is slightly higher and wooded, though rock ledges offer additional views across South Deerfield and the Berkshire foothills.

At the northern end of the range, Rocky Mountain is well-known as the home of the Poet's Seat lookout, so named because it was a favored destination for local 19th-century wordsmiths such as Frederick Goddard Tuckerman, who, in addition to his sonnets, was also an authority on Franklin County flora. After Tuckerman's death in 1873, a wooden lookout tower was erected on the summit, followed in 1912 by the current Poet's Seat Tower, a hefty sandstone structure with fine views of Greenfield and the upper Connecticut Valley. Roughly one mile south of the tower at the southern end of the ridge are the rugged cliffs, ledges, and caves of "Sachem's Head," which offer additional views of scenery and unusual rock formations.

Looming above the east banks of the Connecticut River opposite the Pocumtuck Ridge is the highest point of the Connecticut Valley in Massachusetts, the 1269-foot summit of Mount Toby. Ever since the first known climb by settler Elnathan Toby, for whom the eminence is believed to be named, its views from the nearby Connecticut River and Holyoke Range to the distant profiles of Mounts Greylock and Monadnock have drawn hikers and tourists, including guests of yet another popular 19th-century summit hotel. In 1916, the University of Massachusetts established a 750-acre research forest on the mountain that has been used for a variety of forestry and ecological studies; other recent land additions have created a 1500-acre preserve that extends to the river.

On the lower slopes of Mount Toby, the mossy ravine of Roaring Brook Falls is home to spring wildflowers and a picturesque seasonal cascade.

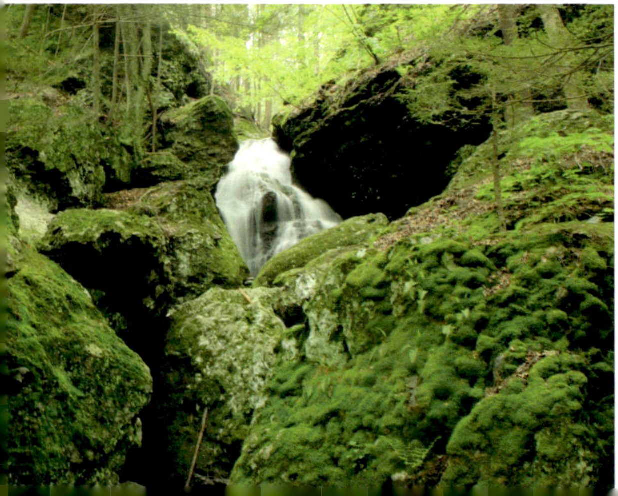

The mass of Mount Toby, the highest point of the Connecticut Valley in Massachusetts, rises high above the east banks of the river near Sunderland.

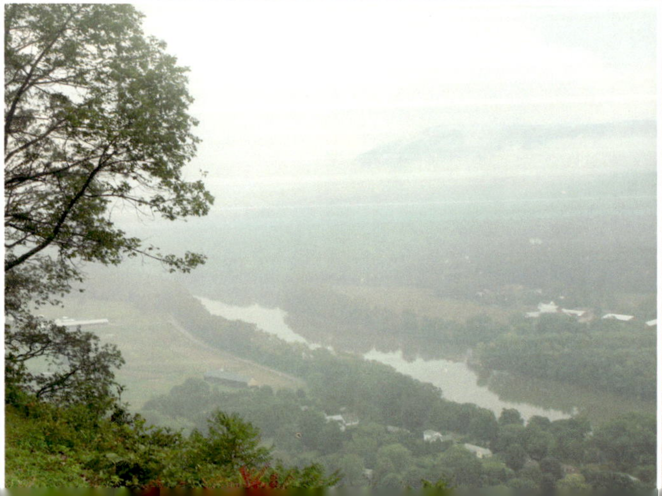

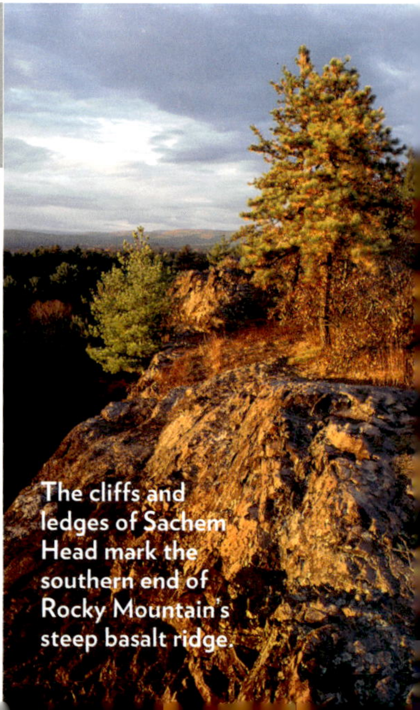

The cliffs and ledges of Sachem Head mark the southern end of Rocky Mountain's steep basalt ridge.

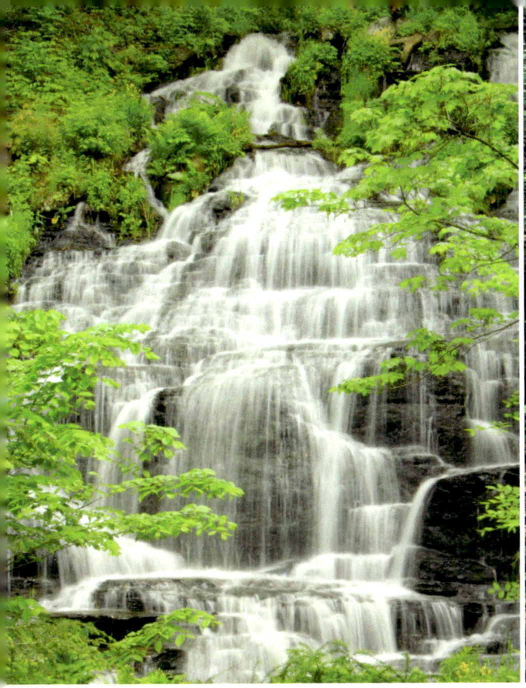

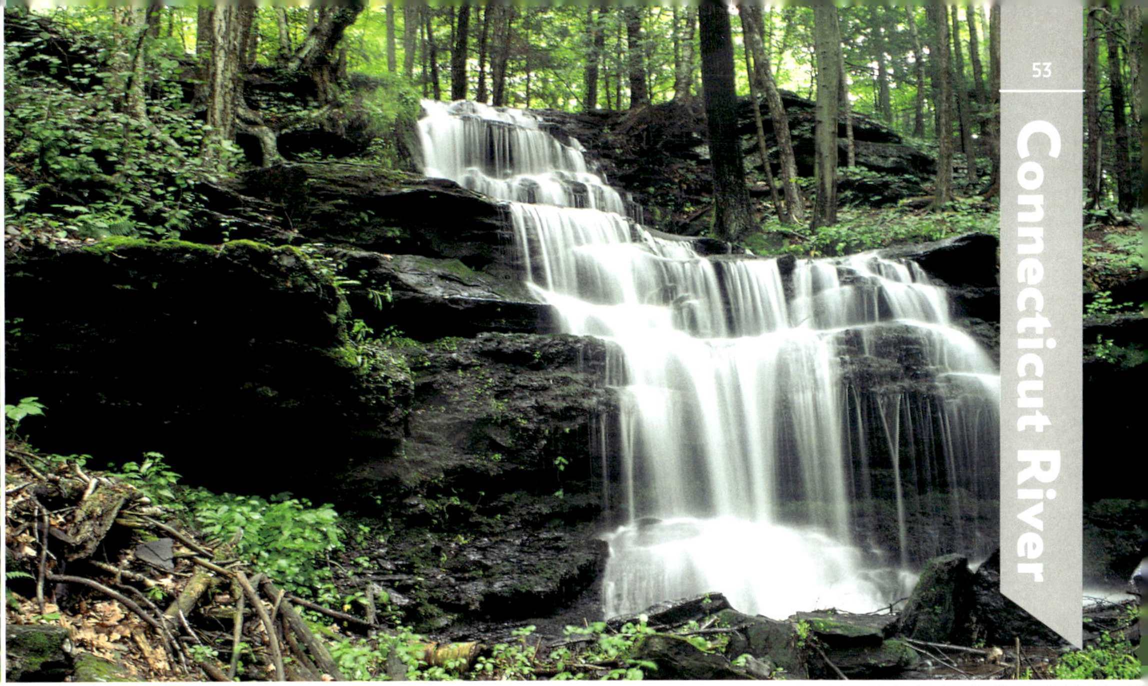

The cascades of Gunn and Slatestone Brooks are part of a cluster of waterfalls along the east banks of the Connecticut River in Sunderland.

At the base of Mount Toby's east slopes is Roaring Brook Falls, where a seasonal stream cascades through a ravine of mossy boulders. A variety of spring ephemerals, including colorful orchids, grows out of the bedrock, which is geologically similar to that of nearby Mount Sugarloaf. Several additional waterfalls, cascades, and pools are clustered at the base of the east slopes outside of the reservation, including Gunn Brook Falls, where another seasonal brook makes a 35-foot drop over mossy ledges. The larger cascades of nearby Slatestone Brook Falls make for an especially picturesque sight as they fan into a 40-foot drop just before the brook empties into the Connecticut River.

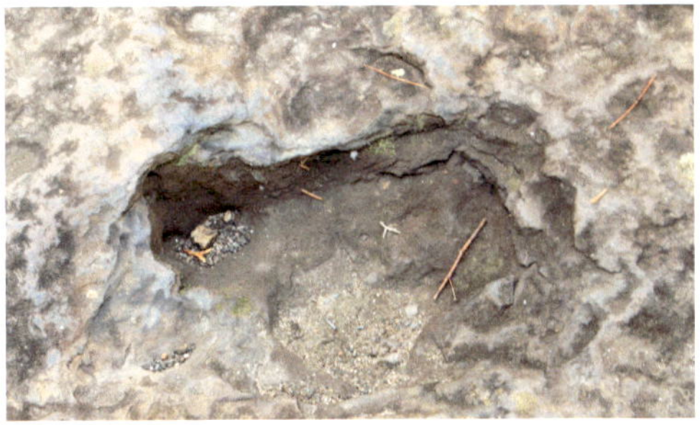

The Connecticut Valley is home to one of the world's largest concentrations of dinosaur tracks.

More insight into the earth's distant past lies at the base of Mount Tom, where a slab of sandstone on the west banks of the Connecticut River near Holyoke preserves a large cluster of dinosaur tracks made hundreds of millions of years ago. Indeed, ever since a teenager named Pliney Moody unearthed a strange series of bird-like prints while plowing his family's farm in South Hadley in 1802, the valley

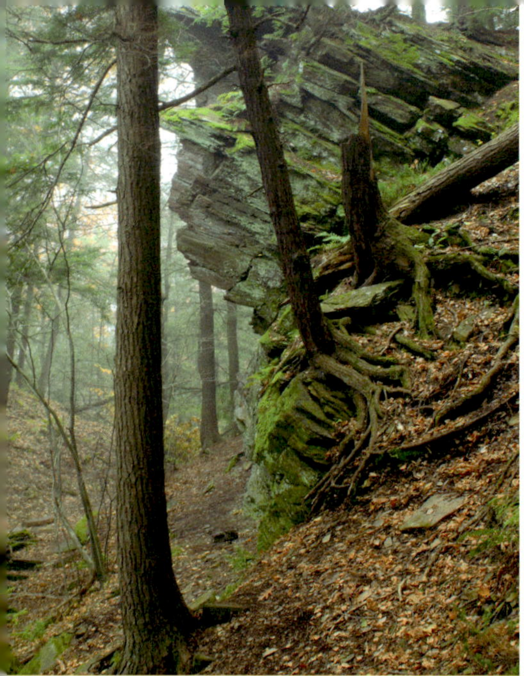

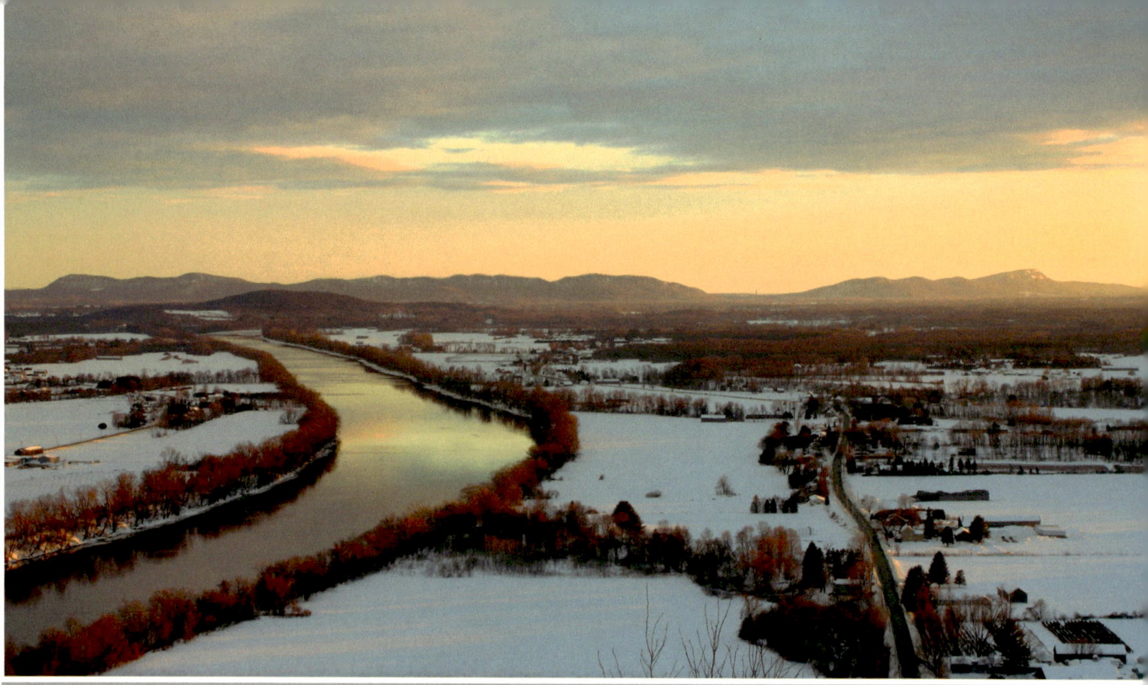

The rocky outcroppings above Barton Cove were the site of an important early dinosaur track find.

Mount Sugarloaf and the other hills and ridges of the Connecticut Valley were once islands and peninsulas in glacial Lake Hitchcock.

has been one of the world's most important areas for dinosaur track and skeleton finds and research, with a stream of significant discoveries over the past two centuries. At the time of Moody's discovery, dinosaurs were still an unknown concept to scientists, and the tracks were initially attributed to a giant bird.

Another key early discovery occurred in 1835, when a construction company extracted rocks from a quarry at Barton Cove in Turners Falls to pave sidewalks in downtown Greenfield. Among the many people who noticed unusual tracks in the new walkway was a local doctor named James Deane, who brought the specimens to the attention of state geologist Edward Hitchcock. Though Hitchcock was initially skeptical, the find proved to be the springboard for his extensive pioneering research in the field. Over the next 30 years he collected more than 10,000 prints throughout the valley, representing more than 150 different species. The sources of the tracks remained a mystery (Hitchcock believed they were from birds) until an 1859 scientist's meeting in Springfield, when Roswell Field, who owned the Turners Falls quarry site, proposed the theory that they were made by prehistoric reptiles, i.e. dinosaurs.

Among the most significant of the many places investigated by Hitchcock was the Holyoke site, where a cluster of 135 prints was uncovered during the construction of the roadway that is now Route 5. According to recent research by Yale University, they were made by three distinct species of carnivorous dinosaurs as they roamed the sandstone shores of the lakes and swamps that characterized the prehistoric valley. Several clusters of tracks, or "trackways," offer the intriguing possibility that some of the dinosaurs may have traveled in packs. In addition to the tracks, also preserved in the rocks along the riverbanks are fossils, plants, and the markings from an ancient pool.

Remarkable discoveries of tracks and skeletons have continued throughout the Connecticut Valley to the present day. In the early 20th century, a Mount Holyoke professor uncovered a small, well-preserved skeleton inside a glacial boulder near the Moody site in South Hadley. Exactly where the boulder came from originally remains unknown, as both it and the skeleton were unfortunately lost in a fire while in storage on the campus in 1916. In 1966, a large concentration of tracks was uncovered at a construction area in Rocky Hill, Connecticut, that is now part of Dinosaur State Park, and during the park's 40th anniversary celebration week in 2006, more tracks were found at a nearby construction site.

When the dinosaurs roamed the valley some 200 million years ago, the land was just north of the equator and was an environment of subtropical lakes, swamps, and pine forests far removed from the landscape of today. Over time, of course, the climate changed markedly as the North American continent gradually drifted to the north. The most recent ice age began approximately 110,000 years ago and lasted for some 90,000 years, burying the Northeast with mile-high ice sheets that enveloped even the highest mountains. The moving ice carved and shaped many of western Massachusetts' familiar features, including the deep valleys of the Connecticut River watershed, the basalt columns of the Metacomet mountains, and the steep south cliff of Mount Sugarloaf.

In the centuries following the last ice age, a visitor to Mount Sugarloaf or one of the valley's other low mountains would be standing atop an island or peninsula in a giant lake high above the level of the present Connecticut River. After the glaciers melted out of the valley roughly 18,000 years ago, sediment deposits were left behind that formed a giant natural dam near present-day Rocky Hill, Connecticut. Over the next 4,000 years, a long chain of lakes, now collectively named for Edward Hitchcock, gradually formed upstream from the dam, ultimately extending for more than 200 miles to northern Vermont. Funneled into the valley lowlands, the finger-like lakes had a maximum width of just 15-20 miles and bottlenecked around eminences such as the Holyoke and Pocumtuck

Ranges and the French King Gorge. Samples taken during a recent study by researchers at the University of Massachusetts indicate that Lake Hitchcock's waters reached the present-day Hadley-Amherst area around 15,800 years ago and lasted for nearly 1,500 years.

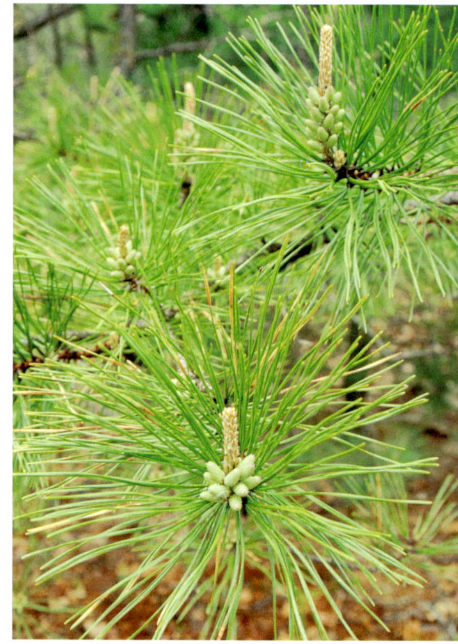

Regionally uncommon pitch pine trees grow out of the acidic sands of the Montague Plains, which were formed by glacial deposits on Lake Hitchcock's floor.

After painstakingly measuring thousands of annual sediment deposits called "varves" during the early 1920s, scientist Ernst Antovs estimated that the older, southern portion of Lake Hitchcock lasted for 4,100 years, which is a relatively small fraction of geologic time, but a surprisingly long period for the Rocky Hill dam to hold back the force of the Connecticut Valley waters. A likely explanation for this is that the valley floor was slow to rebound from the weight of the ice, resulting in a relatively level lake bottom that reduced pressure and erosion to the dam. Recent research indicates that the draining of the lake may not have been a sudden event followed by great floods as one might expect, but instead a more gradual process as the earth's crust slowly returned to its pre-glacial levels and angled the valley towards Long Island Sound.

While Lake Hitchcock's waters are long gone, its legacy remains evident throughout the valley. The rich alluvial soils of the former lake bottom have been prized for agriculture since the first Natives arrived in the valley, and wetlands such as Lawrence Swamp near Amherst were also formed as the lake drained. Beginning in the 17th century, clays that accumulated on the lake floor were mined for brickmaking by colonists. In 1984, when water wells in Whately became contaminated, the town was able to tap and utilize groundwater that was sheltered by the clay.

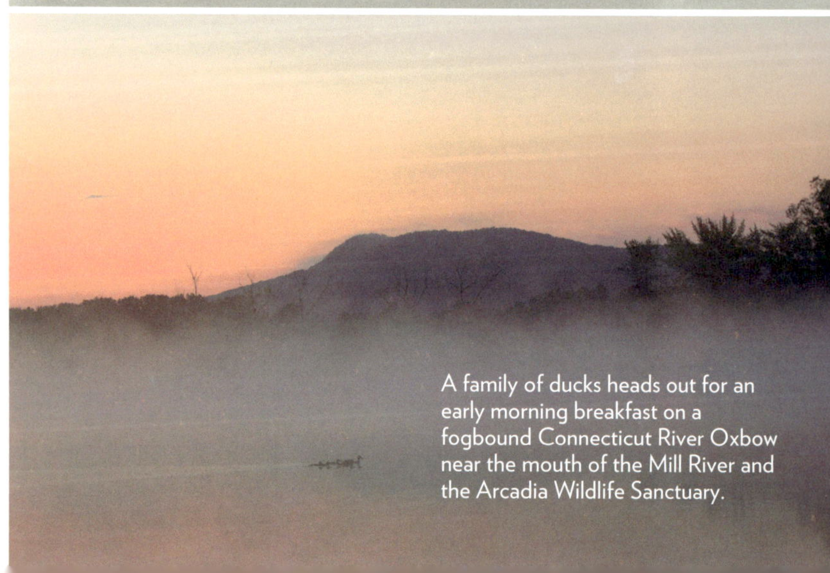

A family of ducks heads out for an early morning breakfast on a fogbound Connecticut River Oxbow near the mouth of the Mill River and the Arcadia Wildlife Sanctuary.

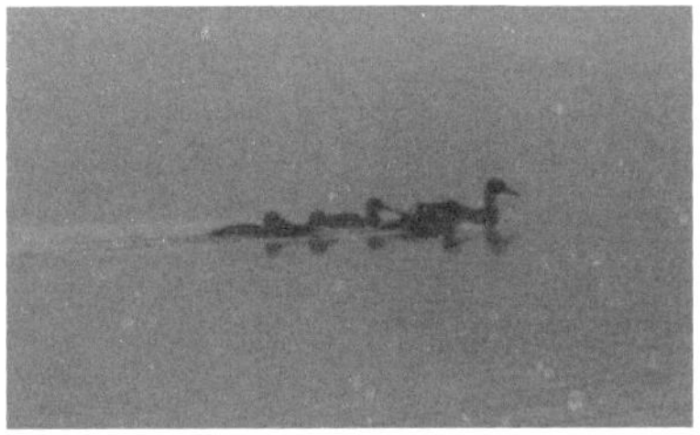

An especially unique and ecologically significant remnant of Lake Hitchcock is the Montague Plains, a large sand barren near Turners Falls. While walking over the sands beneath groves of scrub oak and pitch pine trees here, a visitor might wonder if they had inadvertently detoured to Cape Cod or the New Jersey pine barrens. The plains were originally formed on the floor of Lake Hitchcock by sediments deposited by glacial meltwater streams, then exposed after the lake drained. Many rare plants and animals that are otherwise uncommon in western Massachusetts now call this area home, including grasshopper and vesper sparrows and Karner blue butterflies. Though 1500 acres of the Montague barrens are protected as a state wildlife area, other similar sand plains in the Connecticut Valley have unfortunately been lost to development.

Finally freed from the glaciers and Lake Hitchcock, the revitalized Connecticut River carved a series of sweeping bends through sand and mud sediments on the former lake floor, including the aforementioned Oxbow between Northampton and Hadley. Log drivers once used the Oxbow as a giant yarding area for timber that was floated downstream from areas as far away as the northern mountains of New Hampshire and Vermont. The last long logs were driven in 1915, though pulpwood drives continued until 1948. In 1840, just four years after Thomas Cole completed his celebrated painting, the river finally broke through the neck of the Oxbow, straightening its course and effectively turning the bend into a crescent-shaped, three-mile lake.

Another event of note in the aftermath of the last Ice Age was the arrival of the first known human inhabitants of the valley, known as "paleo-Indians," some 12,000-14,000 years ago. There is presently no known evidence of Native settlements along the shores of Lake Hitchcock, though one legend makes an intriguing reference to a large lake associated with Mount Sugarloaf and the Pocumtuck Range. The animals they hunted on the tundra included large, cold-weather game such as caribou, woolly mammoths, mastodons, and beavers.

As the climate warmed, the landscape shifted from a boreal-tundra setting to the more hospitable environment of today, as evidenced by the arrival of deciduous forests and a greater diversity of plants and animals. Around 2,000 years ago, Natives began to practice agriculture by planting vegetables, corn, and other crops at favorable sites, including villages that established along the fertile, nutrient-rich riverbanks at present-day Westfield, Northampton, Hadley, Deerfield, and Northfield.

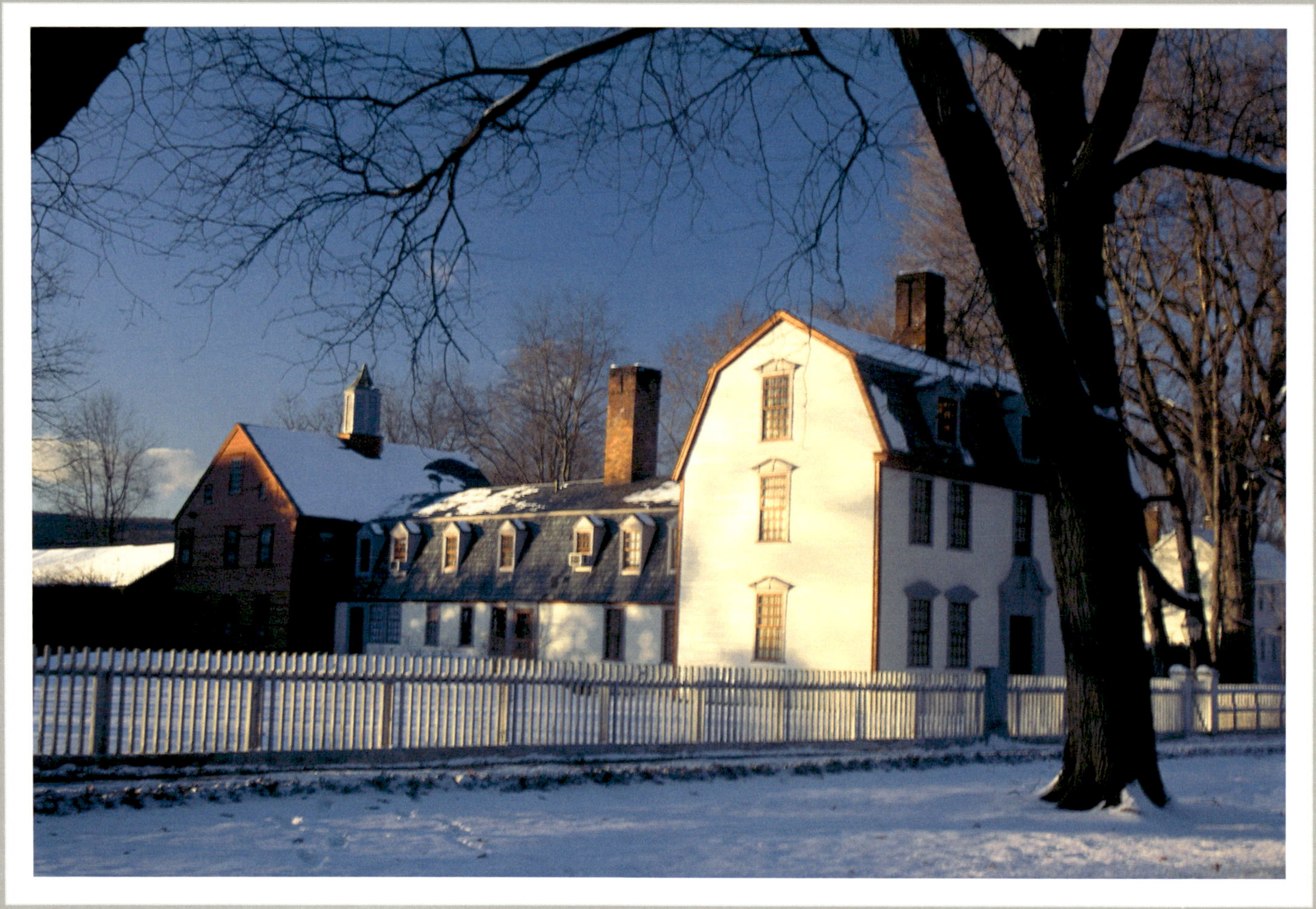

Dwight House is one of 11 historic buildings on a 330-year-old street at Historic Deerfield, an open-air museum that preserves the history of the Connecticut Valley and New England's historic villages.

The first European explorer to visit the Connecticut River was Dutchman Adraien Block, who came across the tidal flats at the river's mouth while leading an expedition in Long Island Sound during the spring of 1614. The seasonal high water enabled Block to navigate as far north as the rapids near present-day Enfield and Windsor, Connecticut, where he noted Native corn plantations and villages. Some 20 years later, a party of English colonists from eastern Massachusetts, led by William Pynchon, scouted and then established the valley's first colonial settlement at Springfield. The river was known to the Dutch as the "Versche River," and was depicted on a 1688 French map as the "Conitic."

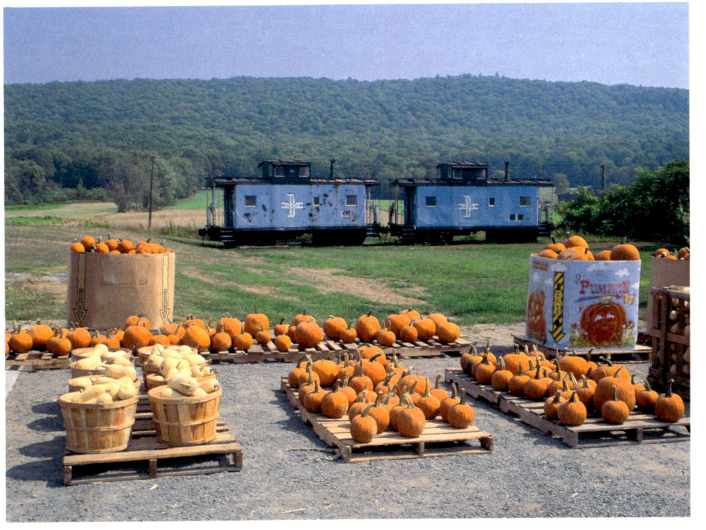

Two former Boston and Maine Railroad cabooses serve as a distinctive landmark for the M and M Green Valley Produce Farm in South Deerfield.

As the 17th century progressed, the colonists gradually expanded north past the falls at Holyoke to the fertile lands of Northampton, Hadley, Deerfield, and Northfield. One consequence of the European settlement was the spread of diseases such as smallpox, which rapidly decimated the Valley's Native populations. While differences in cultures had precluded truly amicable relations between the colonists and the surviving Natives, both sides existed in relative peace until 1675, when Deerfield and Northfield were raided during King Philip's War. Deerfield was again the center of battle in 1704, when an attack by the combined forces of the French and Pocumtucks left 44 colonists dead, 109 taken prisoner, and nearly half of the settlement's homes destroyed. The last conflict between Natives and colonists in the area was in 1748.

After having long provided fertile agricultural land and a trade route for Natives and early settlers, the Connecticut River was tapped for yet another means of sustenance during the 19th century: energy for manufacturing during the Industrial Revolution. In 1795, the country's first canal was opened at South Hadley to afford an easy passage around the river's largest single drop of 60 feet. Neighboring Holyoke was a quiet, sparsely populated settlement until 1847, when the construction of the Holyoke Dam and a canal system prompted its rapid ascent to the world's largest paper manufacturer, with as many as 25 active mills. The Holyoke Dam essentially marks the Valley's transition from the largely rural upper region to the heavily developed and populated industrial greater Holyoke and Springfield areas.

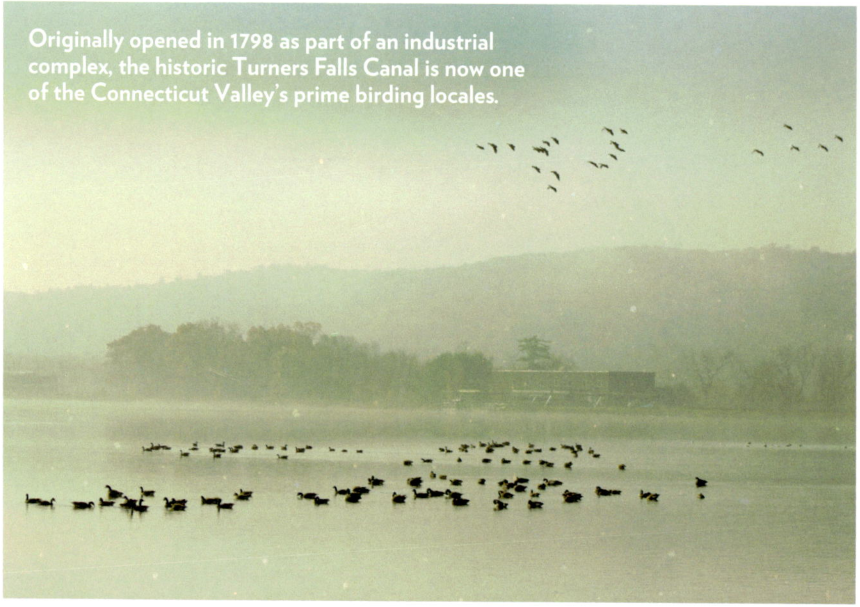
Originally opened in 1798 as part of an industrial complex, the historic Turners Falls Canal is now one of the Connecticut Valley's prime birding locales.

A similar but smaller industrial community was established upstream at Turners Falls following the Civil War, under the leadership of the same Alvah Crocker who had been the driving force behind the construction of the Hoosac Tunnel. Early planners envisioned an even more extensive network of canals to circumvent the river's dangerous rapids, but this never came to fruition following the advent of railroads by the mid-19th century. Today the canal at Turner's Falls is one of the Valley's finest birding areas; uncommon or vagrant species such as greater pink-footed geese and lesser black-backed and Kumlien's Iceland gulls have been observed amidst the familiar Canada geese, swans, mallards, goldeneyes, mergansers, and other waterfowl that frequent the waters.

Though the mills were the cornerstone of the valley's economy, with them came pollution, a problem that was first recognized by late 19th-century conservationists but would continue to plague the river deep into the 20th century. In 1963, a federal researcher provided this unsettling evaluation of the water near Chicopee: "Clumps and rafts of sludge boil to the surface, buoyed by the gas bubbles of decomposition." Fortunately, following the passage of the Clean Water Act, millions of dollars were invested in cleanup efforts and the establishment of sewage treatment plants, and restrictions were implemented on future development. Thanks to these efforts, the river is now classified as a "Class B" waterway, meaning it is suitable for fishing and swimming.

Another consequence of the dams at Holyoke and Turners Falls was the barrier they posed to anadromous fish such as Atlantic salmon and American shad. These species make long migrations from inland freshwater breeding grounds to the

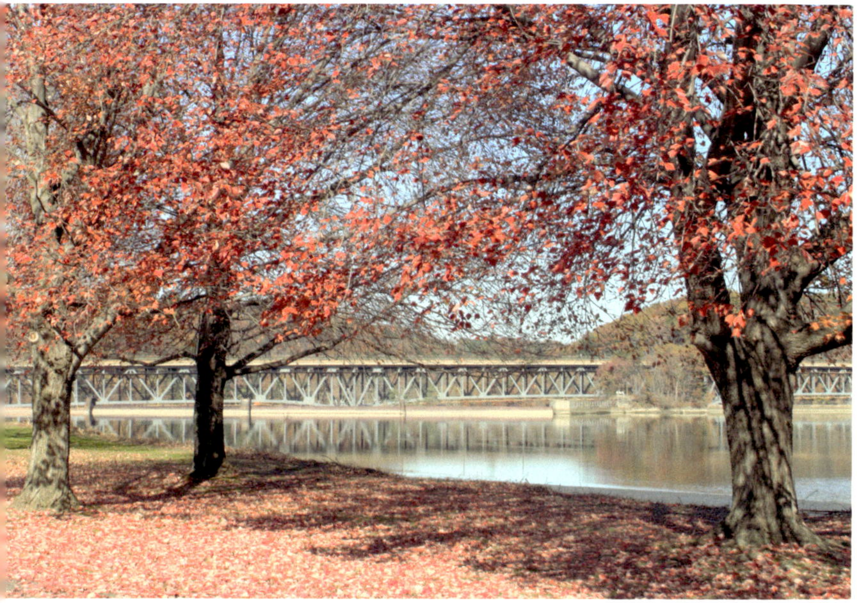

Community Park in Turner's Falls offers recreational trails and views of Barton Cove, the Connecticut River, and the Gill-Montague Bridge.

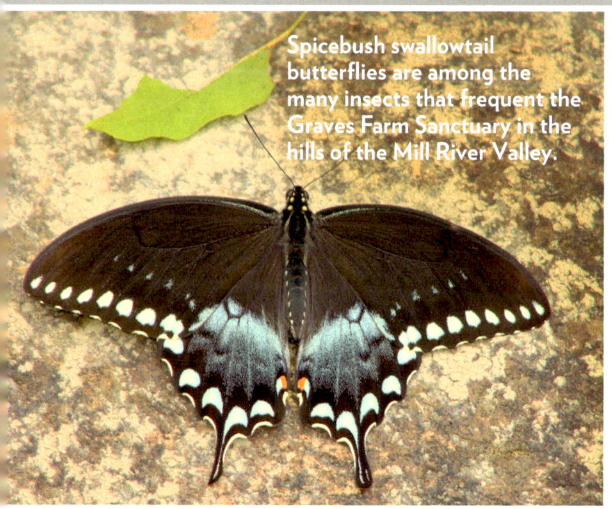

Spicebush swallowtail butterflies are among the many insects that frequent the Graves Farm Sanctuary in the hills of the Mill River Valley.

ocean and back, and as such are dependent on free-flowing, unimpeded passages. During the 19th century, development on the Connecticut River and New England's other rivers effectively eliminated many once-prolific salmon runs. Beginning with the construction of a fish elevator in Holyoke in 1955, more than $60 million dollars' worth of ladders and lifts have been built in an attempt to allow shad and salmon to reclaim their former travel routes.

The variable, often steep topography of western and central Massachusetts also made the Connecticut River's smaller tributaries ideal sources of industrial power. One of the valley's hardest-working waterways was the aptly named Mill River, which originates from two branches in the hills of Goshen and Williamsburg. It offered abundant waterpower, as its West and East branches drop 700 and 300 feet respectively before their confluence, and then the main stem falls another 400 feet along its 15-mile course. However, it is also a seasonal stream with a low volume during the summer months, when a mere 12 percent of New England's average annual precipitation of 45 inches falls. In order to ensure a more consistent flow year-round, mill owners commissioned the construction of the Williamsburg Dam and a large reservoir, similar to those that were built on many other New England rivers during the 19th century, on the East Branch during the mid-1860s.

From the time of its construction onward, there were signs of a potential disaster involving the new dam. While excavating the trench for the

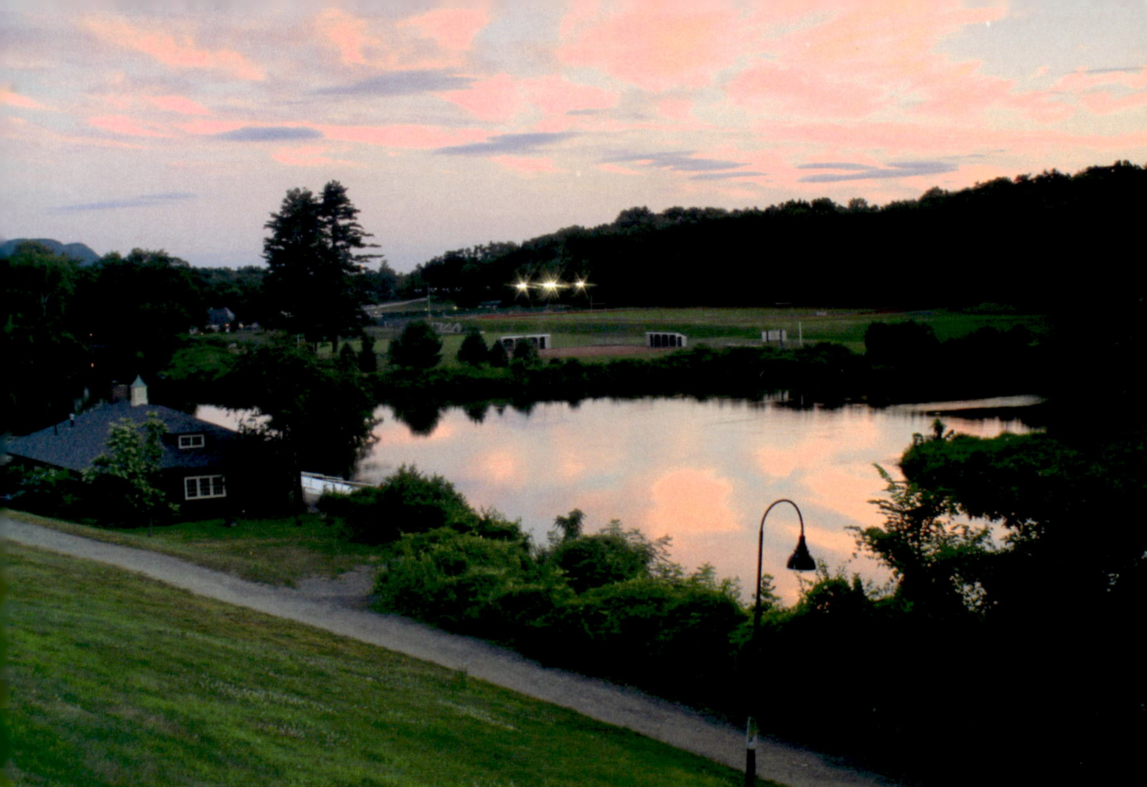

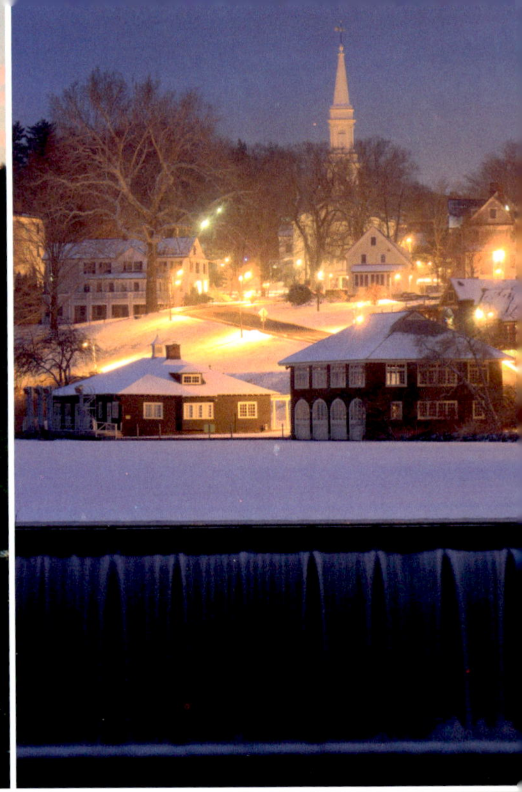

The Mill River is the source for scenic Paradise Pond on the Smith College campus in Northampton. The ridge of Mount Tom is barely visible above the trees on the left.

Winter twilight settles over the Smith College boathouse and Helen Hills Chapel upstream from the Paradise Pond dam on the Mill River.

giant stone wall, the builders encountered soft dirt and gravel, rather than the solid earth that was necessary for a firm foundation. Shortly after its opening in 1866, the reservoir banks displayed noticeable wear after the spring rains and snowmelt, a substantial piece of earth eroded off of the dam, and a worrisome series of leaks were addressed through patchwork repairs. The condition of the dam was a constant concern for the valley residents, and on a sunny spring day in 1874 their worst fears were realized.

On the morning of May 16, George Cheney, the dam's gatekeeper and watchman, was startled to see a giant piece of earth burst out of the banks. Recognizing that a catastrophic failure was imminent, he made a desperate dash on horseback ahead of the rising waters to warn the villages downstream, where he initially met with skepticism from the townsfolk. This wishful thinking was soon proven erroneous when, as related by historian Elizabeth Sharpe in *In the Shadow of the Dam*, "a convulsive boom echoed through the Williamsburg hills and was heard as far away as

Goshen" as the dam broke. Six hundred million gallons of water were abruptly unleashed into the narrow valley, forming a giant wave carrying what one witness described as "a great mass of brush, trees, and trash" through Haydenville, Williamsburg, and Northampton. In the wake of the 11-mile long path of destruction were 140 fatalities, 750 survivors without homes, and a news story that shocked the entire nation. It was the country's first major dam disaster, and underlined the dangers of America's rapidly developing industrial era.

The Mill River is a well-known landmark of Northampton, as it winds through Look Park and the Smith College campus before emptying into the Connecticut River Oxbow at a wildlife-rich floodplain below Mount Tom. The Massachusetts Audubon Society's Arcadia Wildlife Sanctuary encompasses nearly 800 acres of the diverse habitats here, including marshes, swamps, uncommon floodplain forests, and old fields and orchards. During colonial times, the sanctuary's Old Coach Road Trail was part of the main stage road between Northampton and Springfield. The adjacent fertile floodplain was prime agricultural land, and today the old farm fields are maintained as grasslands to benefit bobolinks, meadowlarks, bluebirds, and other species that favor open habitats.

Posted near the top of the sanctuary's two-story marsh observation tower—at a level that's difficult to fathom when looking over the scene below—is a sign marking the high water from the great flood of 1936. With its length, many tributaries, and location in a climate that averages 45 inches of precipitation annually, the Connecticut River has indeed long been prone to flooding, including annual spring high waters and significant floods in 1826, 1840, 1862, and 1927. However, none of these matched the sheer volume and destruction of the 1936 flood, which was the highest on record and one of the Northeast's greatest natural disasters.

As a hard winter drew to a close, a prolonged pattern of heavy snowfall and abnormally cold temperatures was abruptly interrupted by several unusual late winter rainstorms. On March 9, the first storm dropped more than five inches of rain in the mountains of northern New England, causing widespread flooding and an ice jam that tore a 1,000-foot long section off of the Holyoke Dam. It turned out to be a mere precursor for the rains of March 18th-19th, which saturated the northern mountains and the valleys of western and central Massachusetts with more than 10 inches of precipitation. The warm temperatures and soaking rains abruptly melted much of the region's snowpack within a matter of hours, unleashing torrents of water through the Connecticut River's extensive network of tributaries.

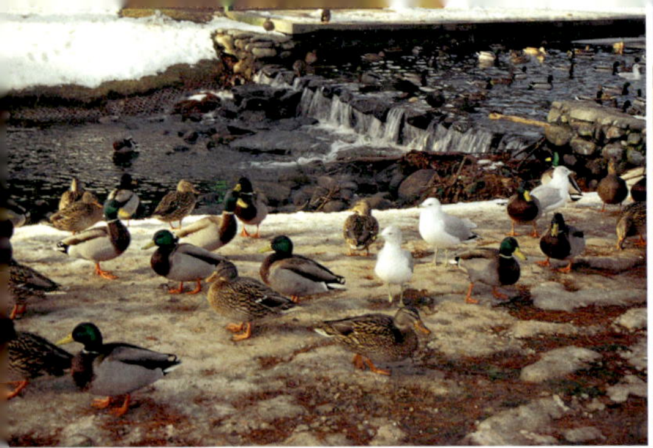

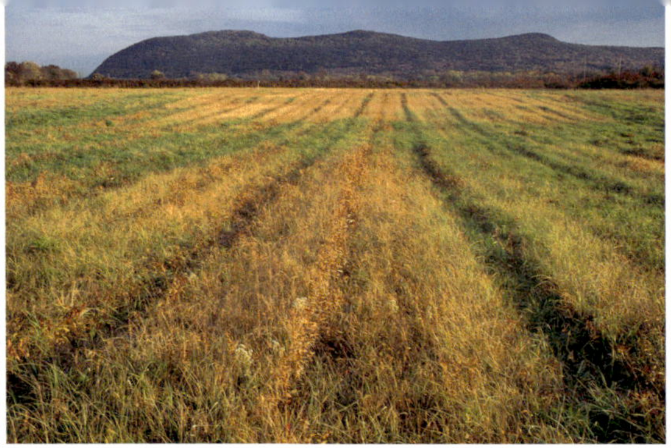

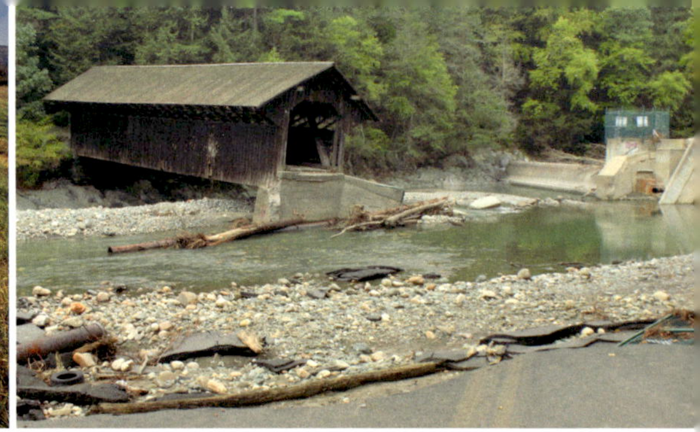

Mallard ducks are familiar residents of Look Park on the Mill River in Northampton, a popular destination for families.

The diverse habitats of the Arcadia Wildlife Sanctuary include expansive open grasslands along the floodplain at the mouth of the Mill River.

The heavy damage to the Greenfield "Pumping Station" covered bridge from Hurricane Irene in 2011 was reminiscent of the destruction caused by the 1930s floods.

The effects of the flooding in western Massachusetts were catastrophic. In Springfield, more than 20,000 people were rendered homeless, and shelters were hastily established at the colleges in Amherst for 3,000 similarly displaced residents of Northampton. In Holyoke, a massive ice jam that was 15 feet high and a mile deep formed in the notch between Mount Tom and the Holyoke Range. After it gave way, roaring torrents of water swept over and around the Holyoke Dam, destroying entire neighborhoods in South Hadley Falls and south Holyoke. After widespread looting broke out, policemen patrolled the inundated streets in boats and canoes with orders to shoot thieves on sight. For an unsettling few hours, there were reports that the giant dam at Vernon, Vermont, was failing, which would have caused even greater destruction, but fortunately it held together.

Much of the Northeast's transportation infrastructure was crippled by the flood, as countless roads, bridges, and railroads were washed away, including many of the region's remaining covered bridges. Among the most prominent of these lost landmarks was the massive Montague City covered bridge, a five-span, 870-foot long structure that was stout enough to support a railroad line on its roof. After it was torn off its supports by the swollen Connecticut River, residents in the nearby town of Sunderland witnessed the startling site of the giant bridge being swept downriver towards the Sunderland Bridge, which it ultimately collided with.

The valley residents had barely come to terms with this unprecedented disaster when the region was struck just two years later by another exceptional storm, the great hurricane of September 21, 1938. While most tropical storms that affect New England follow the coast, an unusual combination of weather fronts steered the 1938 storm inland up the Connecticut River Valley. In addition to another round of torrential flooding, the region's forests were decimated, with an estimated 2 billion trees destroyed in New England and New York alone. To alleviate the sudden threat of fire posed by the downed timber, many ponds and lakes were used as storage yards for fallen logs.

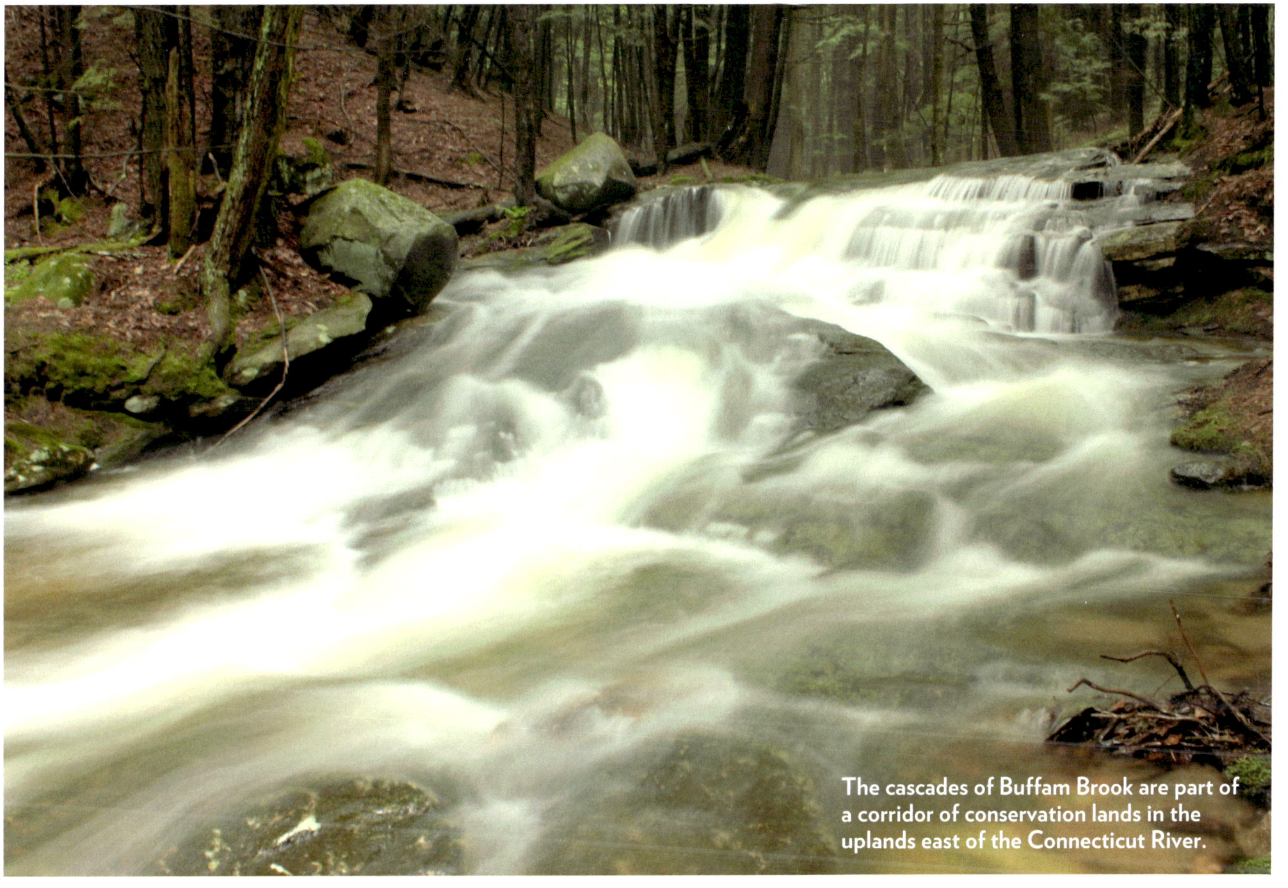

The cascades of Buffam Brook are part of a corridor of conservation lands in the uplands east of the Connecticut River.

East of the Connecticut River Valley, the landscape changes yet again to more rolling, rocky uplands and hilly valleys that characterize the heart of the Commonwealth. The New England National Scenic Trail corridor roughly follows this transition zone from the east end of the Holyoke Range through the rolling Pelham Hills, where waterways such as Hop, Buffam, and Amethyst Brooks cascade beneath groves of mixed evergreen and hardwood forests. The highest peak of this low chain is 1240-foot Mount Lincoln, which is largely owned by the University of Massachusetts Forestry and Wildlife department and abuts a portion of the Quabbin Reservoir watershed lands. The summit fire tower offers views towards the watersheds of the nearby Swift and Millers River Valleys, two of the Connecticut River's key eastern tributaries.

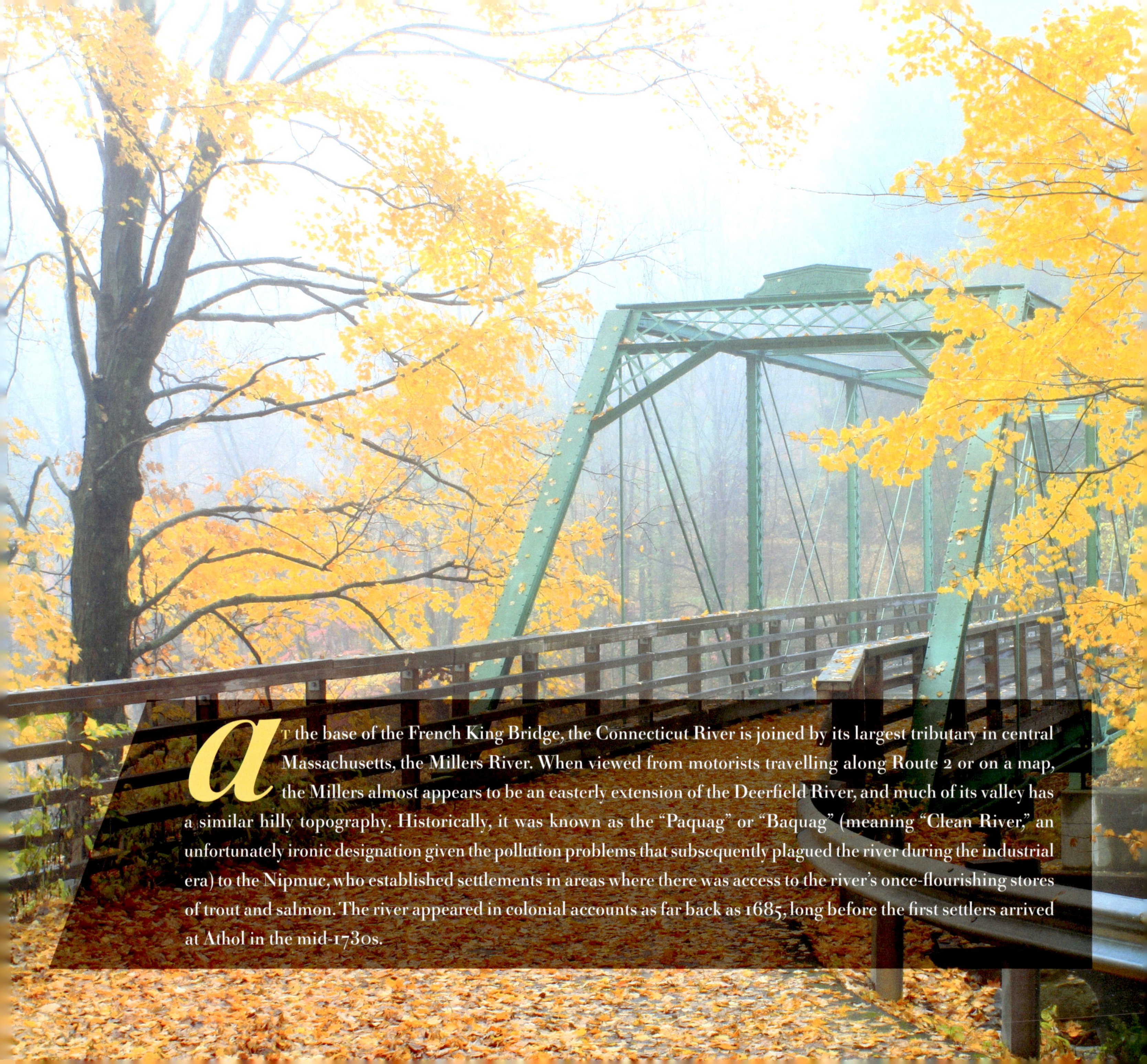

At the base of the French King Bridge, the Connecticut River is joined by its largest tributary in central Massachusetts, the Millers River. When viewed from motorists travelling along Route 2 or on a map, the Millers almost appears to be an easterly extension of the Deerfield River, and much of its valley has a similar hilly topography. Historically, it was known as the "Paquag" or "Baquag" (meaning "Clean River," an unfortunately ironic designation given the pollution problems that subsequently plagued the river during the industrial era) to the Nipmuc, who established settlements in areas where there was access to the river's once-flourishing stores of trout and salmon. The river appeared in colonial accounts as far back as 1685, long before the first settlers arrived at Athol in the mid-1730s.

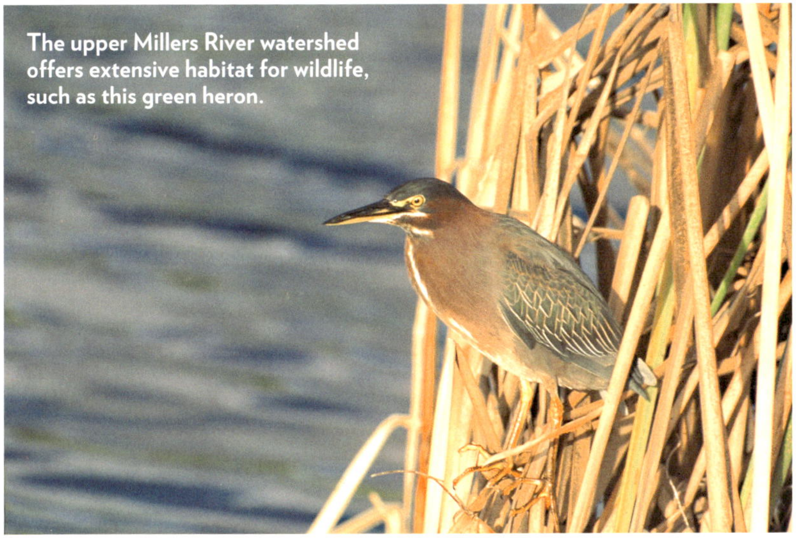

The upper Millers River watershed offers extensive habitat for wildlife, such as this green heron.

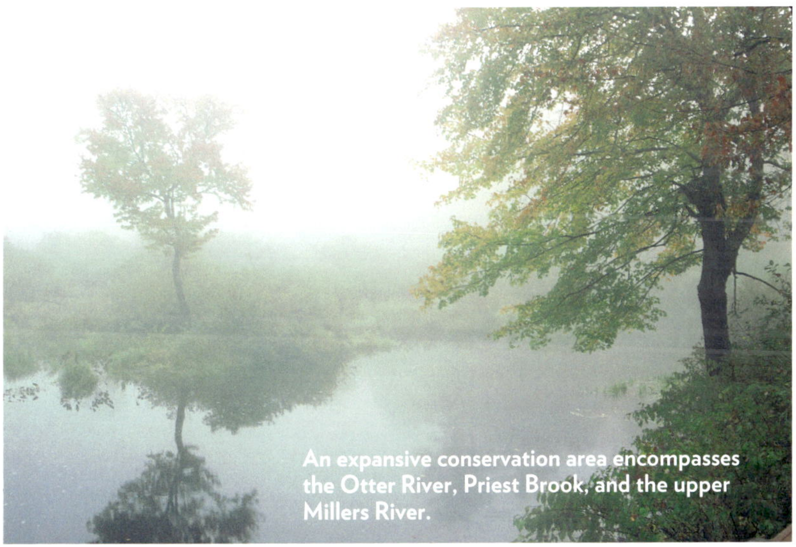

An expansive conservation area encompasses the Otter River, Priest Brook, and the upper Millers River.

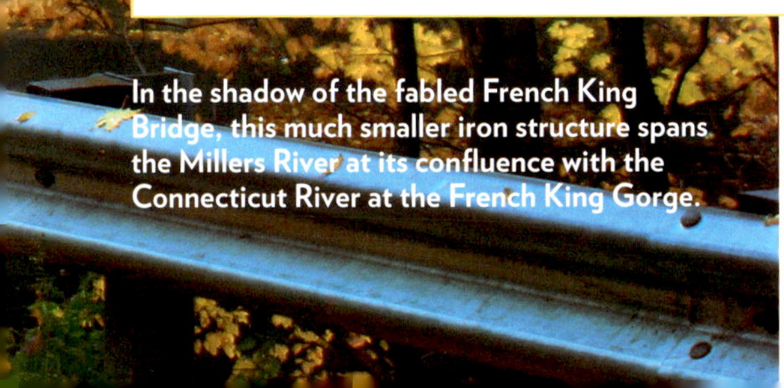

In the shadow of the fabled French King Bridge, this much smaller iron structure spans the Millers River at its confluence with the Connecticut River at the French King Gorge.

The main stem of the Millers River originates from wetlands in Ashburnham and Winchendon, while the headwaters of its short north branch are at Mountain Pond on the west slopes of the Wapack Range in southern New Hampshire. As the river assumes its 52-mile course to the west, it passes through a mosaic of more than 20,000 acres of protected land, where it meets several tributaries, including the Otter River and Priest Brook, in a large complex of wetlands.

Within this expanse lies the Birch Hill Dam, which was one of the first flood-control impoundments built by the Army Corps of Engineers in New England following the storms of the late 1930s that inundated the centers of Athol and Orange. The dam was completed in 1941 and has mitigated the effects of subsequent floods throughout the watershed; it is estimated to have saved $9 million dollars of damage alone during April 1987, when storms added six inches of rain to the perennially high spring waters.

The surrounding wetlands and forests are part of a large corridor of more than 20,000 acres of protected land that includes the Otter River State Forest, Birch Hill Wildlife Management Area, and Lake Dennison. This mosaic of wetlands and woodlands benefit a variety of both wildlife and human

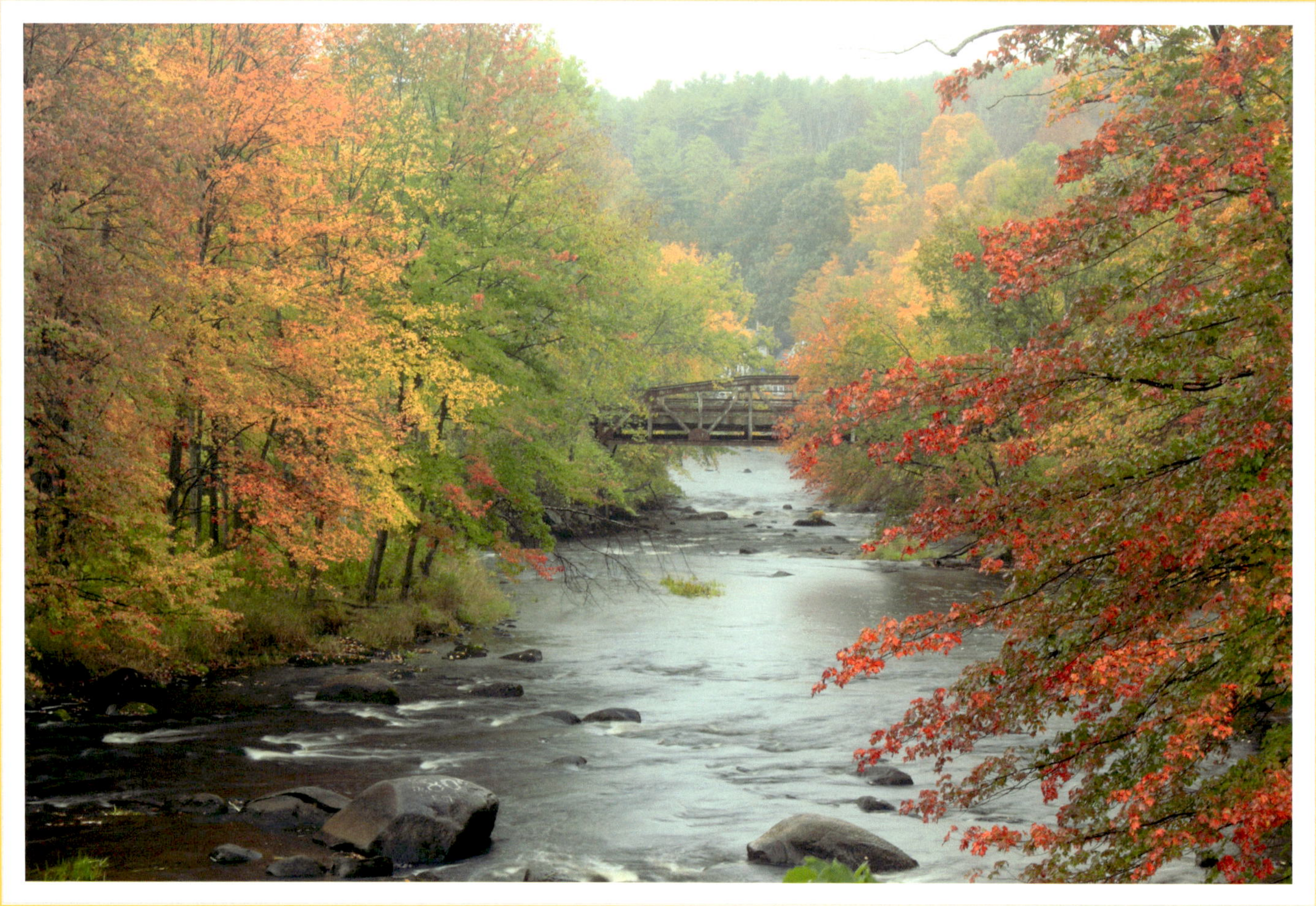

In South Royalston and Athol, the Millers River slices through a scenic glacial valley largely protected by the Millers River Wildlife Management Area and Bearsden Conservation Area.

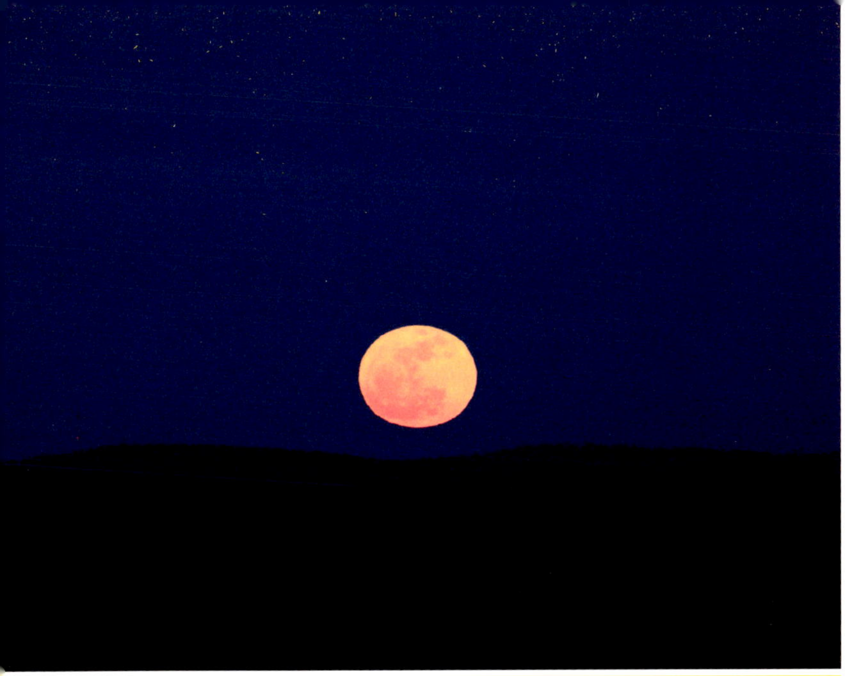

A full moon rises over the countryside of north-central Massachusetts, as seen from the summit of Round Top Hill at the Bearsden Conservation Area in Athol.

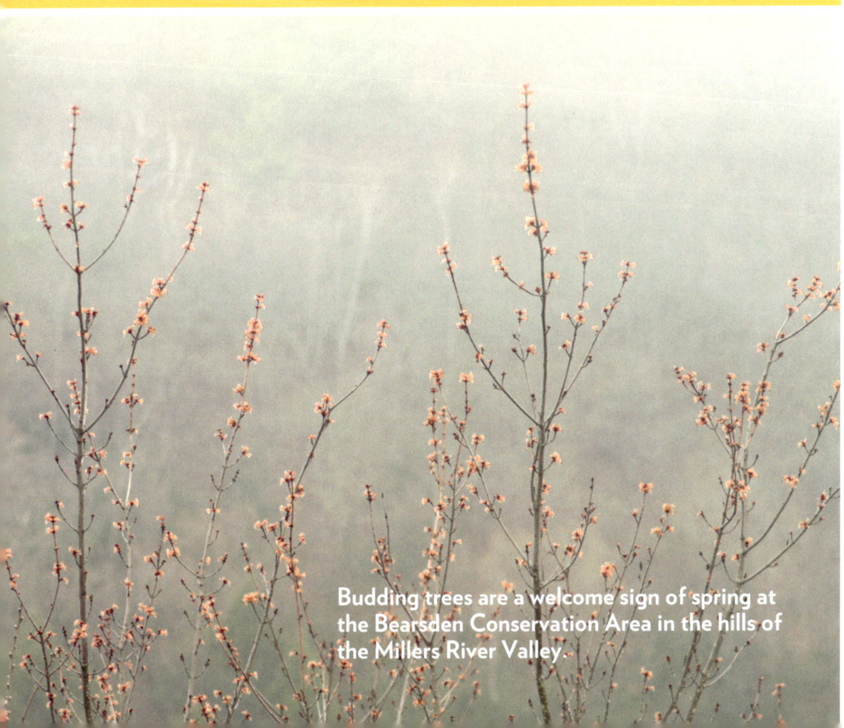

Budding trees are a welcome sign of spring at the Bearsden Conservation Area in the hills of the Millers River Valley.

users: moose, beavers, river otters, wading birds, and dragonflies are among the wildlife that use the wetlands, while anglers, paddlers, skiers, hikers, and snowmobilers enjoy miles of land and water trails. In historic times, these routes led past a number of thriving farms, mills, and villages. A well-known summer camp and cottages once lined the shores of Lake Dennison, where one can glimpse the summit of Mount Monadnock on clear days.

A few miles downstream, the character of the Millers changes as it enters some of the watershed's steepest and most rugged terrain. A short distance east of the center of Athol is the Bearsden Conservation Area, a 1,000-acre expanse of rocky hills, wetlands, and unbroken woodlands that have been cited as one of the finest examples of interior forest in Massachusetts. Visitors to the overlook at Sheep Rock, a partially exposed ledge in a former high-elevation sheep pasture, enjoy a panoramic perspective of the valley's hilly topography. The 1,278-foot summit of nearby Round Top Hill, which was largely denuded by a fire in 1957, offers more views across the forested countryside to the familiar profile of Wachusett Mountain. Thanks to the thermal lift provided by the valley hills, Round Top is a good place to view large flocks of raptors during their spring and fall migrations.

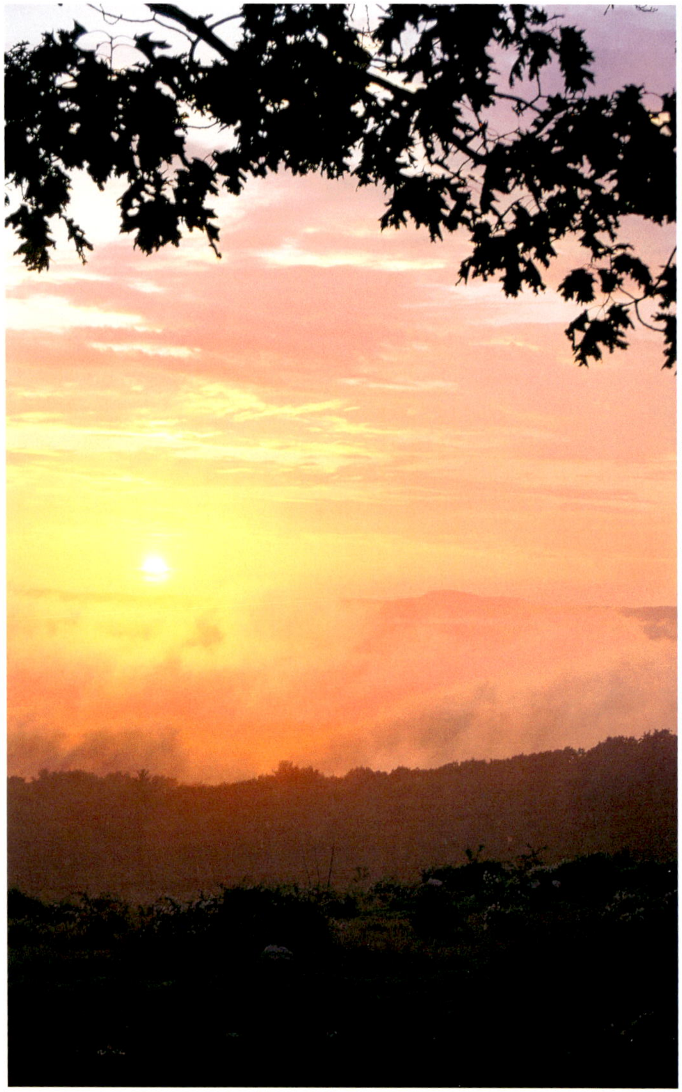

Sunset over Athol and the Millers River Valley, as seen from Adams Farm near the Bearsden Conservation Area. The sloping profile of Mount Grace is visible on the horizon.

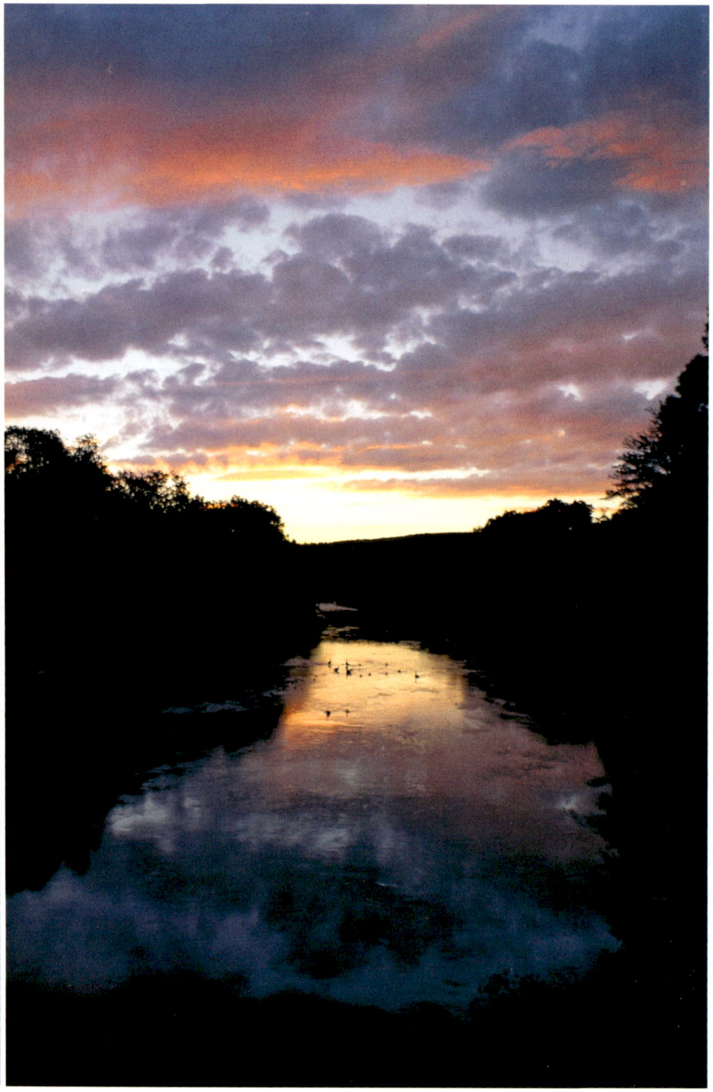

Thanks to cleanup efforts in recent decades, the Millers River, seen here in Orange, offers suitable habitat for ducks, geese, and other wildlife.

Though the Millers River lacks the sheer overall vertical gradient of the Deerfield and Westfield Rivers, it nevertheless produces a considerable amount of energy along its course to the Connecticut Valley and, therefore, has a long industrial history. Mills were built as early as the 1790s in Athol and Orange, and the advent of railroads during the mid-19th century further established the valley as a significant manufacturing center. Though industry has declined in recent decades, it remains an important component of the region's economy. A familiar institution of downtown Athol is Starrett's Tool Company, an internationally renowned toolmaker that serves a variety of clients worldwide. Further downstream is the Erving Paper Mill, which has long been a familiar landmark for travellers along Route 2. During the late 19th century, it was owned by the Stone Company, a highly successful manufacturer of piano cases and legs for pianos and billiard tables. The paper mill began operations in 1905, and continues to be active today after celebrating its centennial anniversary in 2005.

With its concentration of industry, the Millers River inevitably was another of New England's rivers that suffered heavily from pollution. Allen Young, who has authored several books on the North Quabbin region, recalls that the river "stunk, and the color of the water varied so much [due to dyes discharged by the paper mills] that it was almost laughable." Esteemed nature writer Ted Williams was similarly pointed in a 1972 article in *Massachusetts Wildlife:* "Of our many dead and dying rivers few have been more swiftly or savagely desecrated than the Millers."

Fortunately, the passage of the Clean Water Act that same year led to the establishment of sewage treatment plants in the river communities and prompted the mills to treat their wastewater. A decade later, conditions had improved to the point that trout were released into the river at Royalston and Erving in April 1983. As detailed by Young in an article reprinted in his recent book *The Man Who Got Lost: North Quabbin Stories*, the releases were an important symbolic event attended by many area politicians, fishermen, and residents, one of whom was "pleased that fish could return to the river... [and] that the cleanup has also ended the stench that once rose from the waters and compelled residents to keep their windows closed."

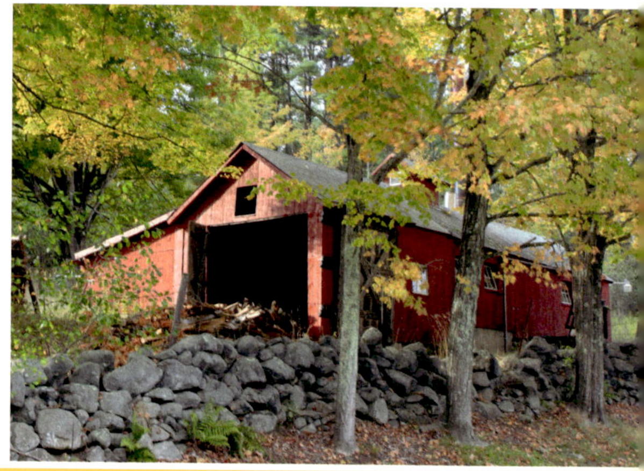

Maple syrup is a popular commodity at many central Massachusetts farms; here the sugar house at Johnson's Farm in Orange makes for a classic New England scene.

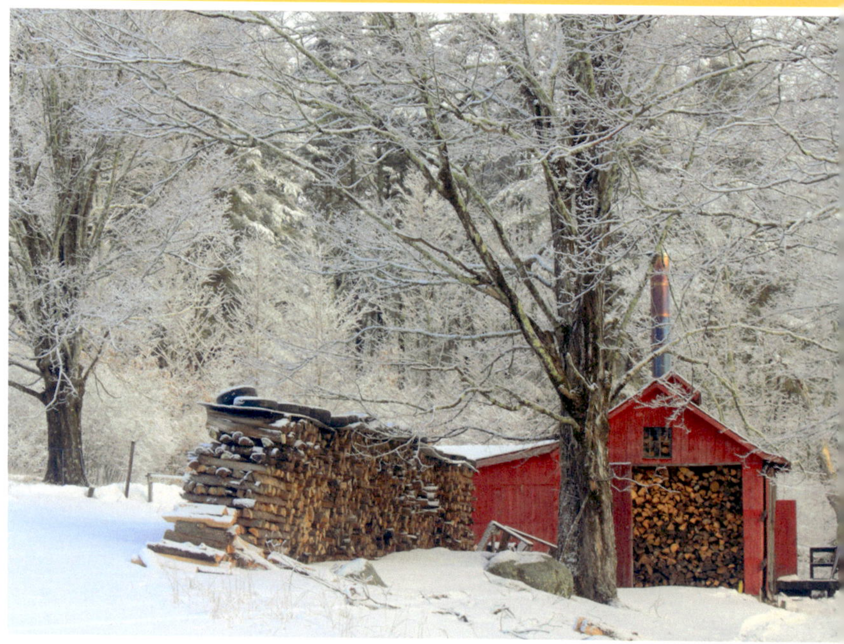

Another of the valley's active manufacturers is the Rodney Hunt Company in Orange, which created Lake Rohunta in 1943 by damming a small tributary of the Millers River on the site of two industrial dams that were casualties of the 1938 hurricane floods. This finger-like waterbody, which was used for electric power through the early 1960s, now serves as a six-mile-long conservation corridor that stretches from the northern tip of Quabbin Reservoir to the Millers River watershed. Its shallow, often weedy waters serve as an important resting and breeding area for ring-necked ducks, mergansers, and other waterfowl, while whip-poor-wills and common nighthawks are among the rare species that may be glimpsed or heard along its shores.

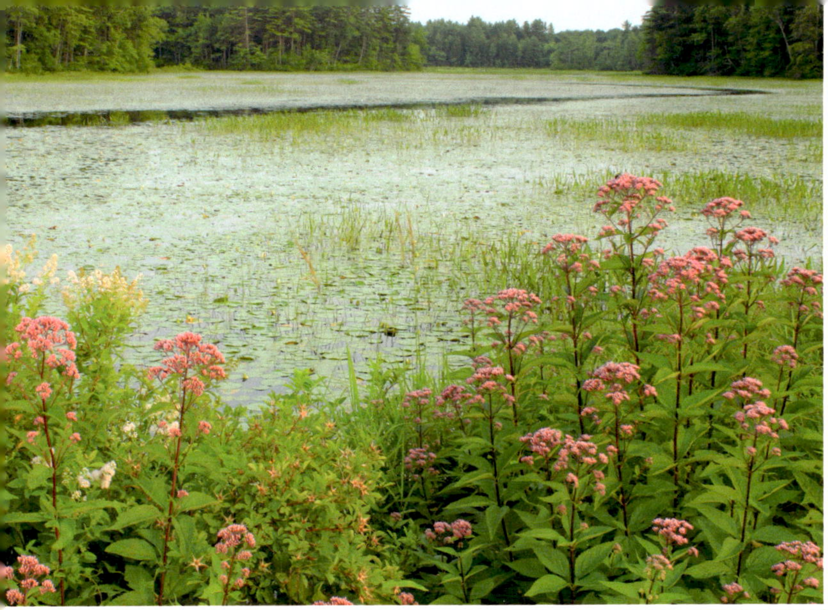

Summer wildflowers bloom along the shores of shallow Lake Rohunta, which is nestled between the Quabbin Reservoir and Millers River watersheds.

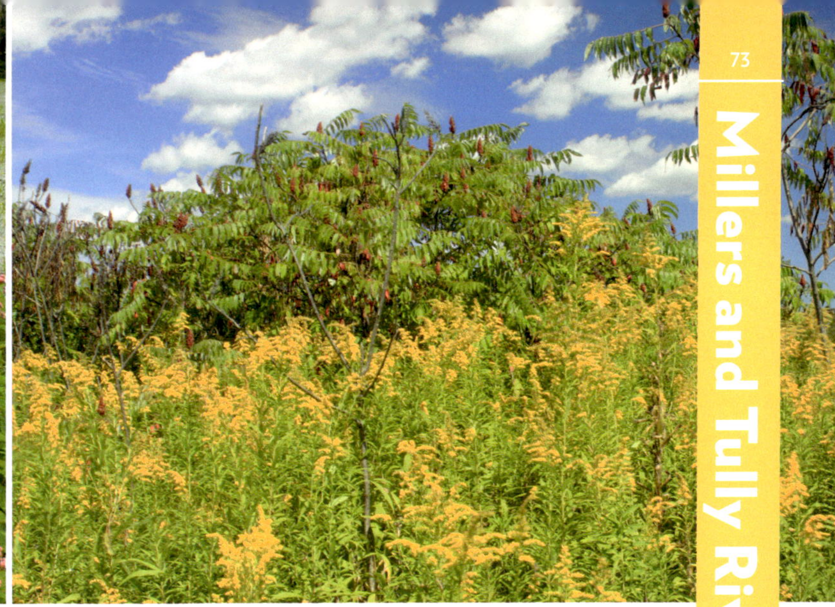

Goldenrod wildflowers add late summer color to Cass Meadow at the confluence of the Millers and Tully Rivers near downtown Athol.

On the periphery of downtown Athol are Cass Meadow Wildlife Management Area and Alan E. Rich Environmental Park, where large open fields offer a glimpse of the valley's agricultural past and habitat diversity for wildlife. The former was one of several sites in the valley where cornfields were planted by the Pequiog, and it briefly was used as an airfield during the 1920s. Among the uncommon species that live here are wood turtles, which are often well-camouflaged along the river bottom, and American rubyspot damselflies, which flitter along the vegetation on the riverbanks in late summer. The unique evening courtship flights of American woodcock are a familiar sight and sound on spring evenings, while monarchs and other butterflies and insects feed on the nectar of abundant wildflowers as the summer progresses.

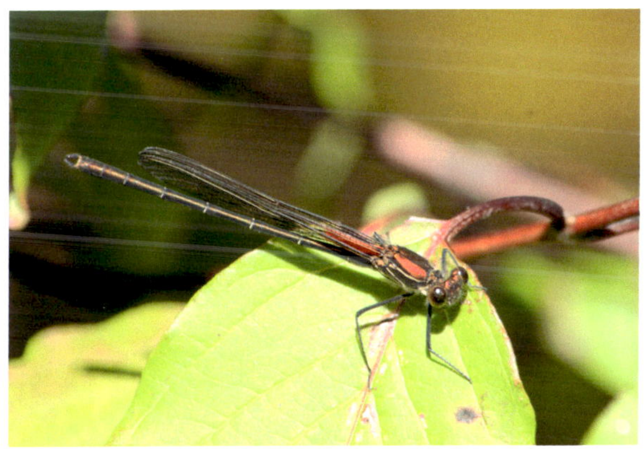

The Millers River offers habitat for uncommon American rubyspots, which are among the roughly 170 species of odenates (dragonflies and damselflies) found in Massachusetts.

For one weekend each April, Rich Park is also alive with hundreds of brightly colored canoes and kayaks when it serves as the starting point for the "River Rat" races, which draw paddlers from across the Northeast and an estimated 10,000 spectators annually. The finish line is five miles downstream, near Butterfield Park and the mills near the center of Orange. This popular community event, which celebrated its 50th season in 2013, is preceded by a parade through downtown Athol. The route is now part of the "Millers River Blue Trail," a paddling route recently dedicated by the Millers River Environmental Center that passes numerous natural and historic sites.

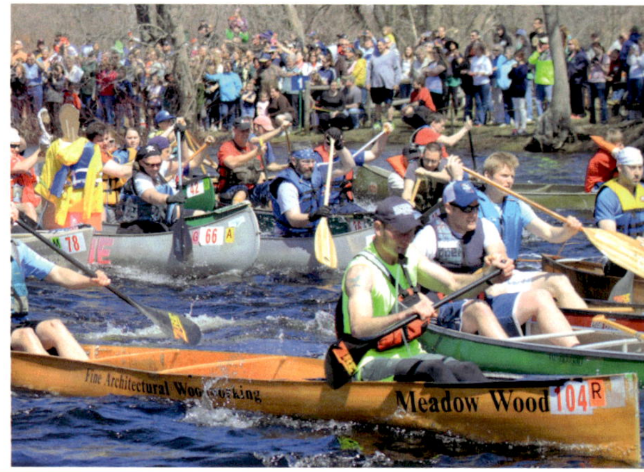

Athol's Rich Park is the starting point for the River Rat canoe race, one of the North Quabbin region's most popular events.

At Cass Meadow, the Millers River is joined by one of its largest sources, the west branch of the Tully River. In 1884, a newspaper described the Tully hills as "approaching the dignity of mountains....of truncated form, with covering of umbrageous trees, wild shrubs and bushes, whose most aggressive inhabitant is the rattlesnake..." The highest of these eminences is beehive-shaped Tully Mountain itself, which rises abruptly out of the countryside of north Orange. Once quarried for soapstone (a practice that ended when an overly ambitious prospector destroyed the useful rocks with dynamite), its rocky talus slopes offer habitat for bobcats, coyotes, porcupines, ravens, and the occasional black bear. Rock ledges adjacent to the summit offer one of the region's finest views, a 180-degree panorama across the valley to Mounts Monadnock and Wachusett.

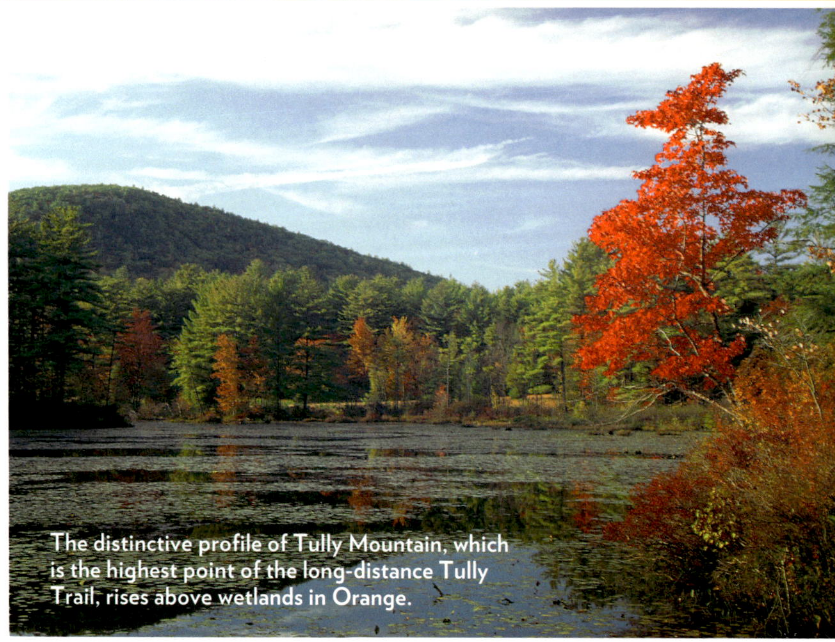

The distinctive profile of Tully Mountain, which is the highest point of the long-distance Tully Trail, rises above wetlands in Orange.

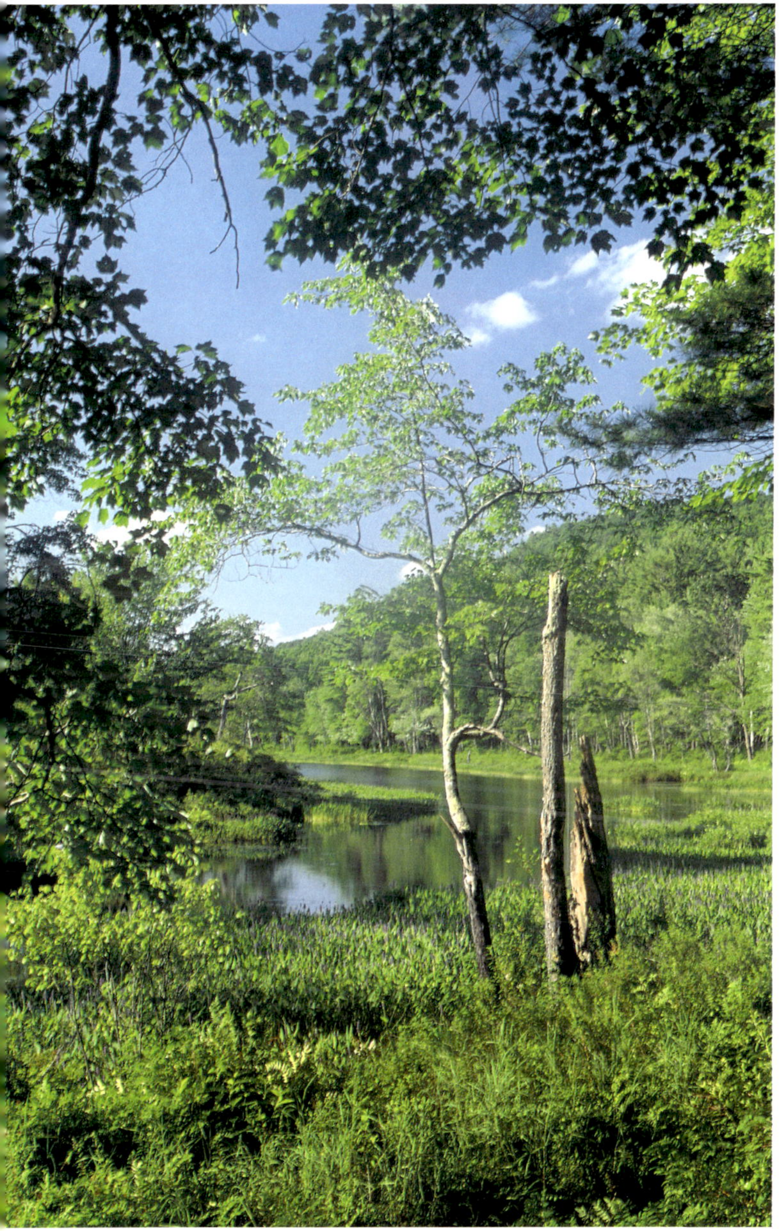

Much of the land that unfolds beneath this vista lies in the heart of the North Quabbin Bioreserve, one of only a handful of such designated areas in Massachusetts. Bioreserves are large areas that are managed chiefly to protect the region's natural resources, in the process balancing economic development, cultural resources, recreation, and other human activities. The North Quabbin Bioreserve encompasses more than 120,000 acres in 19 towns in a 60-mile radius, forming a crucial link between the protected lands of the Quabbin Reservoir watershed and southern New Hampshire's Monadnock region. It was dedicated in December 2002 at a ceremony at Tully Meadow, a large, wildlife-rich wetland at the base of Tully Mountain's northwest slopes.

The Tully River Valley is the centerpiece of the North Quabbin Bioreserve, one of only five such designated areas in Massachusetts.

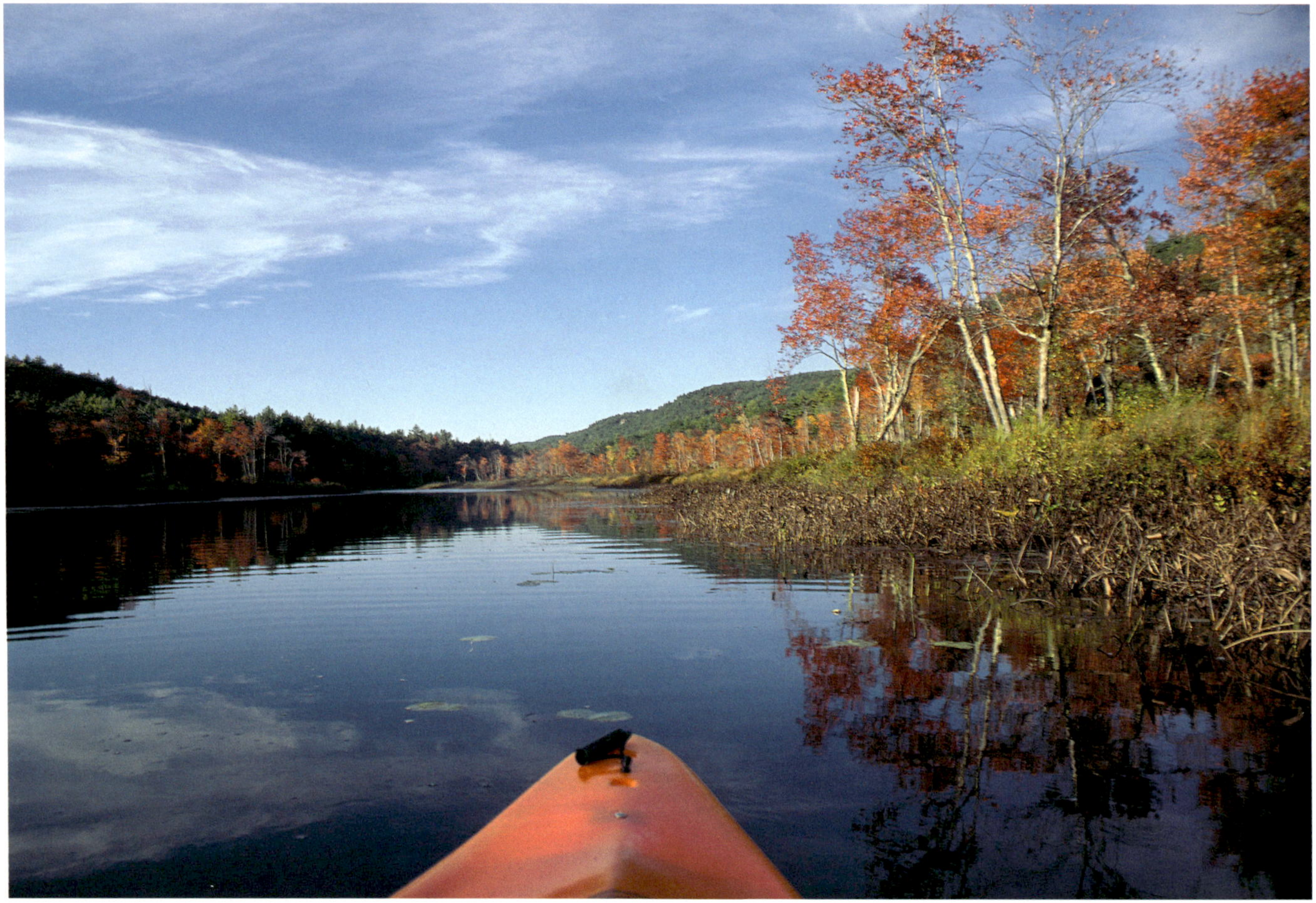

The many recreational opportunities at Tully Lake and Long Pond include hiking, biking, and paddling trails, a disc golf course, fishing, and a popular campground.

In lobbying for the bioreserve, Senator Stephen Brewer evoked memories of the controversial creation of Quabbin Reservoir, which will be discussed shortly, when four communities of the nearby Swift River Valley were taken over by the state: "I explained to them what happened seventy years ago. You need to gain the trust of the people. They love their land up here. They know the land is the only thing that matters."

The project owed much of its success to the efforts of the Mount Grace Land Conservation Trust, which, starting with a two-person staff and a decidedly modest budget, successfully brokered more than 100 deals with valley landowners during 2001 and 2002.

Executive director Leigh Youngblood recalls: "Beginning with the bequest of a modest ranch house near the Tully River in Athol to our historic partnership with Massachusetts Secretary of the Environment Bob Durand, many individuals have contributed to Mount Grace's protection of the Tully River Watershed. The initiative in particular set the course for partnerships and landscape-scale conservation that has continued to the present day." Indeed, over the past quarter-century the Trust has been involved in nearly 300 projects that have protected 27,000 acres across north-central Massachusetts.

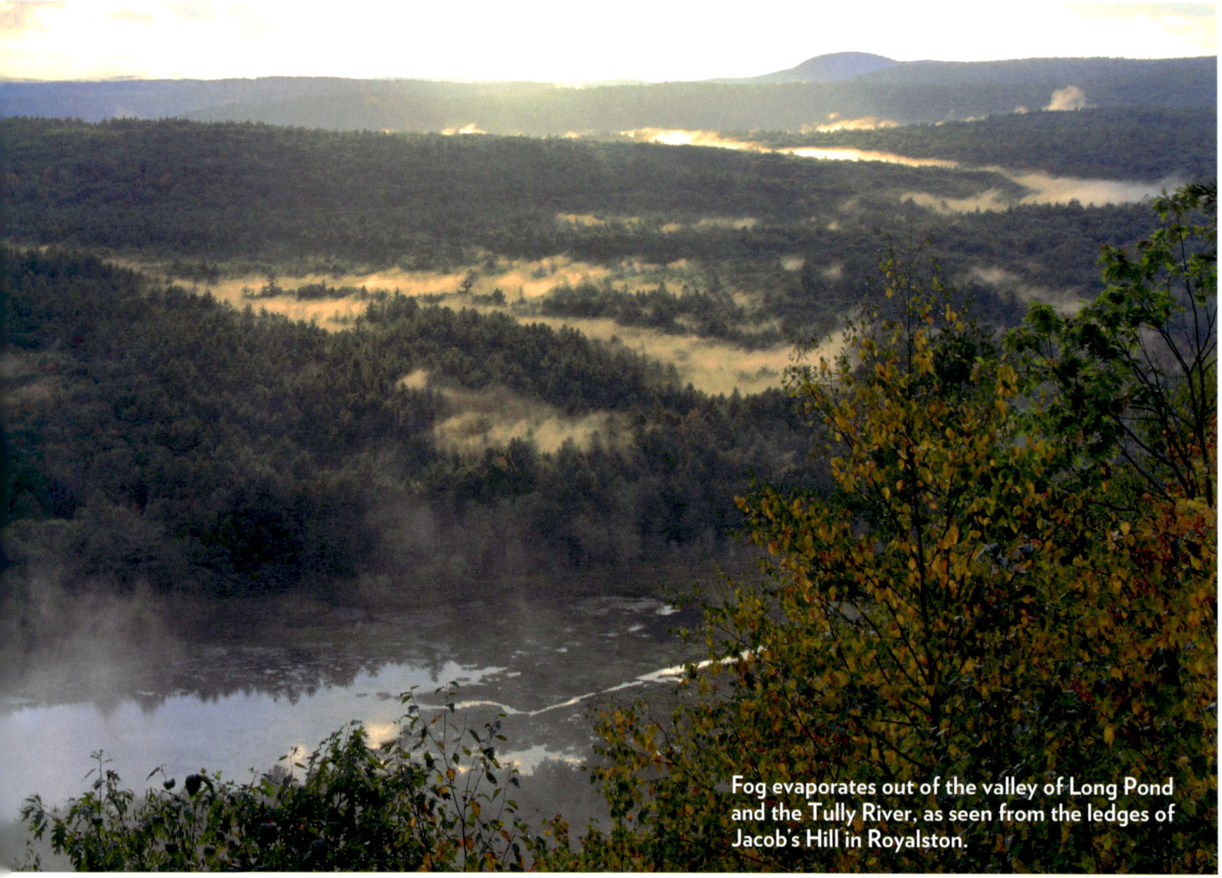

Fog evaporates out of the valley of Long Pond and the Tully River, as seen from the ledges of Jacob's Hill in Royalston.

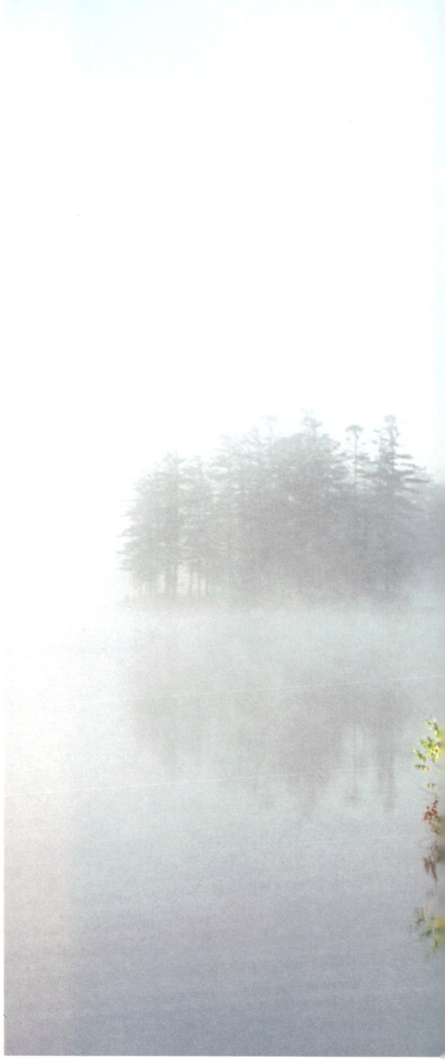

Marking the eastern extent of the Tully watershed is the long wall of Jacobs Ridge, which has been called "the backbone of Royalston." Hikers enjoy fine westerly views across the valley of Long Pond and the Tully River from rocky lookouts at Jacobs Hill and the Ledges, while paddlers on the pond negotiate quiet waters and beaver dams against this scenic backdrop. A short distance from the town's historic common, boggy Little Pond serves as the source for Spirit Falls, a seasonal cascade that makes a long descent to Long Pond in the valley below.

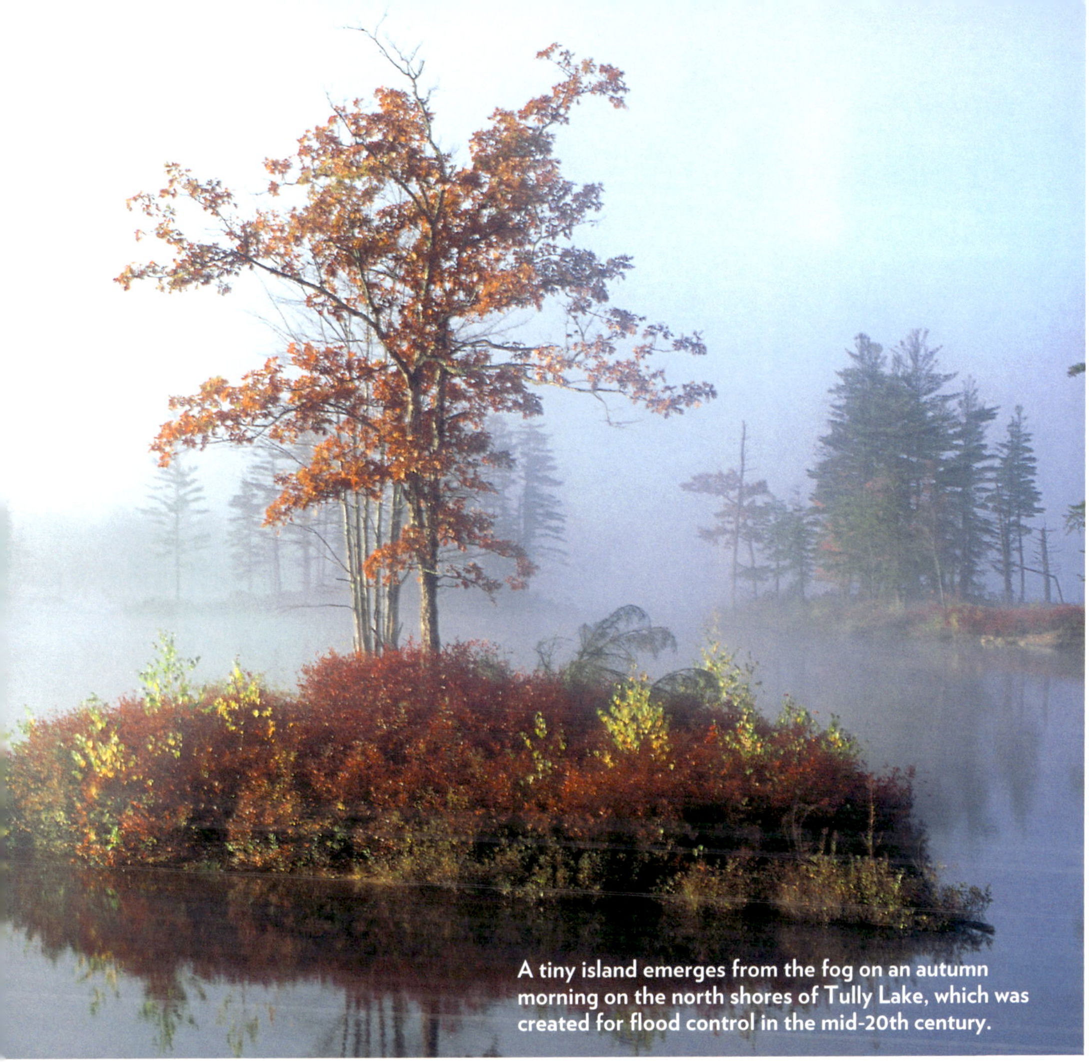

A tiny island emerges from the fog on an autumn morning on the north shores of Tully Lake, which was created for flood control in the mid-20th century.

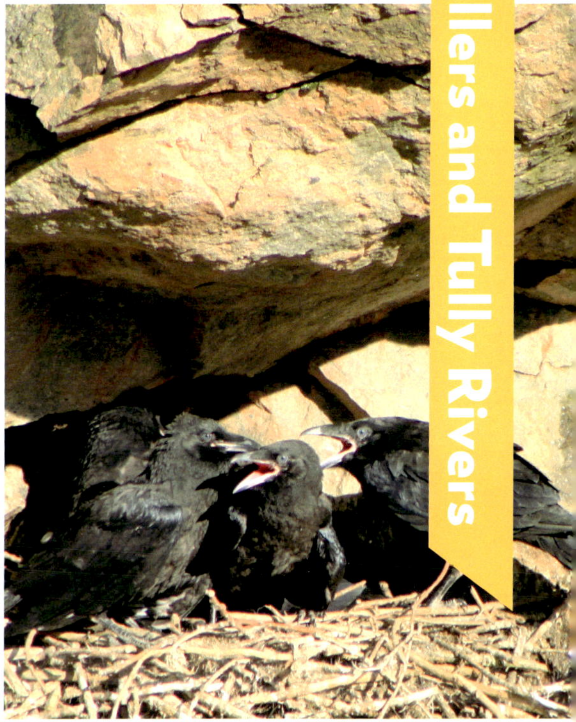

Long revered for their cunning and as a wilderness symbol, breeding common ravens returned to central Massachusetts in the early 1980s.

Long Pond is the finger-like northern arm of Tully Lake, which is part of another flood-control impoundment built in the aftermath of the 1930s floods. In fact, Tully Dam was activated several months before it was completed during the New Year's Day floods of 1949. Tully Lake was created behind the dam in 1964, and is now the centerpiece of a popular recreation area with hiking, mountain bike and paddling trails, a disc golf course, picnic area, and campground. Tully Lake, Birch Hill, Barre Falls, and other flood-control dams in central New England work in conjunction with the Reservoir Regulation Team, which monitors river levels and coordinates water level management when severe storms such as Hurricane Irene in 2011 are forecast.

In describing the Tully region, Edward Hitchcock noted "at least three waterfalls connected with deep gorges in Royalston that are well worth the attention of those who are fond of wild natural scenery." The largest and most-visited of these cascades is Doanes Falls, where Lawrence Brook drops 200 feet to the inlet of Tully Lake over a quarter-mile long rocky slope.

Colonial explorers noted this active waterway's industrial potential as early as the mid-18th century, and a number of mills were built along its banks during Royalston's industrial heyday, including a four-story operation owned by Amos Doane whom the falls are named after.

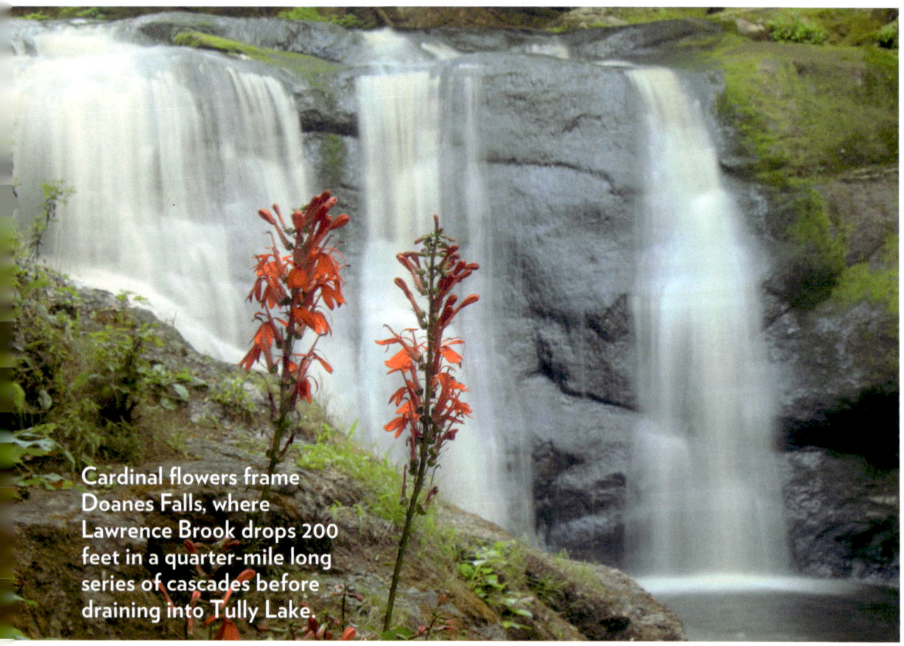
Cardinal flowers frame Doanes Falls, where Lawrence Brook drops 200 feet in a quarter-mile long series of cascades before draining into Tully Lake.

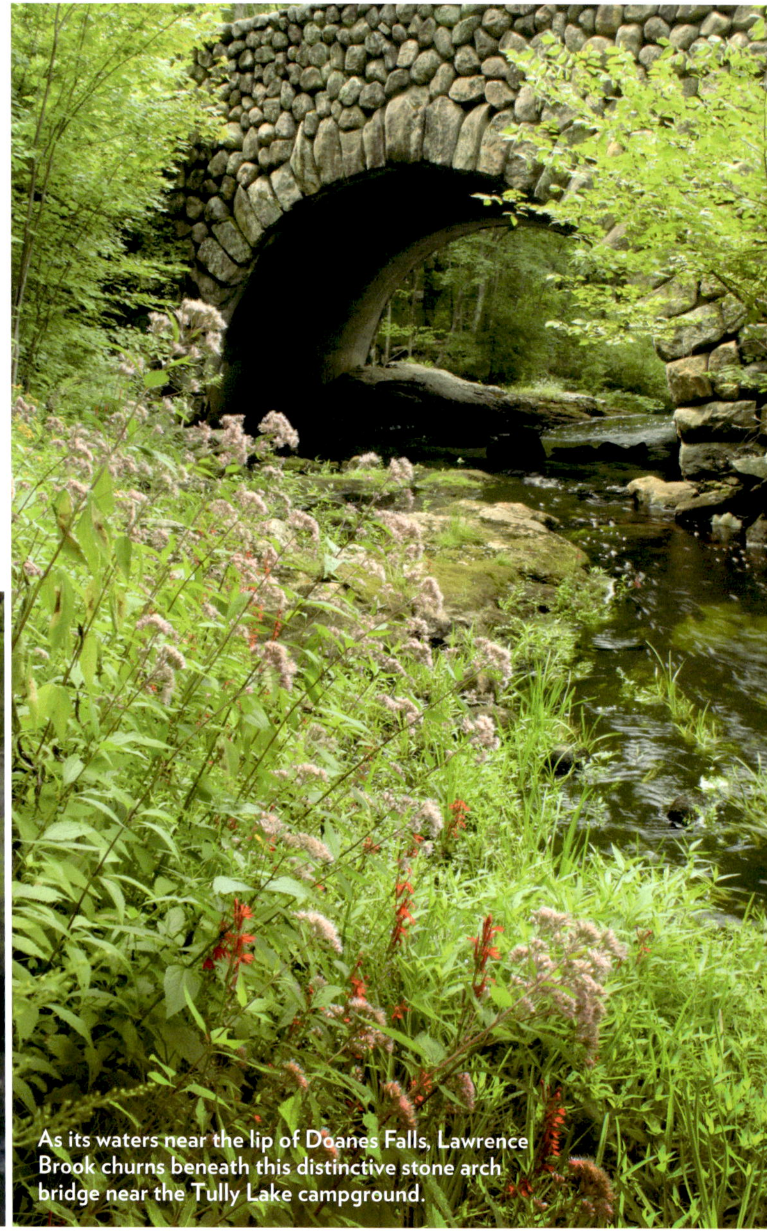
As its waters near the lip of Doanes Falls, Lawrence Brook churns beneath this distinctive stone arch bridge near the Tully Lake campground.

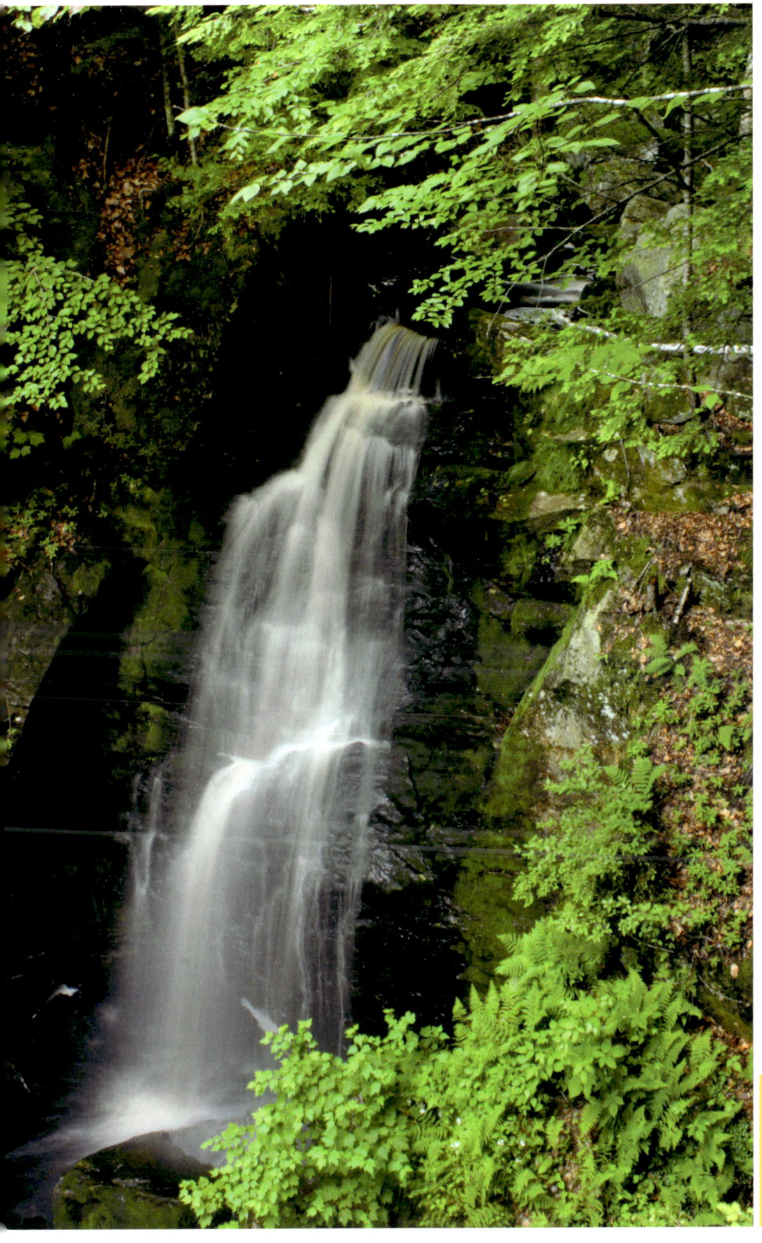

According to local accounts, this had less to do with his products and more with his colorful personality; in the words of one historian, he was "engaged in many law suits...many interesting anecdotes are related of him.

The more secluded Royalston Falls have an entirely different character, as narrow Falls Brook makes a long, graceful plunge into a dramatic gorge lined by evergreen hemlock trees. An early account of the valley by the Trustees of Reservations described the topography as "quite startling," and it indeed is one of the region's most unusual natural areas. In addition to the falls and gorge, upstream are pools, rocks, and a tiny natural bridge that have also been shaped by the brook's continual carving power. When hiking to the falls through the valley's quiet, remote woods, it's hard to imagine that this area was once the site of popular town festivals and a casino.

Now surrounded by dense woodlands along the Tully Trail corridor, picturesque Royalston Falls was once the site of town festivals and a casino.

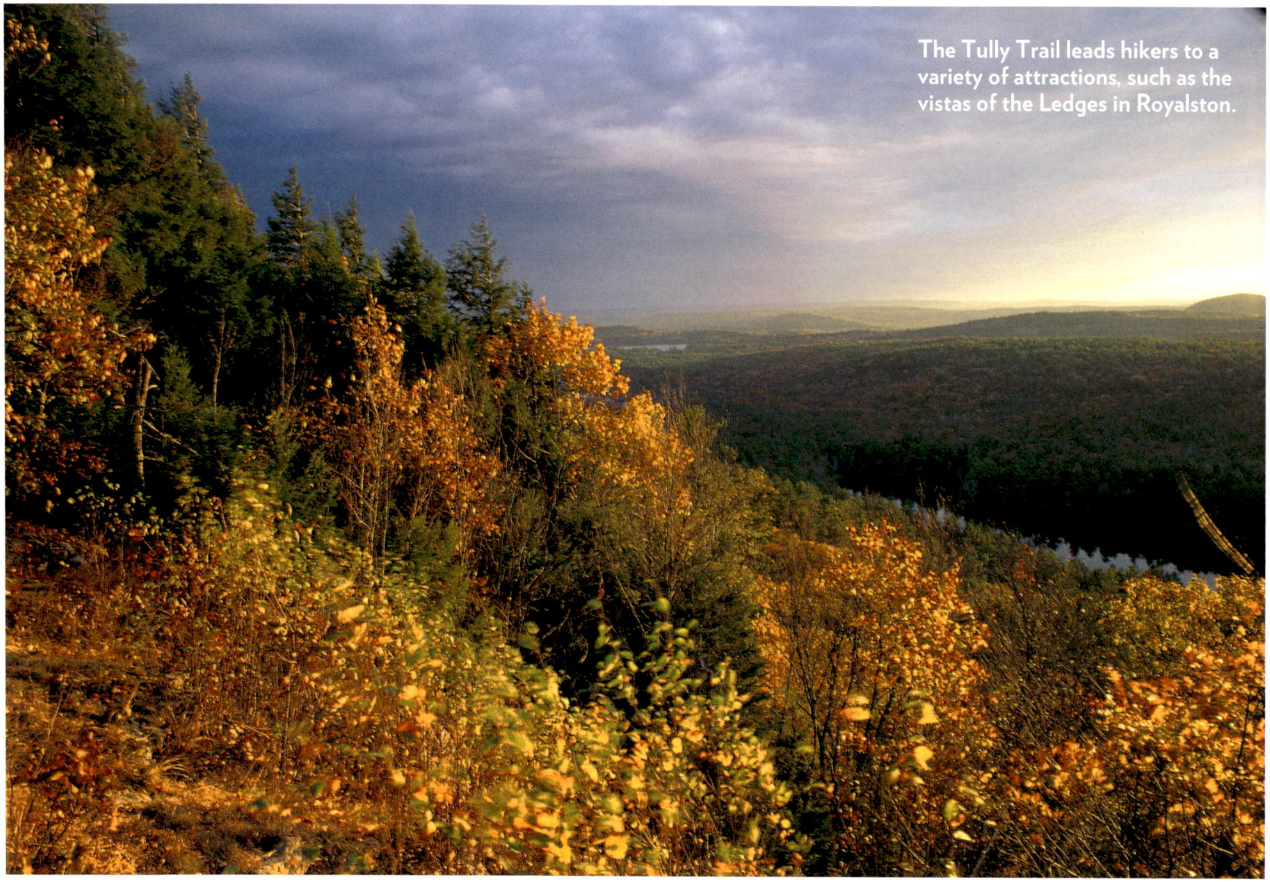

The Tully Trail leads hikers to a variety of attractions, such as the vistas of the Ledges in Royalston.

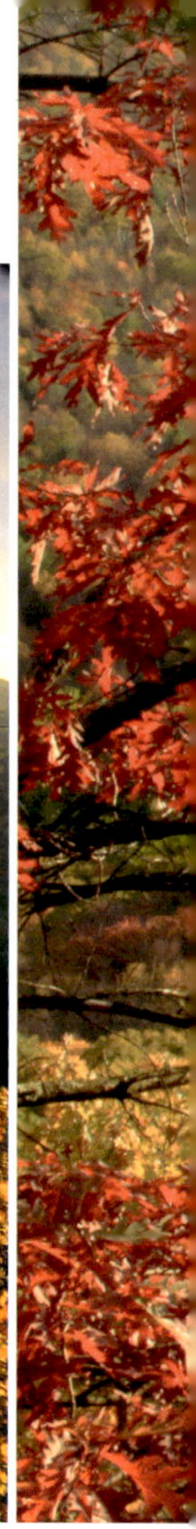

In addition to the bioreserve, the valley is now home to the Tully Trail, a recently created 22-mile-long circuit that passes the aforementioned natural features and other conservation areas. Volunteers completed the first two miles in 1994, and with the support and management of local groups, such as the Trustees of Reservations, the Appalachian Mountain Club, and the Mount Grace Land Conservation Trust, have expanded the route to its present length. Though the loop traverses some rolling and rugged terrain, especially at Tully Mountain and Jacobs Hill, it is generally gentle enough that hard-core hikers can complete it in a long day of walking.

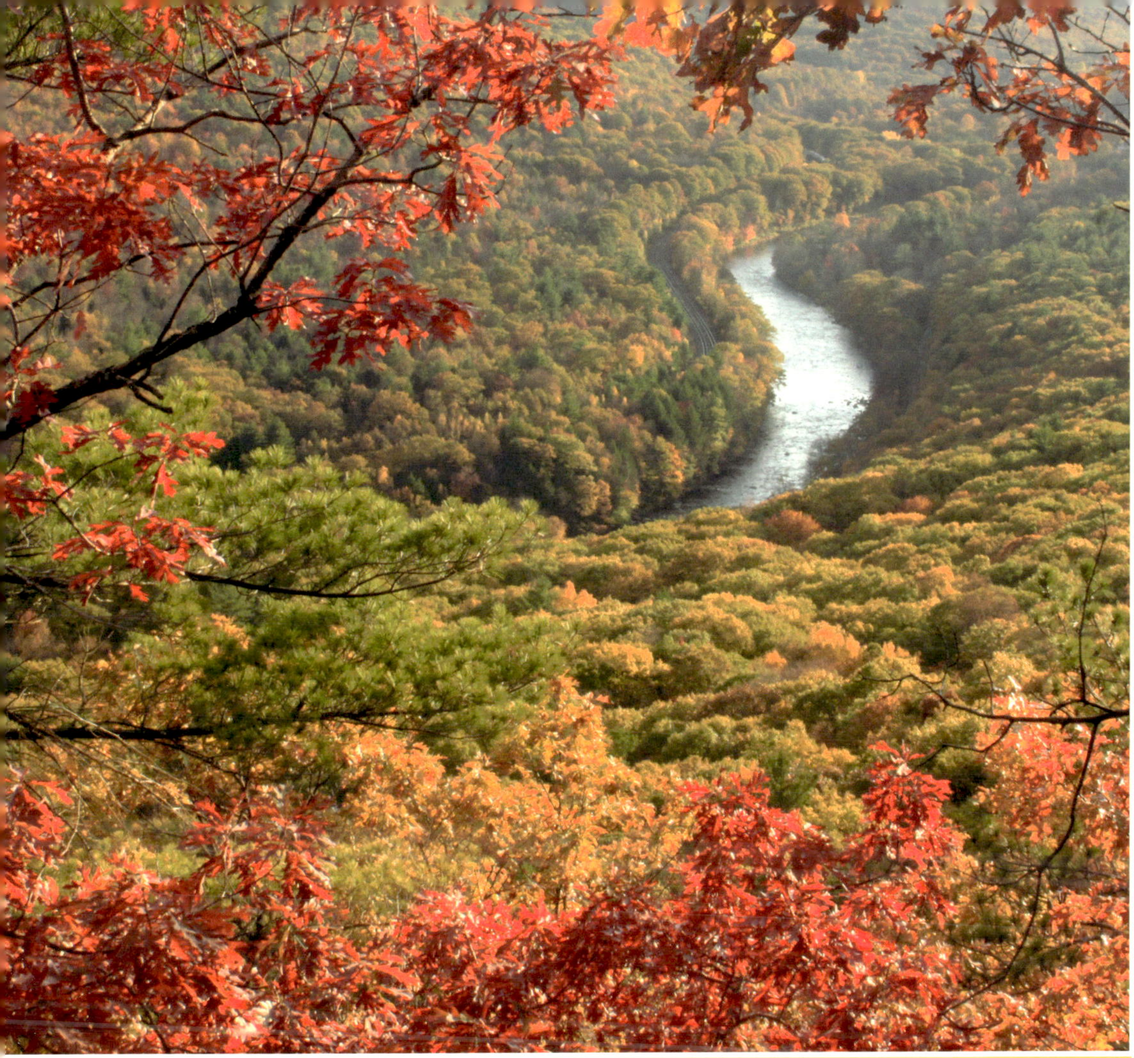

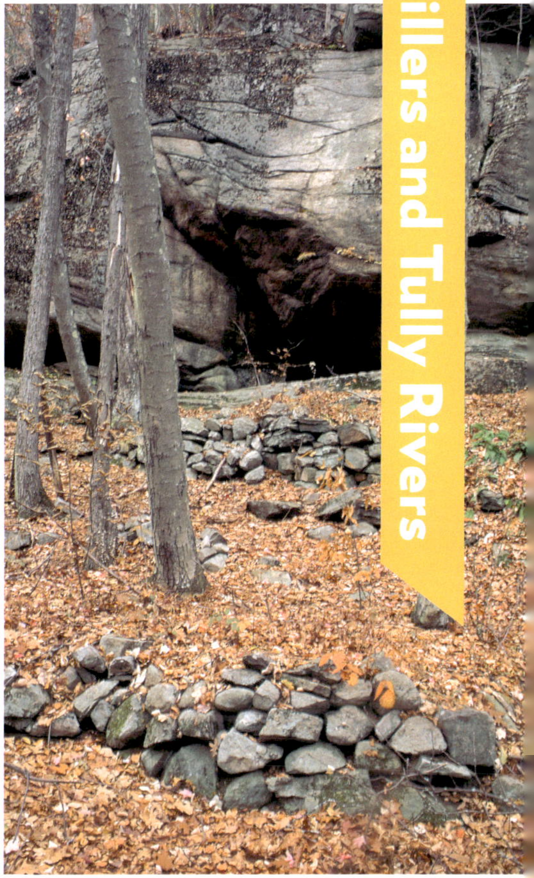

This panoramic overview of the Millers River Valley from the ledges of Hermit Mountain in Erving is one of the finest overlooks along the New England National Scenic Trail.

Once home to John Smith, a Scottish immigrant who entertained thousands of visitors during the late 19th century, the Hermit's Castle is one of the region's most unique historic sites.

The lower portion of the Millers River Valley in Erving and Wendell is especially scenic, as the river and Route 2 wind through a narrow corridor between Northfield and Bear Mountains.

Above the north banks rises the rocky ridge of Hermit Mountain, a shoulder of Northfield Mountain so named for one John Smith, a Scotsman who made his home in a rock cave known as the "Erving Castle" in the late 19th century.

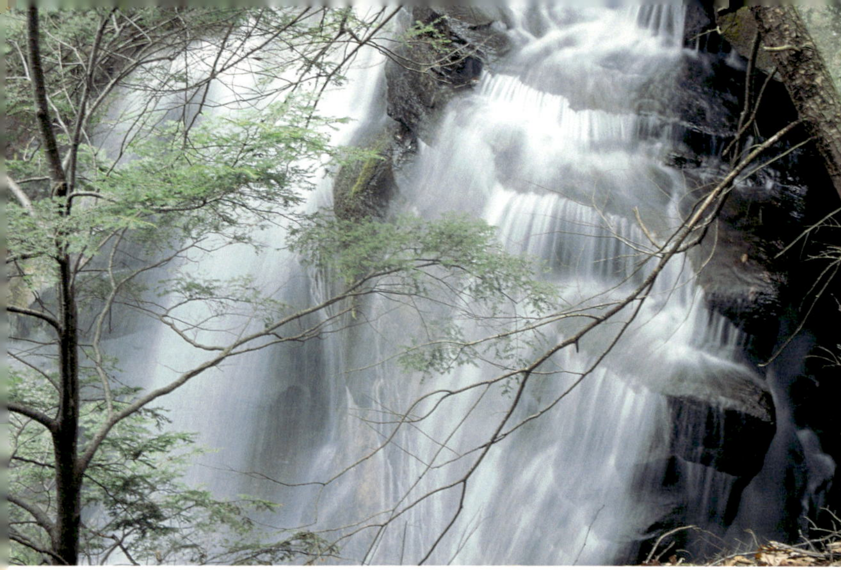

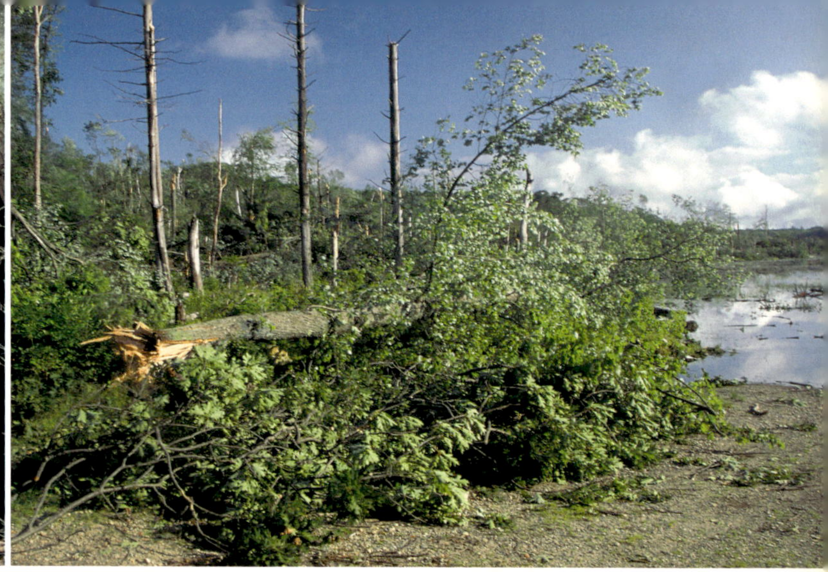

Fed by the outflow from the Northfield Mountain reservoir, seasonal Briggs Brook cascades over steep rock ledges on Hermit Mountain near Erving.

A considerable portion of the Wendell State Forest, including the area around Wickett Pond, was damaged by a tornado in July 2006.

As detailed by naturalist John Foster in a history of Smith and the Castle, in the context of the time a "hermit" was not a total recluse from society, but instead someone who lived on the estates of nobility and entertained lords and their guests. Indeed, after Smith left such a life in his native Scotland to move to central Massachusetts in 1866, he actively promoted both himself and the Castle and entertained thousands of visitors, including the Count and Countess of Prussia. The low stone walls adjacent to the cave site likely mark his former vegetable and flower gardens. After relocating down the slope following the arrival of a periodically contentious fellow hermit, Smith continued to live at the ledges until 1899, when he became ill and moved to Montague for the final year of his life. Today the Castle continues to be visited by hikers, who arrive via a short side trail off of the New England National Scenic Trail. Above the cave site are 800-foot high ledges with outstanding panoramic views of the heavily forested valley.

The Erving and Wendell State Forests combine to form yet another large block of protected land here, more than 11,000 acres worth of forests, rocky outcroppings, and wetlands that shelter moose, bears, bobcats, peregrine falcons, and other wild creatures. A popular attraction of the former is Laurel Lake, where a swimming beach lies

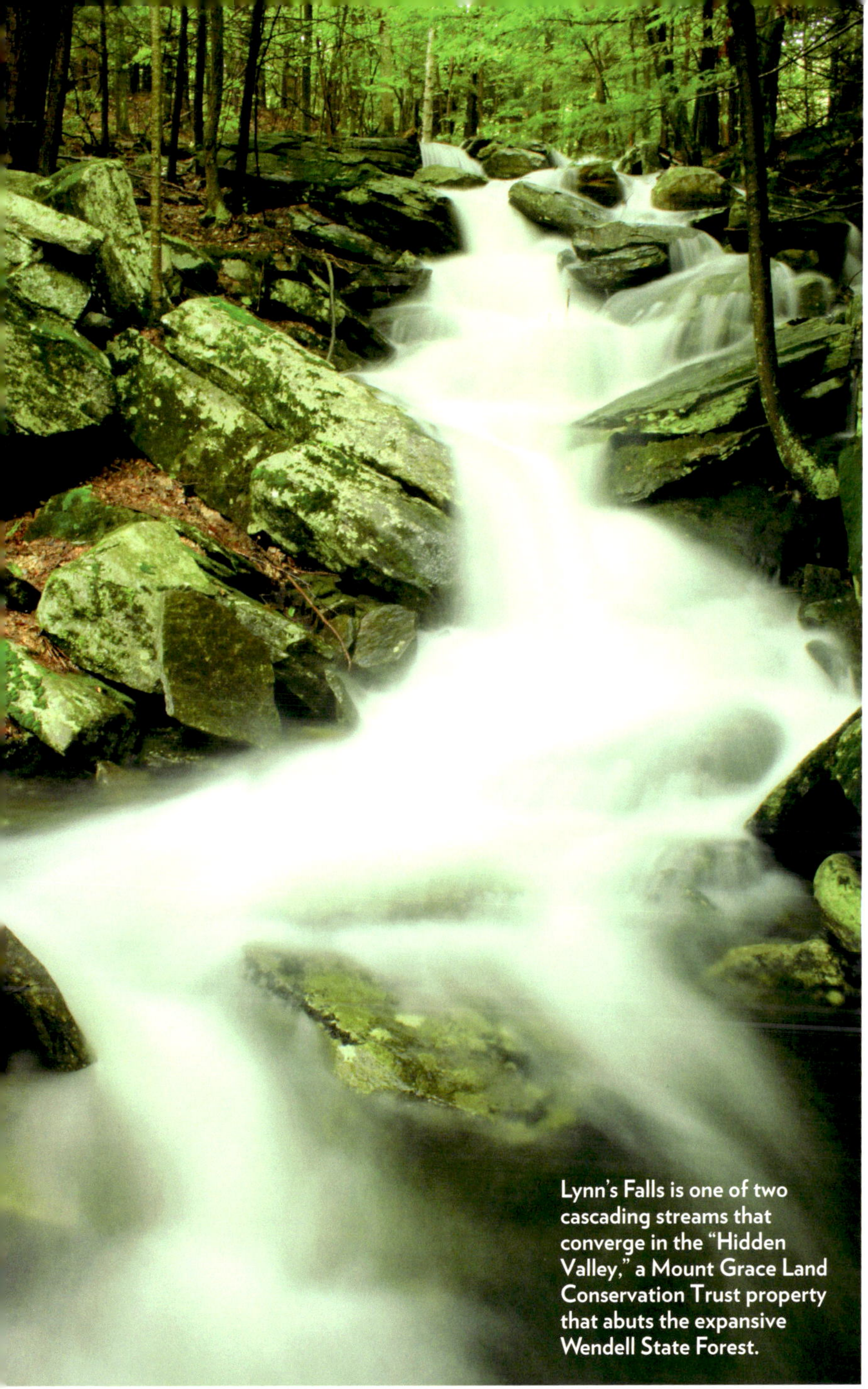
Lynn's Falls is one of two cascading streams that converge in the "Hidden Valley," a Mount Grace Land Conservation Trust property that abuts the expansive Wendell State Forest.

nestled beneath a ridge cloaked with groves of mountain laurel. Lookouts offer views of the valley topography and a glimpse of Mount Monadnock, which rises through the trees to the north.

Across the valley to the south are the mixed forests, rocky ridges, cascading streams, and ponds of the Wendell State Forest, which is another link in the New England National Scenic Trail corridor. A wide swath of fallen timber is the legacy of a powerful F2 tornado that destroyed thousands of trees and damaged several homes and barns in Wendell in July 2006, though fortunately there were no human fatalities. One doesn't think of central New England as tornado country, but they do occur periodically, as evidenced by the storms that caused extensive forest and property damage in southern Hampden County on June 1, 2011. An even more devastating twister was the 1955 category F5 storm that originated at the northern tip of Quabbin Reservoir. After killing two people in Barre near the onset of its southwesterly course, the tornado touched down in downtown Worcester, killing more than 100 people. The towering top of the massive storm was visible to weather observers as far west as Schenectady, New York.

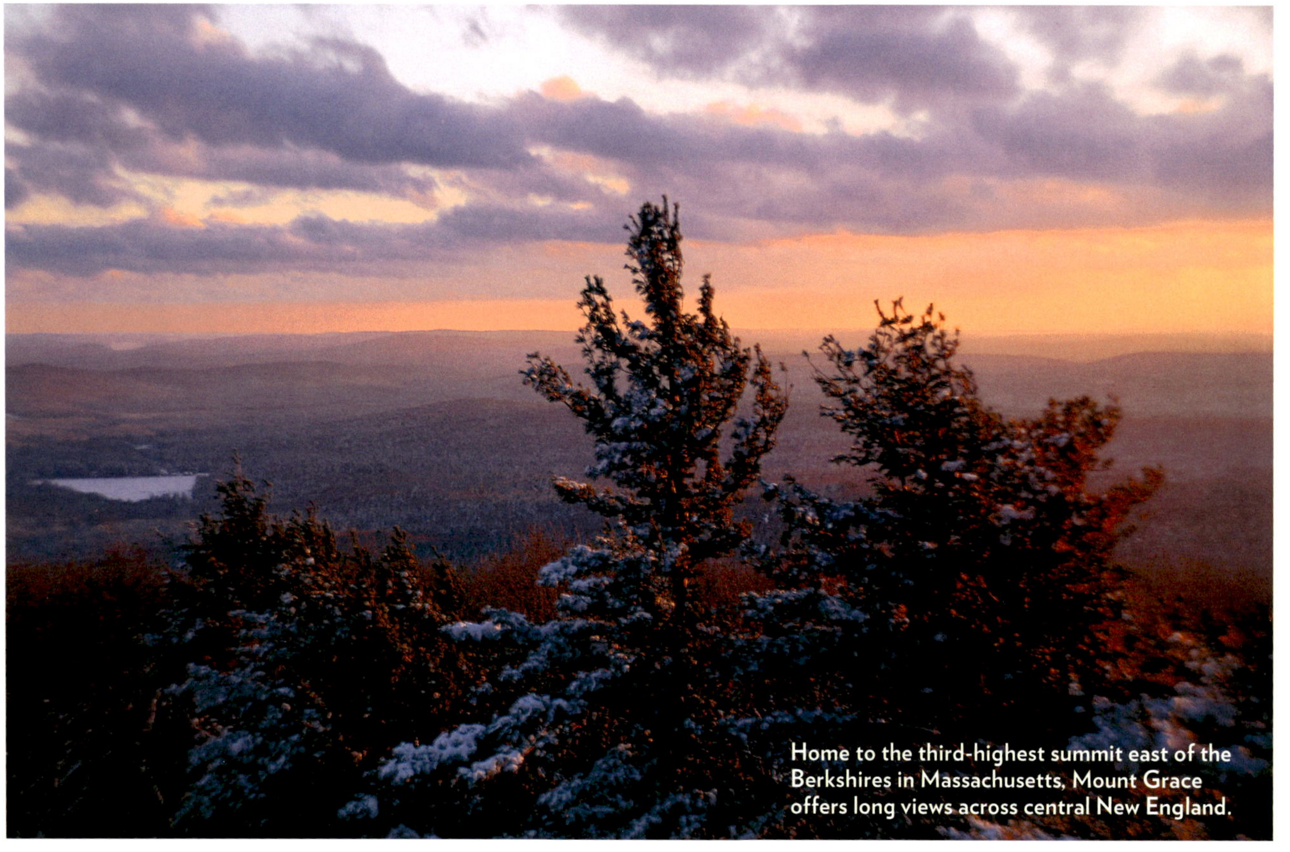

Home to the third-highest summit east of the Berkshires in Massachusetts, Mount Grace offers long views across central New England.

Just east of the confluence of the Millers and Connecticut Rivers are more low mountains and hills that mark the transition from the central uplands to the Connecticut Valley. The highest of these eminences is Mount Grace in Warwick, which, at 1,617 feet, is the third-highest summit east of the Berkshires, after only Wachusett Mountain and Mount Watatic. It is the centerpiece of one of the oldest state forests in Massachusetts, a 1,700-acre tract established during the early 1920s. The 40-foot high summit fire tower, which is part of a regional network of fire-control lookouts that also includes Wachusett Mountain and Mount Toby, was first erected on the summit in 1911 and rebuilt after the hurricane of 1938. The mountain was once an active ski area with several trails, but it suffered from insufficient facilities and ceased operations by the early 1960s.

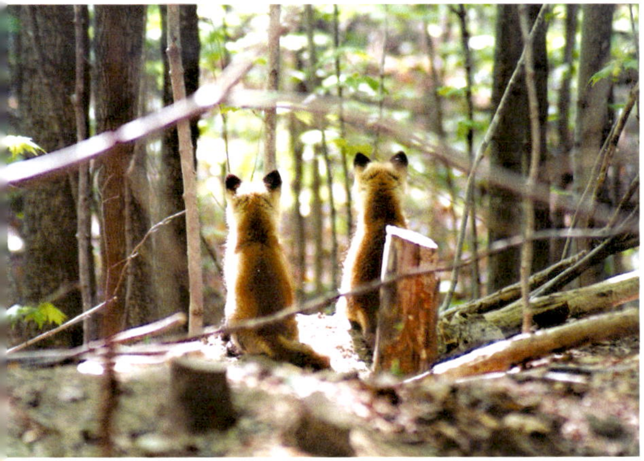

"Watching:" Two young red fox kits await the return of their mother to their den at the edge of a farm field.

Today, the mountain's primary recreational users are hikers, who enjoy long views from the highest point on the New England National Scenic Trail in Massachusetts and Connecticut. Like Wachusett Mountain, Mount Grace has a relatively modest elevation, but is sufficiently isolated to afford long, 360-degree views that include the Quabbin and Connecticut Valleys, the Berkshires, Mount Monadnock and southern New Hampshire, and Vermont as far north as the pyramid-shaped profile of Mount Ascutney.

Nestled below the rocky, hemlock-capped ridge of nearby Brush Mountain is a small wetland of regionally uncommon black gum trees, a southern species that arrived in the region during a postglacial climate warming period. At the base of the east slopes are the stone foundations from the homestead of Calvin T. Swan, an African-American of many talents. In addition to building many of Northfield's prominent homes, he was a farmer, mill operator, and a charter member of the Franklin County Anti-Slavery Society.

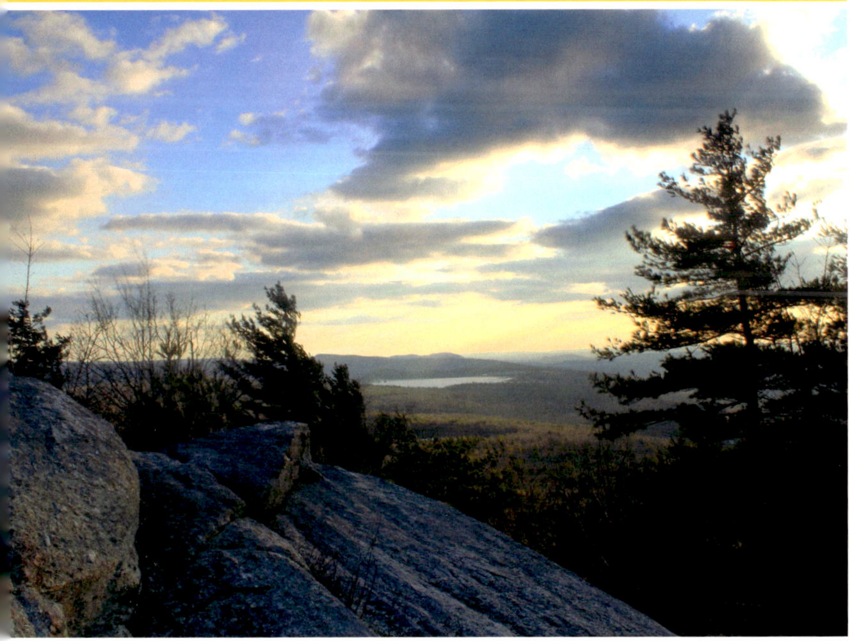

Northfield Mountain, seen here from a nearby lookout, is home to a large recreation area and summit reservoir used for hydroelectric power.

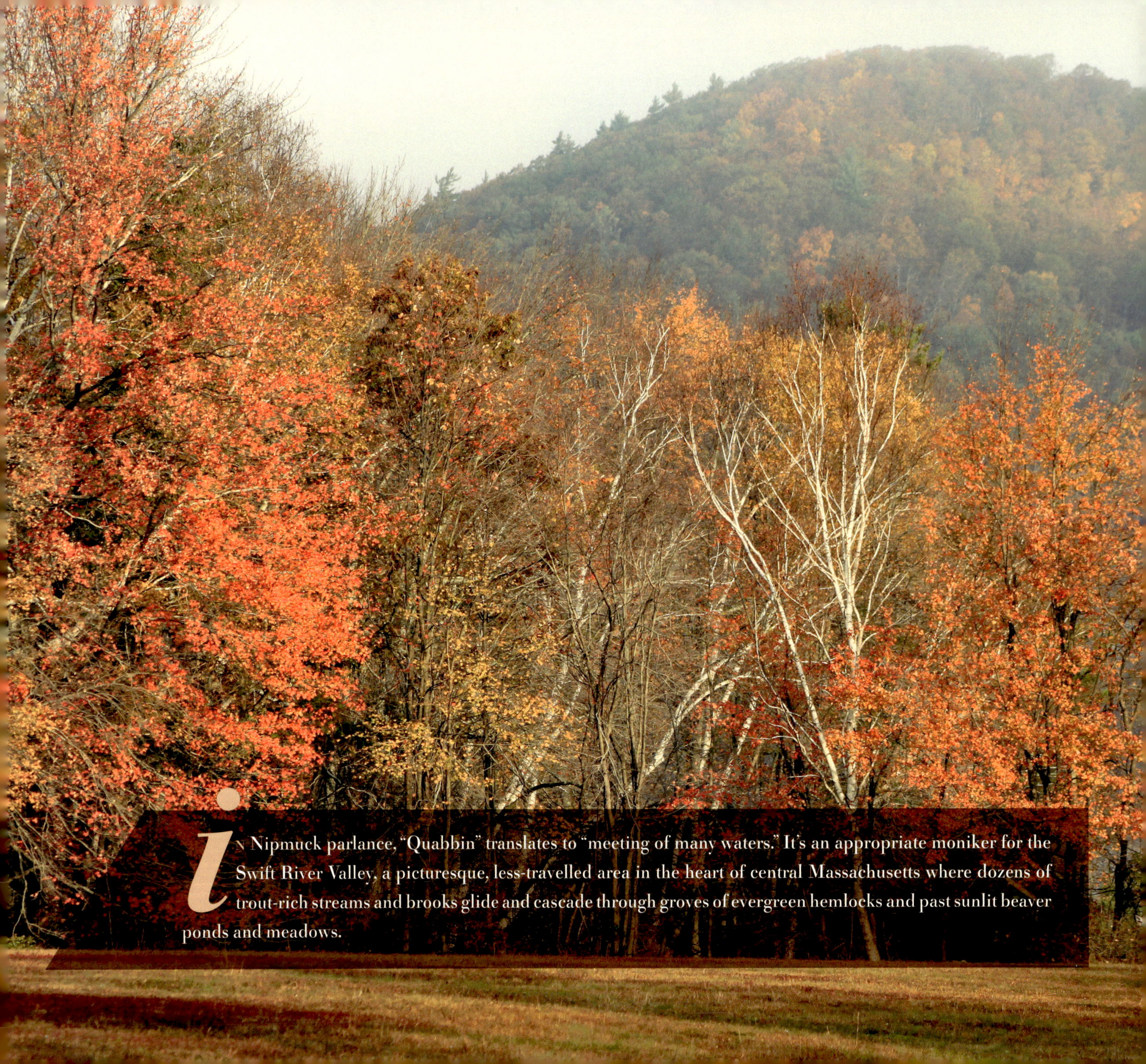

In Nipmuck parlance, "Quabbin" translates to "meeting of many waters." It's an appropriate moniker for the Swift River Valley, a picturesque, less-travelled area in the heart of central Massachusetts where dozens of trout-rich streams and brooks glide and cascade through groves of evergreen hemlocks and past sunlit beaver ponds and meadows.

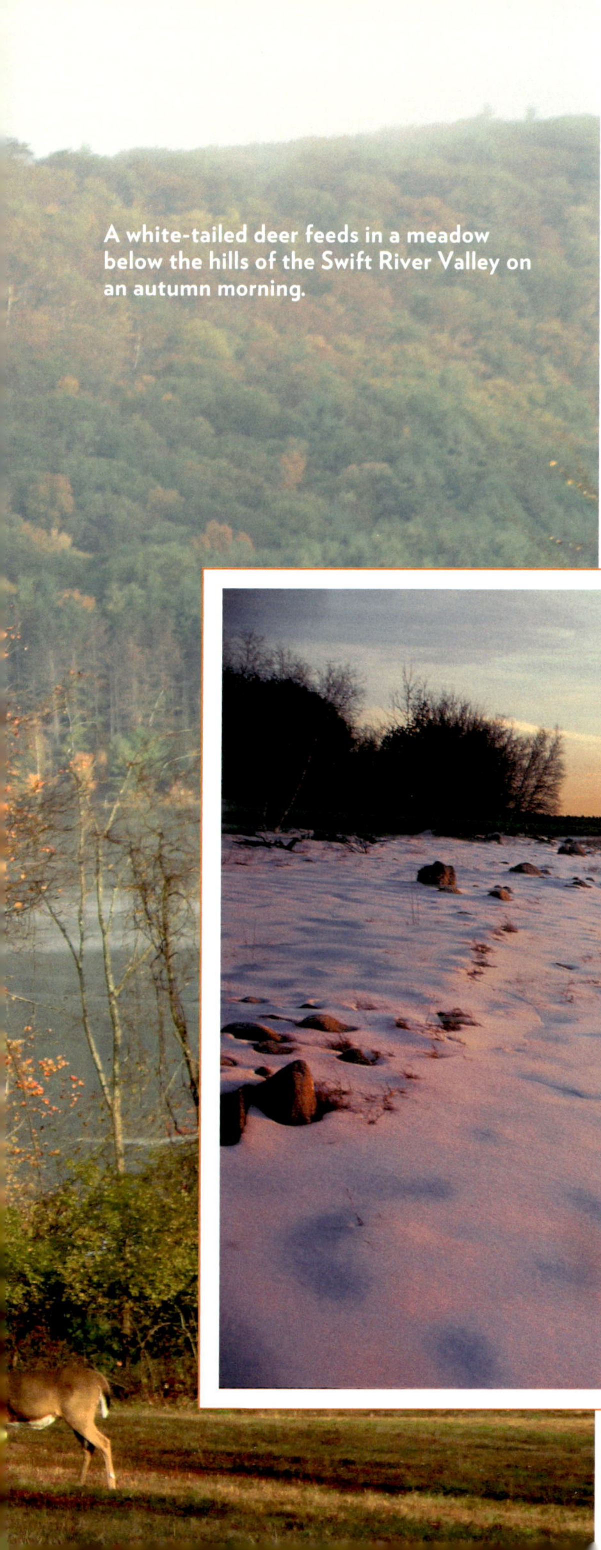

A white-tailed deer feeds in a meadow below the hills of the Swift River Valley on an autumn morning.

Originally the domain of the Nipmuck, from the 1730s onward the valley was home to small towns and villages established by settlers amidst the rolling hills and ridges. The three branches of the Swift River and its larger tributaries provided power for a variety of mills, including modest-sized manufacturing centers at Enfield and Dana, while arable lands such as Greenwich Plains and the hills of Prescott yielded cereals, fruits, and other crops. Summer visitors enjoyed the scenery from the many camps and cottages that were built along the shores of the numerous lakes, ponds, and streams. Many visitors arrived via the "Rabbit Run," a railroad line so named for the many stops, or "hops," it made between Springfield and Athol.

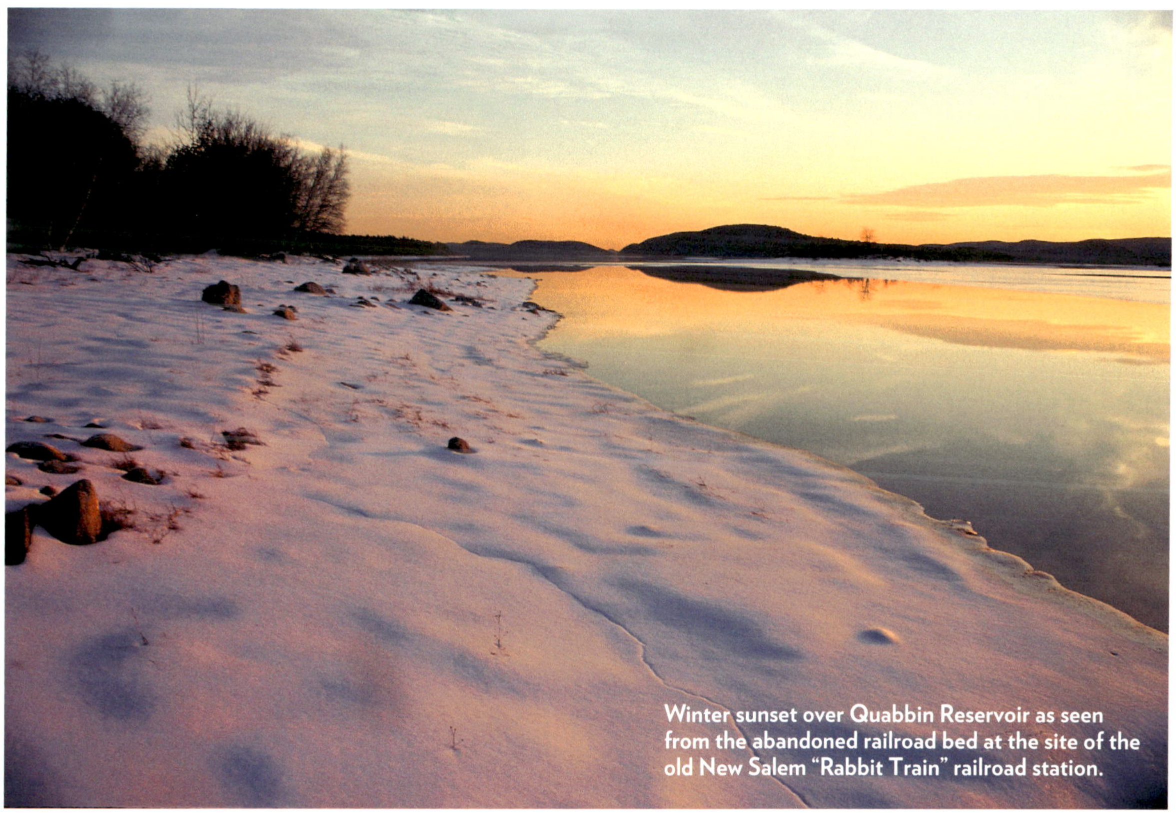

Winter sunset over Quabbin Reservoir as seen from the abandoned railroad bed at the site of the old New Salem "Rabbit Train" railroad station.

The "Rabbit" train's passengers in 1895 likely included a group of engineers sent by planners in Boston to investigate the suitability of the Swift River Valley for a giant artificial reservoir. From nearly the time of settlement onward, water supply was a constant issue for Boston and eastern Massachusetts. As the region's population increased, its local water sources were rapidly depleted, and the city suffered heavily from a series of devastating fires during the 18th century. In response, over the next two centuries planners and engineers undertook a long process of expanding the state water supply network to include sources that were both progressively larger and further to the west, culminating (or so many people thought) with the opening of the Wachusett Reservoir near Worcester as the world's largest artificial reservoir in 1905.

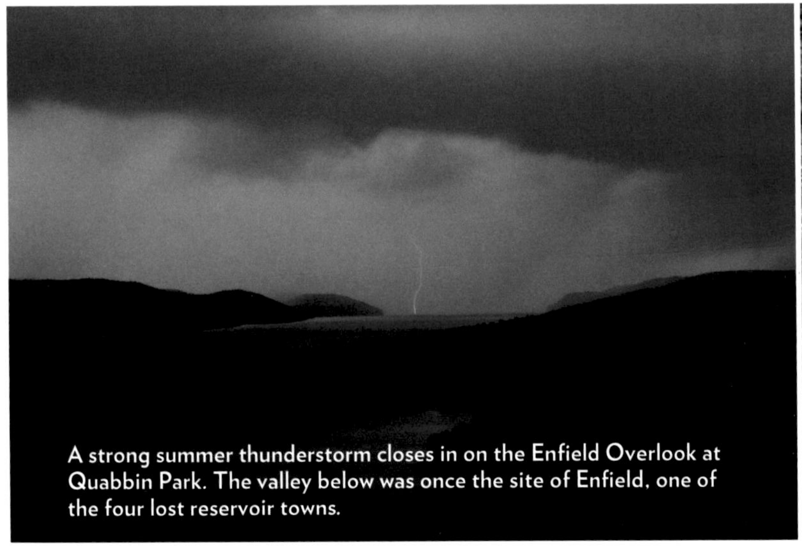
A strong summer thunderstorm closes in on the Enfield Overlook at Quabbin Park. The valley below was once the site of Enfield, one of the four lost reservoir towns.

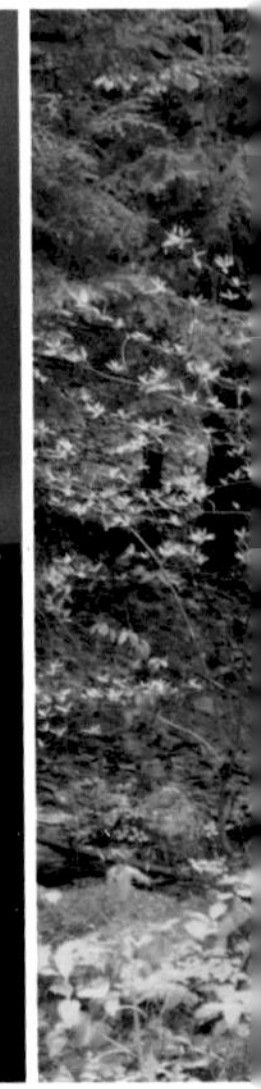

However, within a decade after the opening of Wachusett Reservoir, droughts and the ongoing demand of the greater Boston and Worcester areas prompted planners to pursue the Swift River project in earnest. From an engineering perspective, the valley was a logical location for a reservoir on several counts: its bowl-shaped topography was well-suited to hold a large body of water behind a simple dam, its waters were relatively clean and unspoiled during an era when many other New England rivers were heavily polluted, and it had a light human population with few manufacturing areas or landmarks. The last point was especially significant and controversial, as the proposed reservoir would necessitate the flooding of four towns and their associated villages. As rumors of the impending project gathered strength, the affected communities predictably fell into rapid decline, as property values plummeted and businesses closed, and, by 1920, the specter and reality of the impending reservoir loomed heavily over the valley.

Though there was naturally resistance from the residents of the doomed towns of Enfield, Greenwich, Prescott, and Dana, as well as some mill owners with interests downstream from the proposed dam site, the valley interests were essentially powerless against the political clout of eastern Massachusetts, and the state formally authorized the Swift River, or "Quabbin" project in April 1927. Prescott, whose population had dwindled to a mere 250 residents by 1927, was disincorporated shortly after the project was approved, while Enfield, Dana, and Greenwich retained their

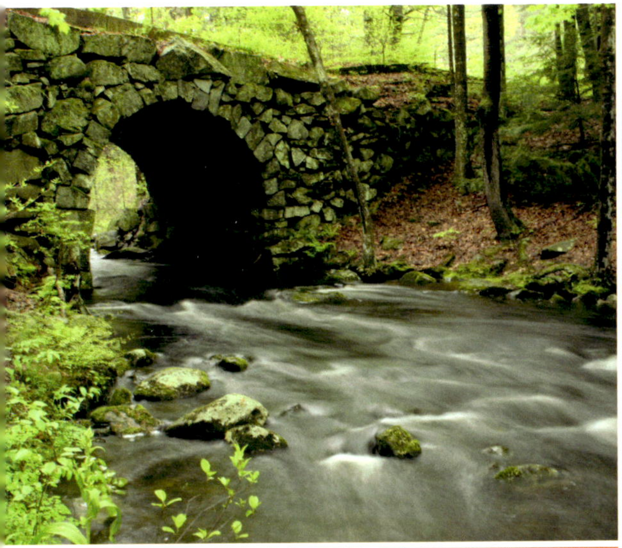

One of the most distinctive historic landmarks in Quabbin Reservation is the Keystone Bridge, which has spanned the Middle Branch of the Swift River since 1866.

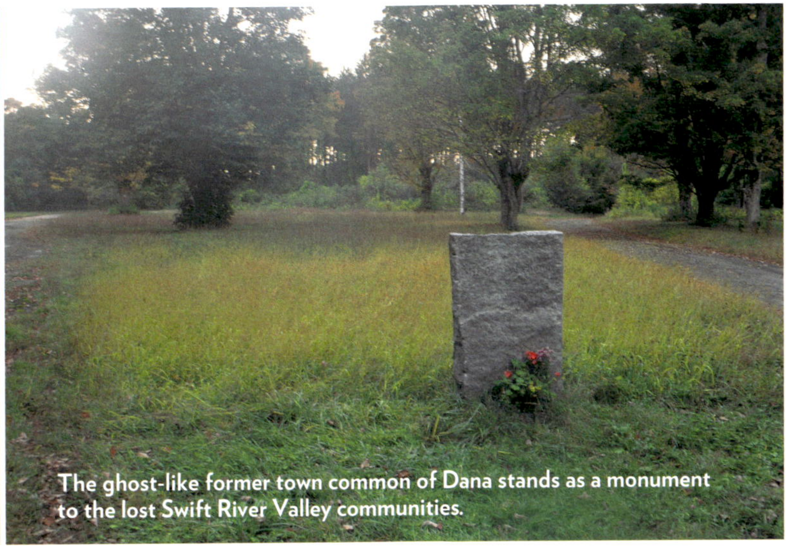

The ghost-like former town common of Dana stands as a monument to the lost Swift River Valley communities.

government through 1938. Portions of New Salem and Pelham were also taken over by the state.

One can imagine the emotions the residents of the lost towns must have felt as their formers neighborhoods and town centers were abandoned and razed (some buildings were moved to the surrounding towns), and the forests clear-cut and burned. The valley somewhat appropriately resembled a war zone, as global tensions increased during the 1930s, and at night the skies glowed with smoke from burning brush and trees. One of the last holdout residents was Guy Marvel of Dana, a farmer and fish hatchery owner who, unsatisfied with the offer for his property, took the state to court several times. After finally leaving in late 1941, two years after the reservoir began to fill, he bought the land adjacent to the reservation boundary to spite the water commission.

Though the town buildings are long gone, many historic markers, such as stone foundations and walls, mill and bridge sites, and old roads, remain as artifacts of the lost communities amidst Quabbin Reservation's extensive forests and wetlands. A well-known historic site is the former town common of Dana, which was abandoned because of its proximity to the watershed but not flooded. The stone foundations of the hotel, stores, and the other buildings that once lined the green are still visible, and the common and adjacent old fields are mowed and maintained for historic value and wildlife habitat. A simple stone monument memorializes the residents who had to leave their homes and change their lives to accommodate the reservoir.

The Swift River's waters were finally released into Quabbin in 1939, and the reservoir's size is evident in the fact that it took no less than seven years to fill to its 512-billion gallon capacity. With its construction, Boston's water needs finally seemed secure for a long time. However, almost unbelievably, within a matter of years the state faced yet another water crisis, after a long drought during the 1960s caused the reservoir to drop to less than half its capacity. Yet again, planners looked west for more sources, and conceived a plan to divert spring flood flows of the Connecticut River to Quabbin via the pumping station and reservoir on the summit of Northfield Mountain.

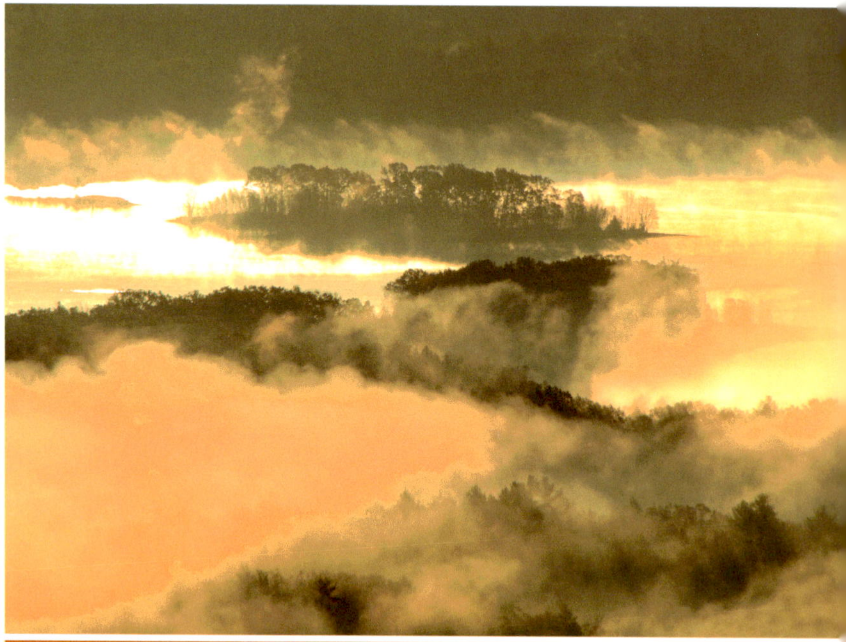

Early morning fog shrouds the hills of the Swift River Valley, which became islands after the creation of Quabbin Reservoir. 120 islands of various sizes are spread across the expansive waters.

Unlike the Quabbin proposal, the Connecticut River proposal ran into a fury of sustained opposition from conservation groups and university researchers in western Massachusetts and Connecticut during the 1970s and 1980s, and it never came to fruition. A fortunate by-product of these debates was that they prompted water conservation initiatives within eastern Massachusetts, such as leak detection, metering, and repairs to the centuries-old delivery pipes. These measures, along with abundant precipitation in recent decades, have proved very successful in reducing and stabilizing demand on the state water supply system.

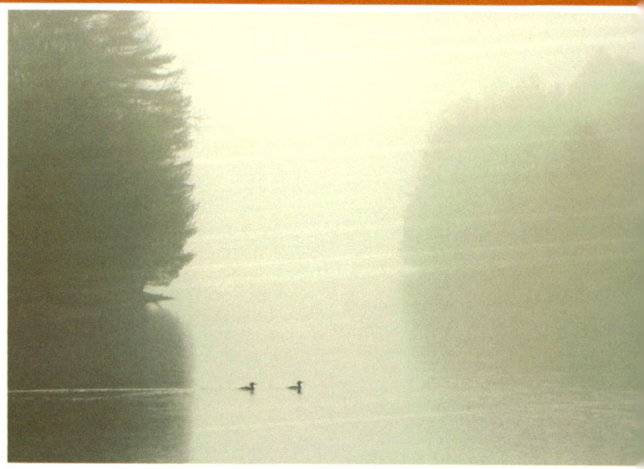

In early spring and late autumn, Quabbin Reservoir and the region's other lakes and ponds serve as crucial resting grounds for common mergansers and other migratory waterfowl.

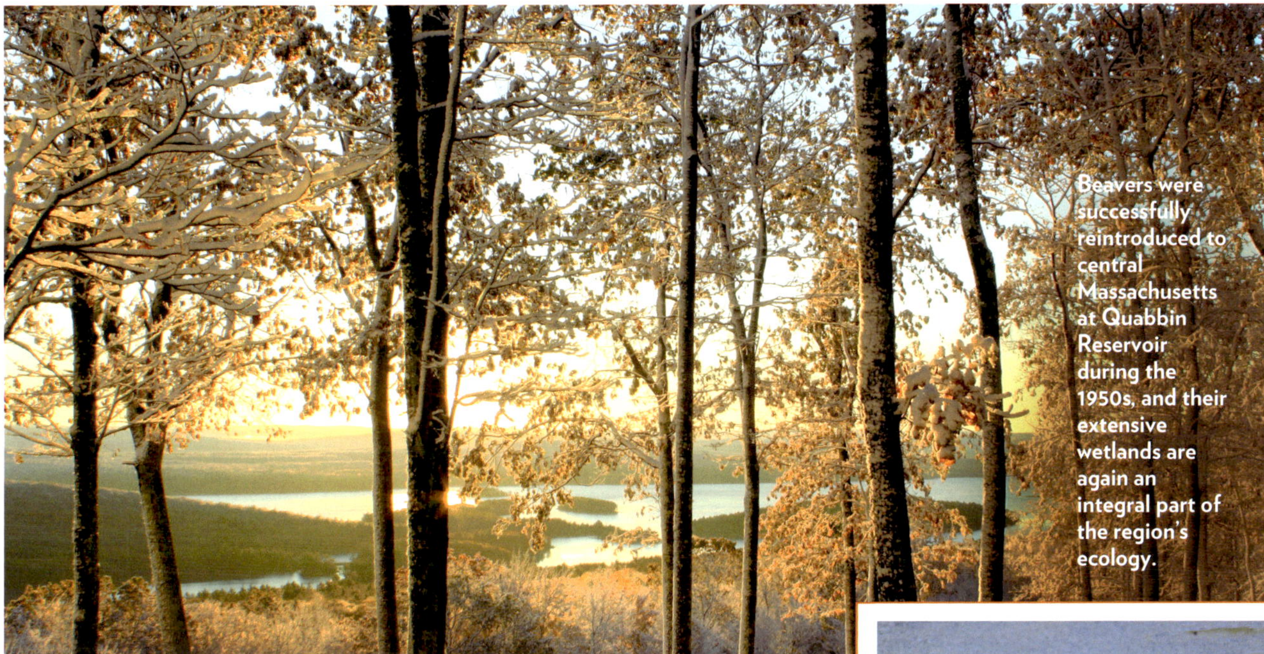

Beavers were successfully reintroduced to central Massachusetts at Quabbin Reservoir during the 1950s, and their extensive wetlands are again an integral part of the region's ecology.

An unusual autumn snowstorm blankets foliage above Quabbin Reservoir in New Salem. An extensive forest buffer helps maintain the quality of the reservoir's numerous source waters.

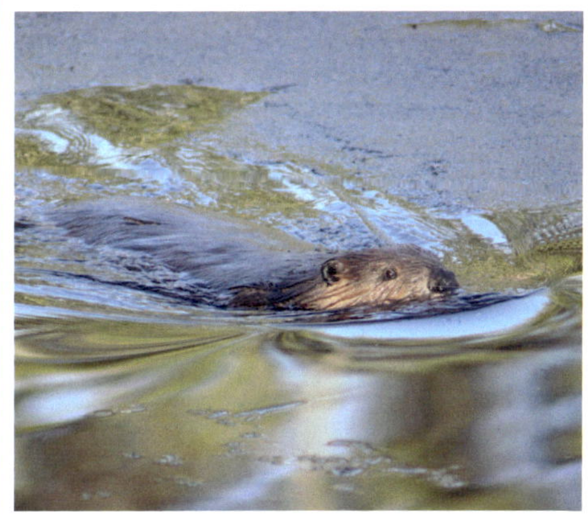

In addition to providing water for more than 2.5 million residents, the reservoir and its surrounding buffer of undeveloped land stand as southern New England's largest expanse of protected land, a 40-square-mile "Accidental Wilderness" (as aptly coined by author Thomas Conuel in his popular book about the reservoir) in the heart of a highly populated region. The diverse habitats include forests, streams, brooks, more than 100 islands, extensive beaver wetlands, old fields, hills, rocky outcroppings, and the reservoir's open water. The reservation has served as a reintroduction area for bald eagles, beavers, and wild turkeys, and after a long absence, moose and fishers have finally returned over the past quarter-century.

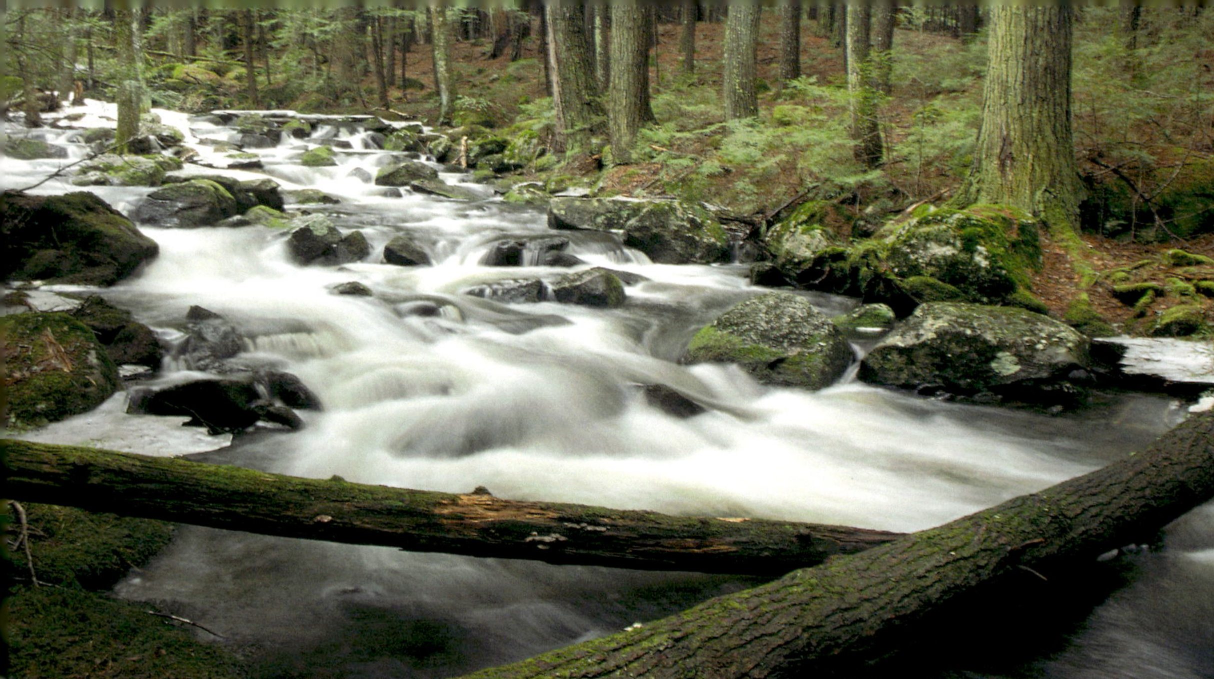

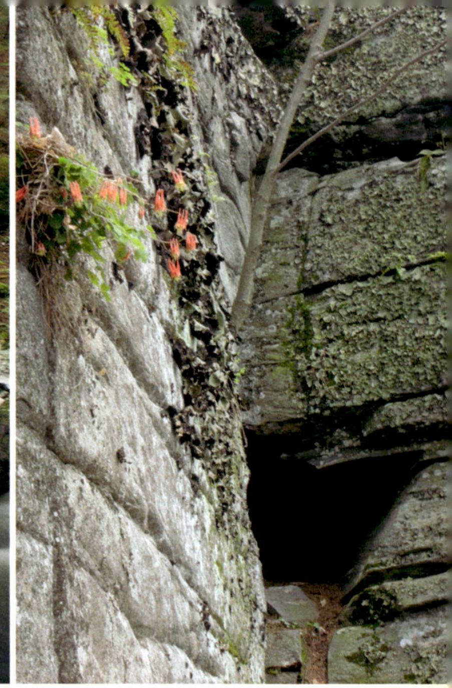

Rutland Brook cascades through a forest of giant hemlocks and pines en route to its confluence with the East Branch of the Swift River at Connors Pond.

In the rocky "Porcupine Ledges" above Rutland Brook, highly adaptable columbine wildflowers grow out of tiny cracks in the bedrock.

Beyond the reservation, the reservoir's source waters are protected by additional networks of conservation areas that extend up the various branches of the Swift River watershed. The largest tributary is the East Branch, which winds for 11 miles to the reservoir's northeast corner. Before meeting the reservoir, it flows through a scenic valley in Petersham, where the Trustees of Reservations, Massachusetts Audubon Society, and Harvard Forest collectively protect nearly 5,000 acres. This is a prime area for anglers, as the river is known as one of the state's premier trout streams.

A popular destination for fishermen and hikers alike is Connors Pond, formed by a dam on the East Branch adjacent to Route 122. This scenic waterbody is fed at its north end by Rutland Brook, which cascades out of an upland beaver pond through a forest of giant hemlocks and pines down the slopes of the valley. At the crest of the valley are the Porcupine Ledges, giant rocky outcroppings so named because of their suitability as den sites for porcupines and other creatures.

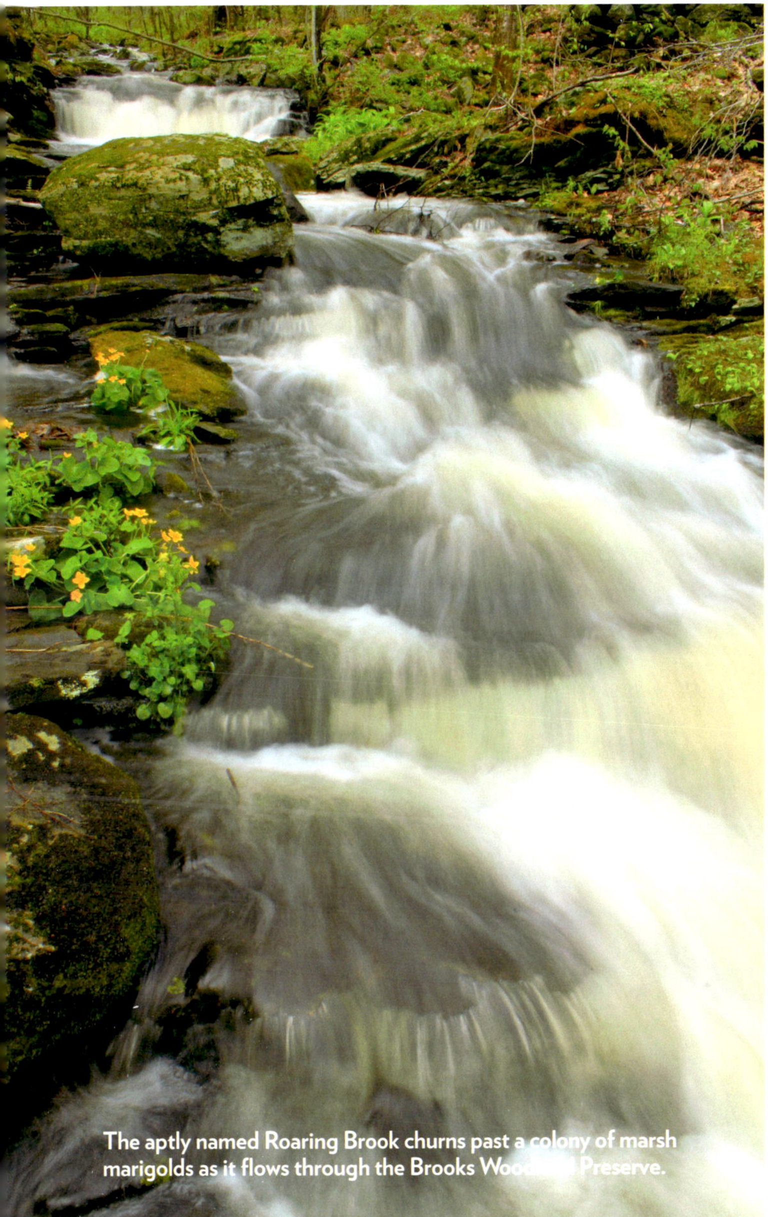

The aptly named Roaring Brook churns past a colony of marsh marigolds as it flows through the Brooks Woodland Preserve.

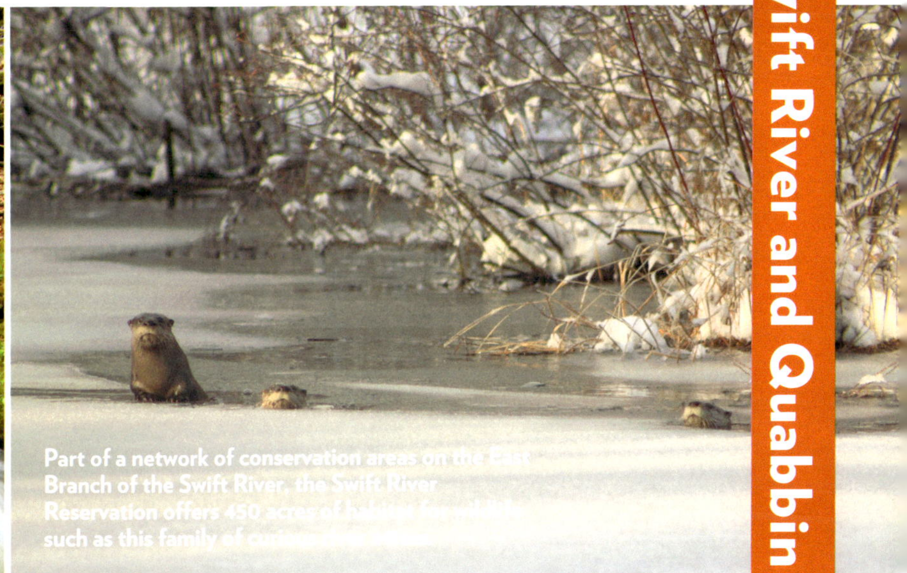

Part of a network of conservation areas on the East Branch of the Swift River, the Swift River Reservation offers 450 acres of habitat for wildlife such as this family of curious river otters.

Downstream from Connors Pond are the three tracts of the Swift River Reservation, where open fields on old mill villages and farm sites offer diversity to the extensive surrounding woodlands. The river itself comes alive with the colorful blooms of bright red cardinal flowers, Joe-pye-weed, jewelweed, and other mid to late summer flowers, especially where beaver dams and wetlands open up sunlit gaps in the dark forest. Earlier in the growing season, the steep valley slopes host colonies of ephemerals such as bloodroot, hepatica, red and painted trilliums, and marsh violets, followed in autumn by the foliage of maples, birches, oaks, and other hardwoods.

The East Branch emanates from headwaters in the quiet woodlands of Phillipston, where one might be as likely to encounter a moose or bear as another human visitor. Another cluster of conservation areas protect these crucial source waters, including the Mount Grace Land Trust's Fox Valley Wildlife Sanctuary and the Popple Camp and Phillipston Wildlife Management Areas. One of the area's most interesting botanical attractions is the nearby Eliot Laurel Reservation, where a hillside comes alive with colorful mountain laurel blooms each June.

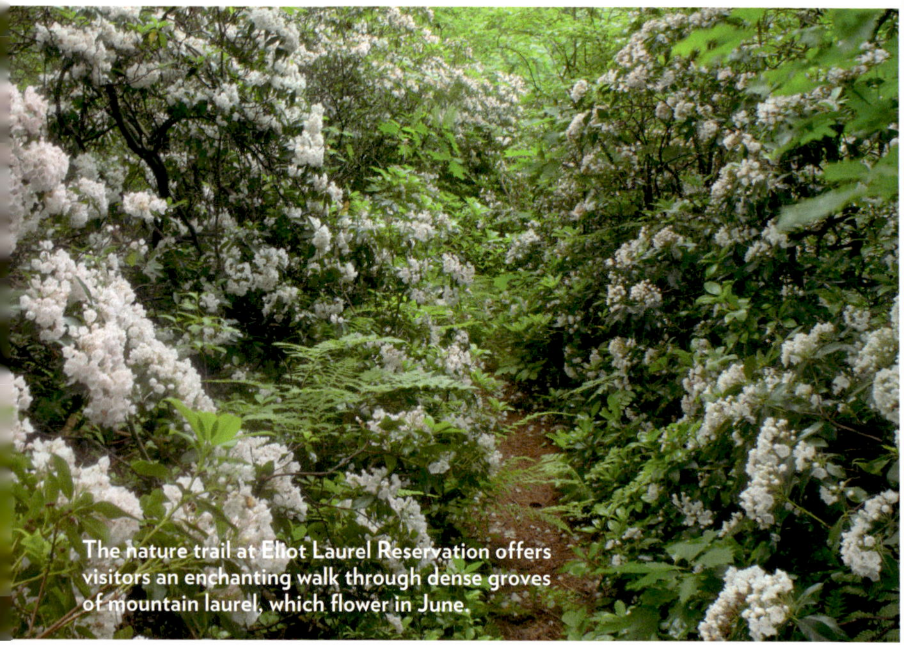

The nature trail at Eliot Laurel Reservation offers visitors an enchanting walk through dense groves of mountain laurel, which flower in June.

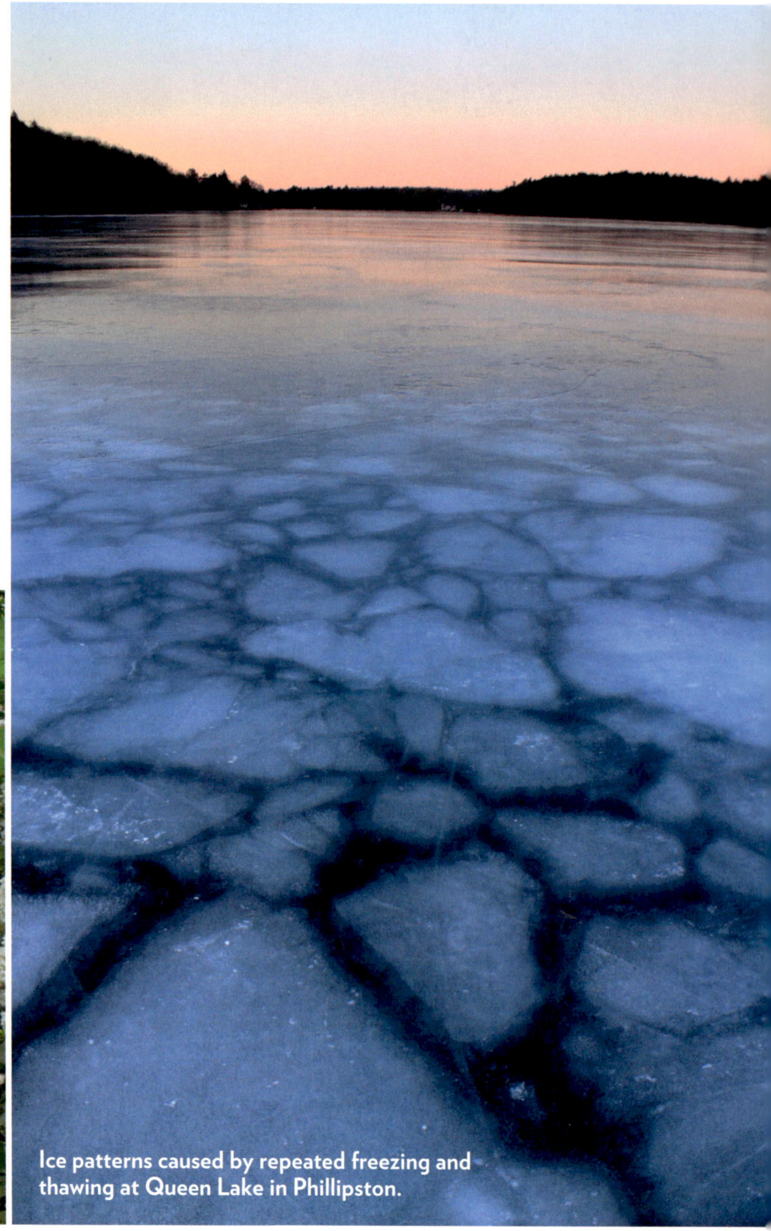

Ice patterns caused by repeated freezing and thawing at Queen Lake in Phillipston.

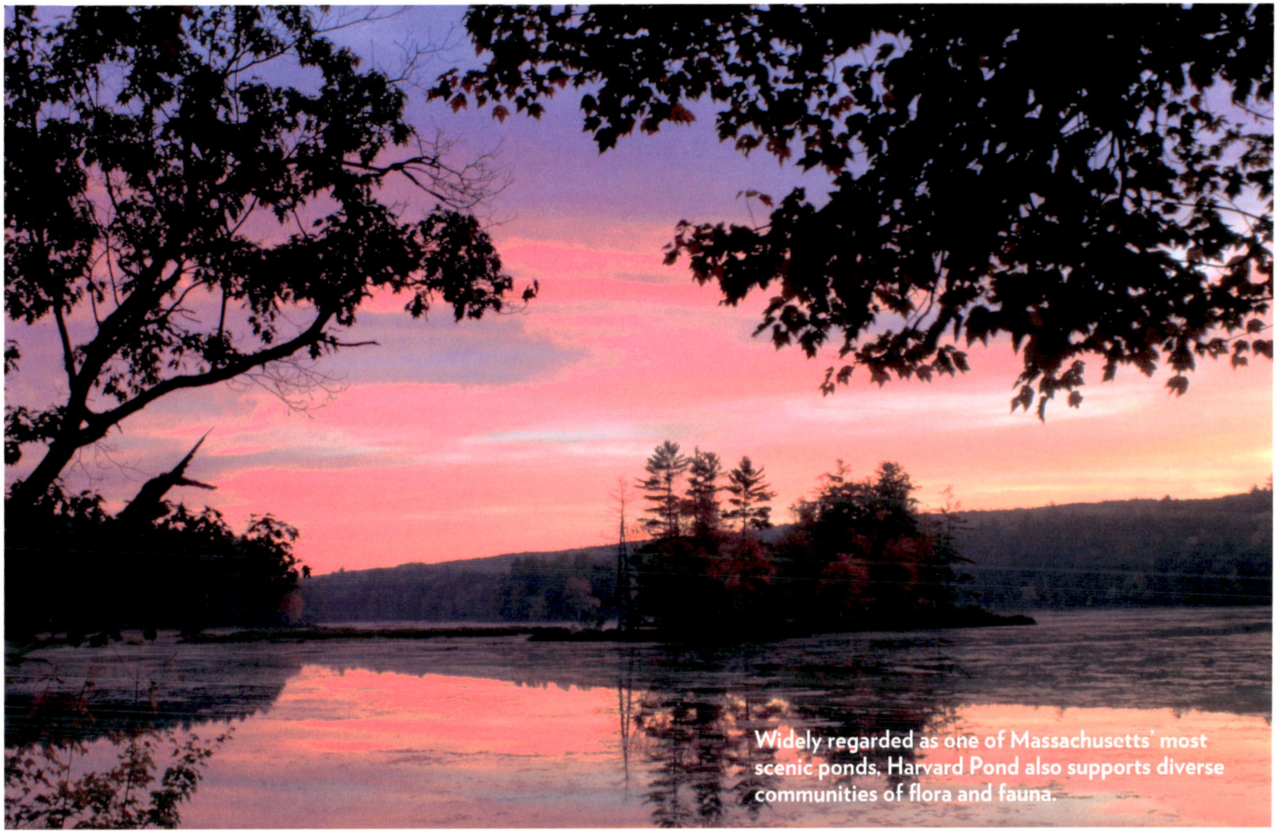

Widely regarded as one of Massachusetts' most scenic ponds, Harvard Pond also supports diverse communities of flora and fauna.

Among the most prominent landowners along the East Branch was James W. Brooks of Petersham, an early conservationist who donated some 3,000 acres of his estate to establish the Harvard Forest as a research station of the university in 1907. Over the past century, Harvard Forest has conducted pioneering forestry and ecological research on a wide variety of subjects, and it is now part of the National Science Foundation's Long Term Ecological Research Network. One of its distinguished early graduates was Bob Marshall, who earned a forestry degree in 1924 before going on to become a renowned wilderness advocate and author. Its outreach includes the Fisher Museum, which is home to a famous series of intricately crafted dioramas that depict the remarkable cycle of change that New England's landscape has undergone over the past 400 years. With long, unbroken views over expansive fields and open horizons, many of the scenes stand in marked contrast to today's largely forested landscape.

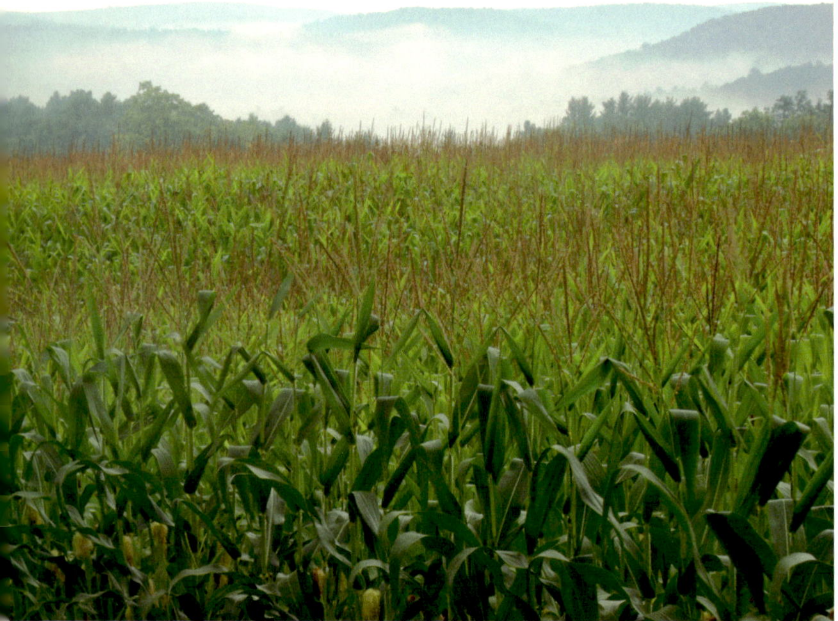

Though the Swift River Valley and central Massachusetts are largely reforested now, open views across this cornfield offer a glimpse of the region's agricultural past.

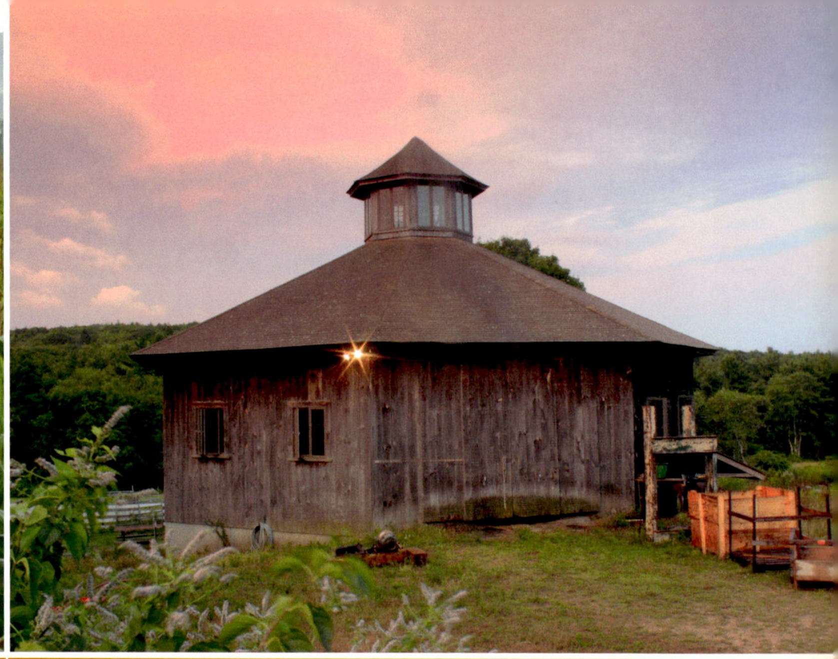

The Sweetwater Farm in Petersham is the site of this uncommon hexagon, or "round," barn.

Before the arrival of European colonists, the various Native groups lived in relative harmony with the land, enjoying abundant natural resources for agriculture, hunting, fishing, and trading. Settlements were concentrated in fertile river valleys, with smaller, scattered groups in the less hospitable uplands. The arrival of European settlers from the early 17th century onwards began the long cycle of transformation, as the once-abundant forests were cleared for agriculture, and by the mid-19th century roughly three-quarters of the landscape was open. Even the rocky, steep slopes of Wachusett Mountain, Mount Watatic, and other hills and ridges felt the axe, as they were cleared for sheep pastures. Still visible amidst the forests of today are miles of stone walls—built with the ubiquitous rocks that were unearthed from the plowed fields—that stand as a permanent artifact of the extent of land clearing.

However, by the late 1800s farmers were rapidly abandoning their rocky lands in favor of the more fertile soils of the Midwest or jobs in factories, which offered higher pay and often an easier alternative to agriculture. As a result, the region's decimated forests began a gradual cycle of recovery. While many woodlots and individual parcels have been cut again over the past century, forests have reclaimed three-quarters of the landscape.

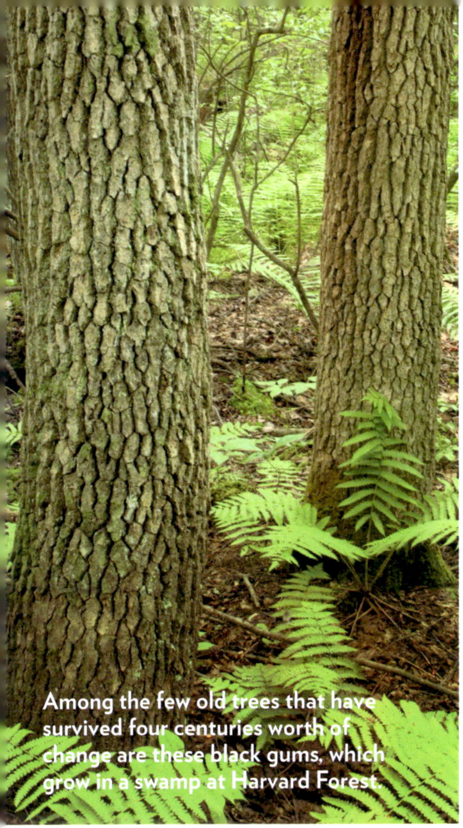

Among the few old trees that have survived four centuries worth of change are these black gums, which grow in a swamp at Harvard Forest.

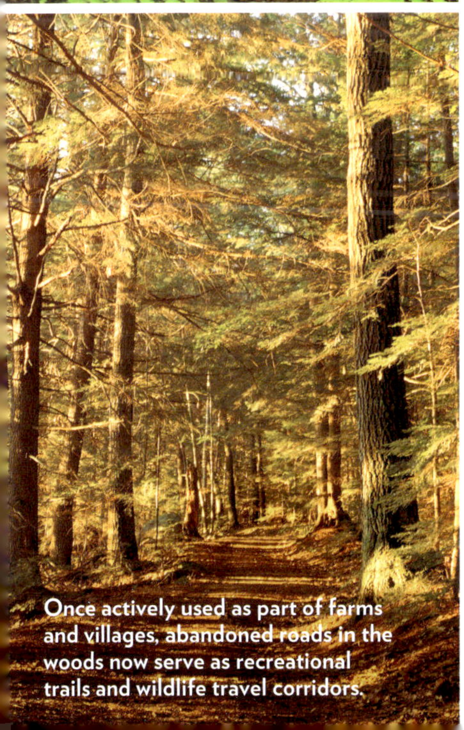

Once actively used as part of farms and villages, abandoned roads in the woods now serve as recreational trails and wildlife travel corridors.

Though the forests are seemingly thriving today, they remain stressed by a variety of natural and human factors. Perhaps the best-known historic example of a forest pest is the loss of the American chestnut during the early 20th century (further detailed shortly) to the blight fungus; other significant outbreaks include Dutch elm disease and oak defoliation by gypsy moth caterpillars. Eastern hemlocks are currently threatened by the hemlock woolly adelgid, a tiny aphid that was accidentally introduced to the eastern states from Asia during the 1920s. Identified by tiny white egg sacs, adelgids gradually kill hemlocks by feeding on the evergreen needles. They have been present in the lower, milder elevations of the Connecticut Valley since the 1980s and have gradually spread across the higher hills over the past 25 years. Though cold winter snaps can slow infestations to some degree, the long-term outlook for hemlocks is of considerable concern.

A potentially significant threat to eastern forests recently emerged in central Massachusetts when the Asian long horned beetle was discovered by a family at a backyard barbeque in Worcester in 2008. This infestation is especially dangerous because, unlike other forest pests such as the adelgid that affect specific species, the beetle has a diverse palette that includes maples, birches, ashes, elms, and other hardwoods, and a widespread outbreak would likely have catastrophic consequences for the region's woodlands. In an urgent effort to quarantine the beetle, nearly 30,000 trees have been removed from the greater Worcester area in recent years.

Unusual natural "disturbances," or significant storms, also affect forests on an irregular basis. The most destructive event over the past century was the hurricane of 1938, which caused widespread forest damage. In recent years, several storms have caused additional stress on trees and area residents alike, including the great ice storm of December 2008. After a night of hearing trees, branches, and power lines break apart with gunfire-like sounds, residents in most central New England hill towns woke up in the cold the following morning to a landscape glazed in thick ice. The extensive damage was a nightmare for utility companies, as crews recruited from across the country scrambled to restore power, and some unfortunate neighborhoods were left in the dark for several weeks.

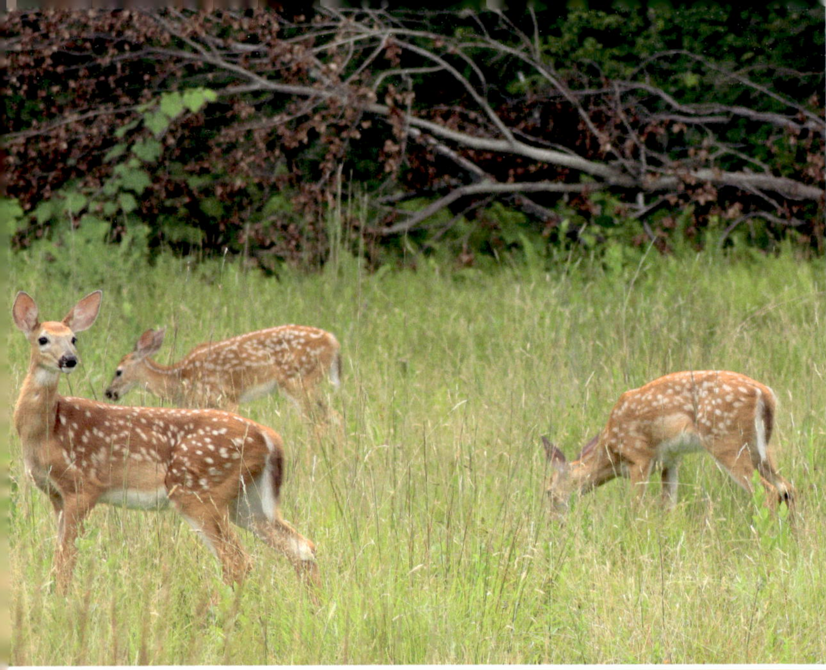

Though their populations are thriving today, even familiar wildlife such as white-tailed deer once suffered greatly from hunting and habitat loss.

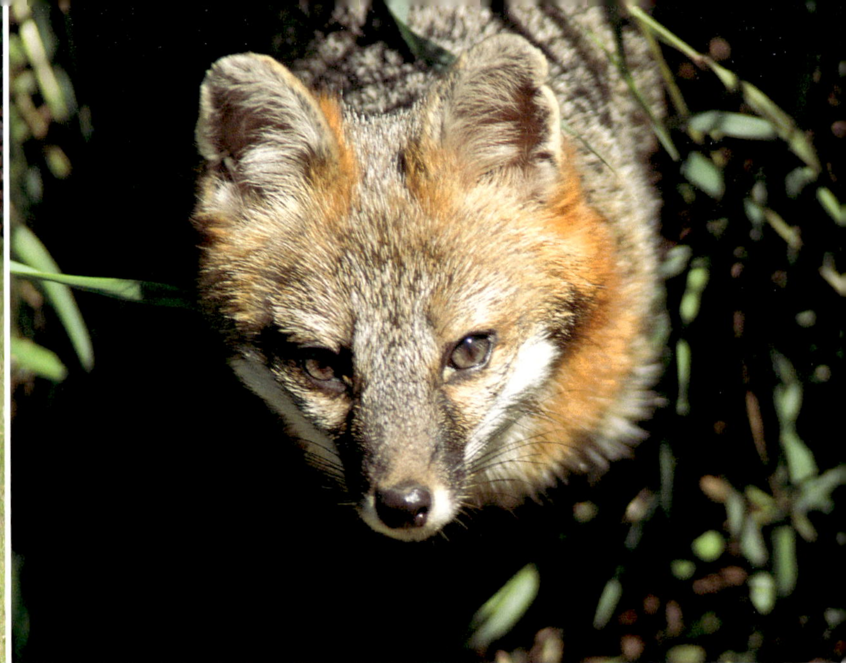

Predator eye: a female gray fox makes morning hunting rounds along the edge of a meadow.

Just four years later, the Halloween weekend blizzard of October 2012 caused another round of forest damage and power outages. A prolonged stretch of unusually mild weather during the previous weeks had delayed the foliage color change and leaf drop, leaving the trees especially vulnerable to the heavy, wet snow. A remarkable snowfall of 32 inches—far greater than any other storm that winter—was recorded near Mount Monadnock in southern New Hampshire. While both events caused considerable hardship and damage to individual trees, their overall effect on the forests was relatively small compared to the 1938 hurricane.

In addition to the effects on forests, land clearing and years of largely unregulated hunting had a profound impact on wildlife. As hard as it may be to imagine the present landscape without white-tailed deer, black bears, moose, wild turkeys, beavers, wood ducks, and great blue herons, these and many other creatures were all temporarily extirpated from the region in historic times. Thanks to the regrowth of mature forests, the implementation of managed hunting seasons, and reintroduction programs such as those conducted at Quabbin, these species are largely thriving again, though moose and fishers have only returned in recent decades.

Yet to be officially confirmed as returning are mountain lions and wolves, though regular sightings, especially of the former, are a frequent and intriguing topic of conversation among area residents. On a recent early spring morning, I was watching a large flock of migratory ducks at the northern tip of Quabbin Reservoir when I heard a startlingly loud and violent series of snarling and fighting noises from a nearby hillside. Shortly afterward, a hiker who was in the vicinity at the same time flagged me down to report that he had witnessed two mountain lions fighting. As he put it, "I feared for my life and didn't know what to do...it was something out of *National Geographic*." The timing was of interest because just a few weeks earlier, two area residents had reported observing a deer carcass that had been unceremoniously wedged into branches high in a tree along the banks of the nearby Swift River.

While the majority of mountain lion sightings have been erroneous accounts of bobcats, feral cats, coyotes, deer, and even domestic dogs, some have been made by highly credible sources. Two of these have been registered by Bob Clark, a former president of the Friends of Quabbin who has extensive experience exploring and documenting the region's natural history. His first sighting was on a crisp early winter day in December 1963, when he observed fresh tracks, a large scrape, and a fur sample in the vicinity of Dana Common in the eastern portion of Quabbin Reservoir. In June 1981, Bob had a firsthand encounter while driving a gravel road in the same general area, as detailed in his own words in a sighting report:

> *I saw a mountain lion leap from the left side of the road to the top of a low bank on the right side (north side) of the road and into the woods about 240 feet in front of me....I went about 50 feet into the woods and stopped.....the cat was behind a patch of huckleberries about 100 feet ahead of me. I watched as it made long, low, graceful leaps away from me up the gradual slope of the hillside toward the north-northeast. It was very fast, much faster than a bobcat....The tail was the most conspicuous feature, appearing as long as the body and head combined and evenly thin throughout. It was held in line with the body, neither high nor low, while the tip was held at an angle and moved as needed for balance.*

Another significant find occurred in July 1997, when professional wildlife tracker John McCarter discovered an unusually large scat that had been covered (a behavior characteristic of felines) next to the remains of a beaver near the northern tip of Quabbin Reservoir; DNA tests subsequently confirmed it was from a mountain lion. What's been lacking so far are follow-up reports or photo documentation, but many feel that it's just a matter of time before mountain lions, wolves, or both are officially confirmed as reclaiming the top of the food chain in New England.

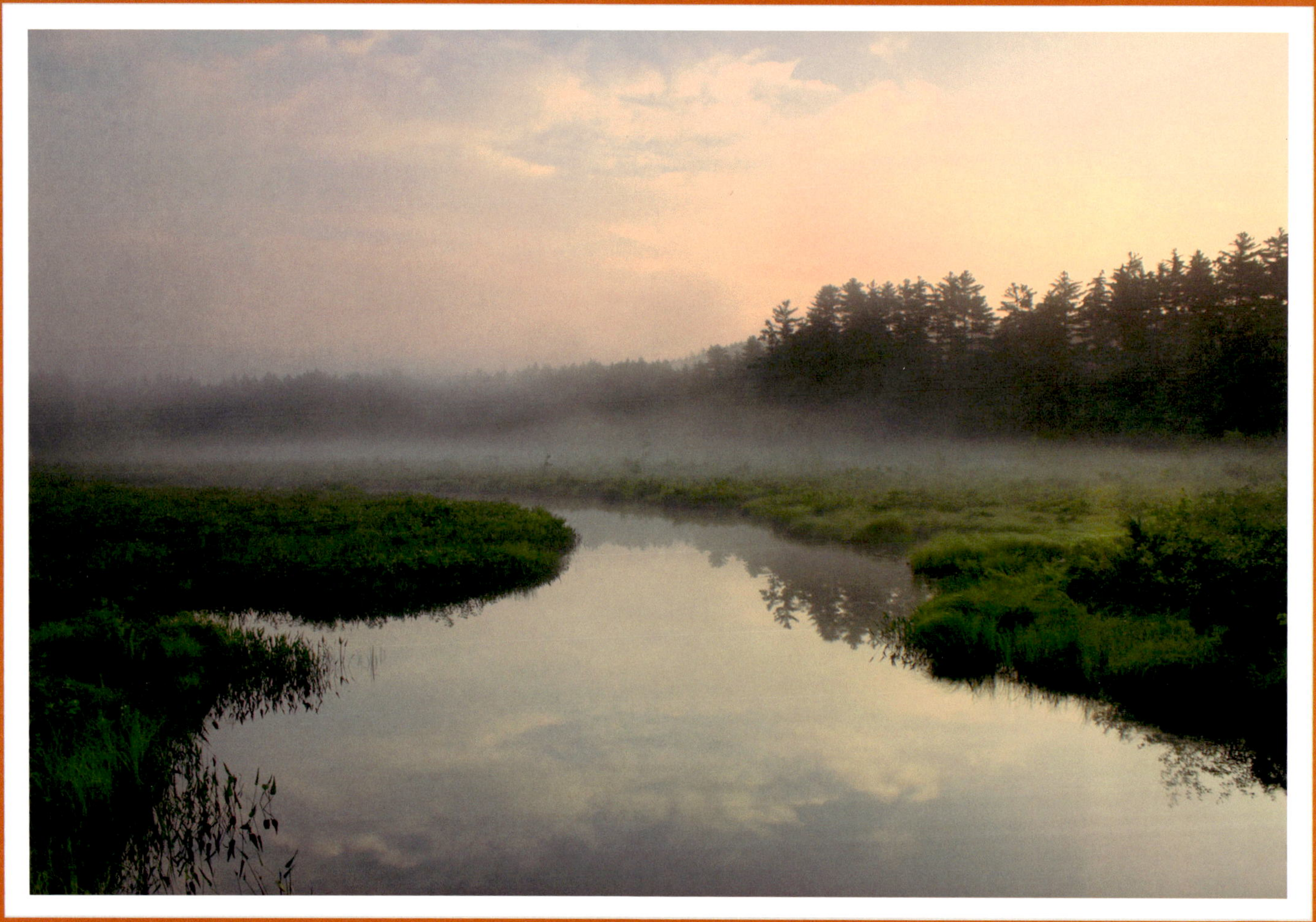

The Middle Branch of the Swift River winds past this open marshy area above its confluence with Quabbin Reservoir.

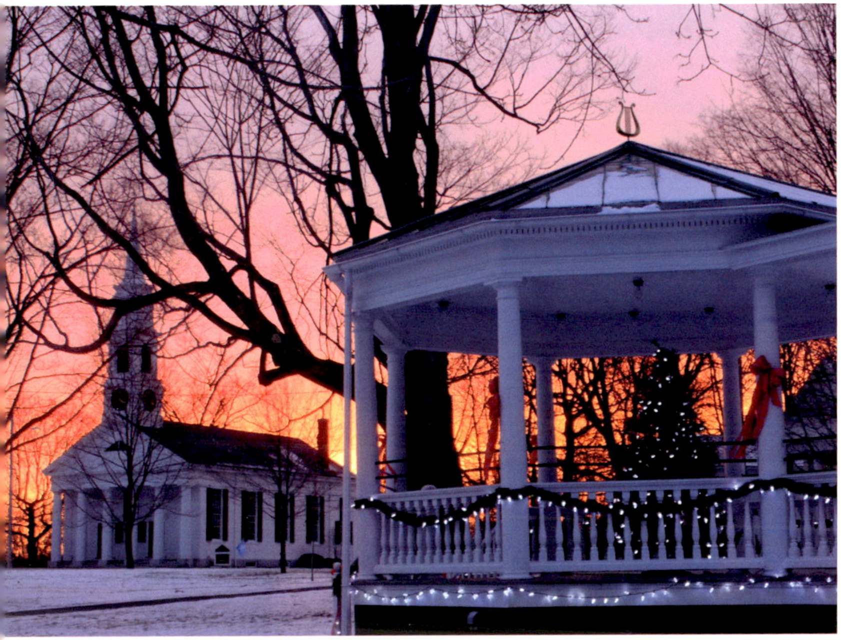

A winter sunset flickers over the Petersham town common, which is part of a historic district surrounded by conservation land.

Petersham is one of several central Massachusetts towns with a largely timeless character, thanks to its historic district, village common, and adjacent conservation lands. Arguably its most prominent landmark—and another inevitable subject of conversation among tourists and townsfolk alike—is the Nichewaug Inn, an elaborate country inn built in 1899 by James Brooks. It hosted visitors from throughout the Northeast for many years, and then was part of the Sisters of the Maria Assumptia Academy before being abandoned in the early 1980s. In a ceremony at Fenway Park in 2001, the deteriorating structure was placed on a list of endangered Massachusetts historic sites.

The nearby North Common Meadow, which was once the inn's private golf course, serves as both a legacy of the town's past and a natural area that benefits a variety of wildlife. Formerly pastureland, it is maintained as a meadow that is home to abundant wildflowers, butterflies, dragonflies, and uncommon grassland birds such as bobolinks and meadowlarks. A small pond offers additional diversity to the preserve, which serves as a gateway to the adjacent forests and wetlands of the Brooks Woodland Preserve and Rutland Brook Wildlife Sanctuary. The long easterly views across the meadow to Wachusett Mountain are reminiscent of the open scenes of the valley's agricultural era.

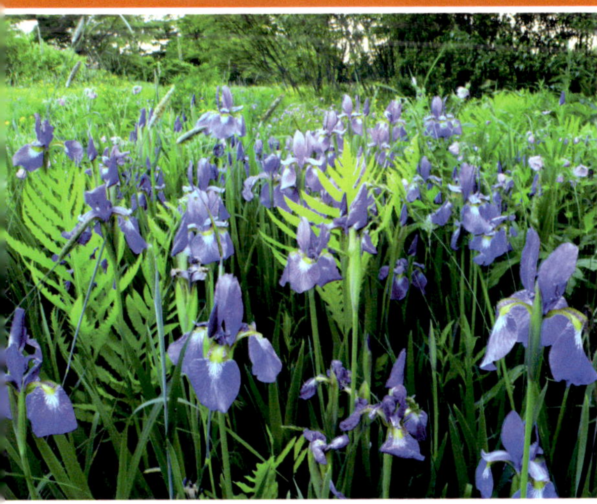

A colorful colony of blue flag iris blooming in the North Common Meadow, a former pasture in Petersham's historic district that is now home to grassland birds and other wildlife.

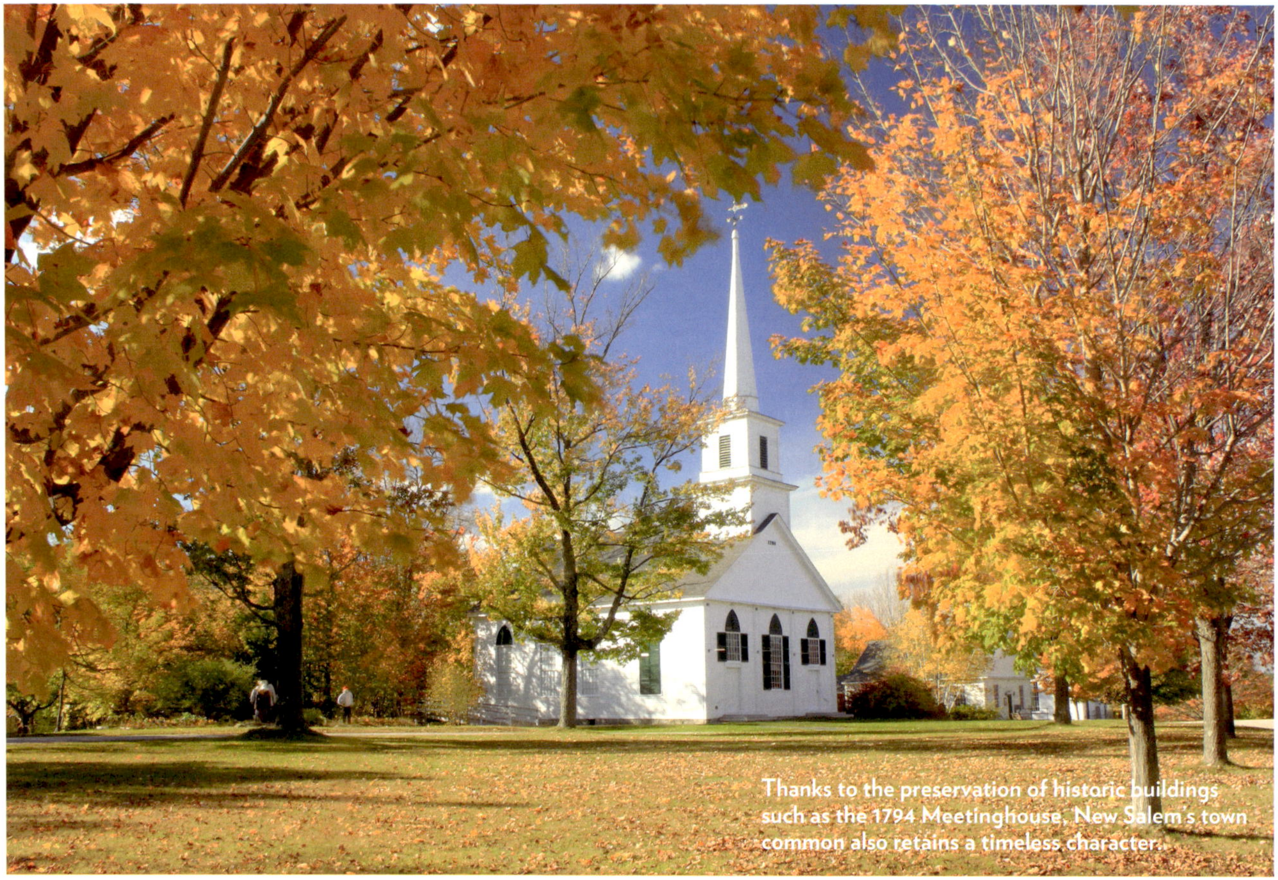

Thanks to the preservation of historic buildings such as the 1794 Meetinghouse, New Salem's town common also retains a timeless character.

Neighboring New Salem boasts a similarly photographic common, as sugar maples line a small green with two twin church steeples. Originally built as the First Church of New Salem, the 1794 Meetinghouse has hosted a long list of civic events over the years, and continues to maintain an active arts program. Another building of note is the former New Salem Academy, a former preparatory and high school with many distinguished graduates. A considerable portion of the town's land was taken by the state during the creation of Quabbin Reservoir; several public roads dead-end at access areas to the reservation.

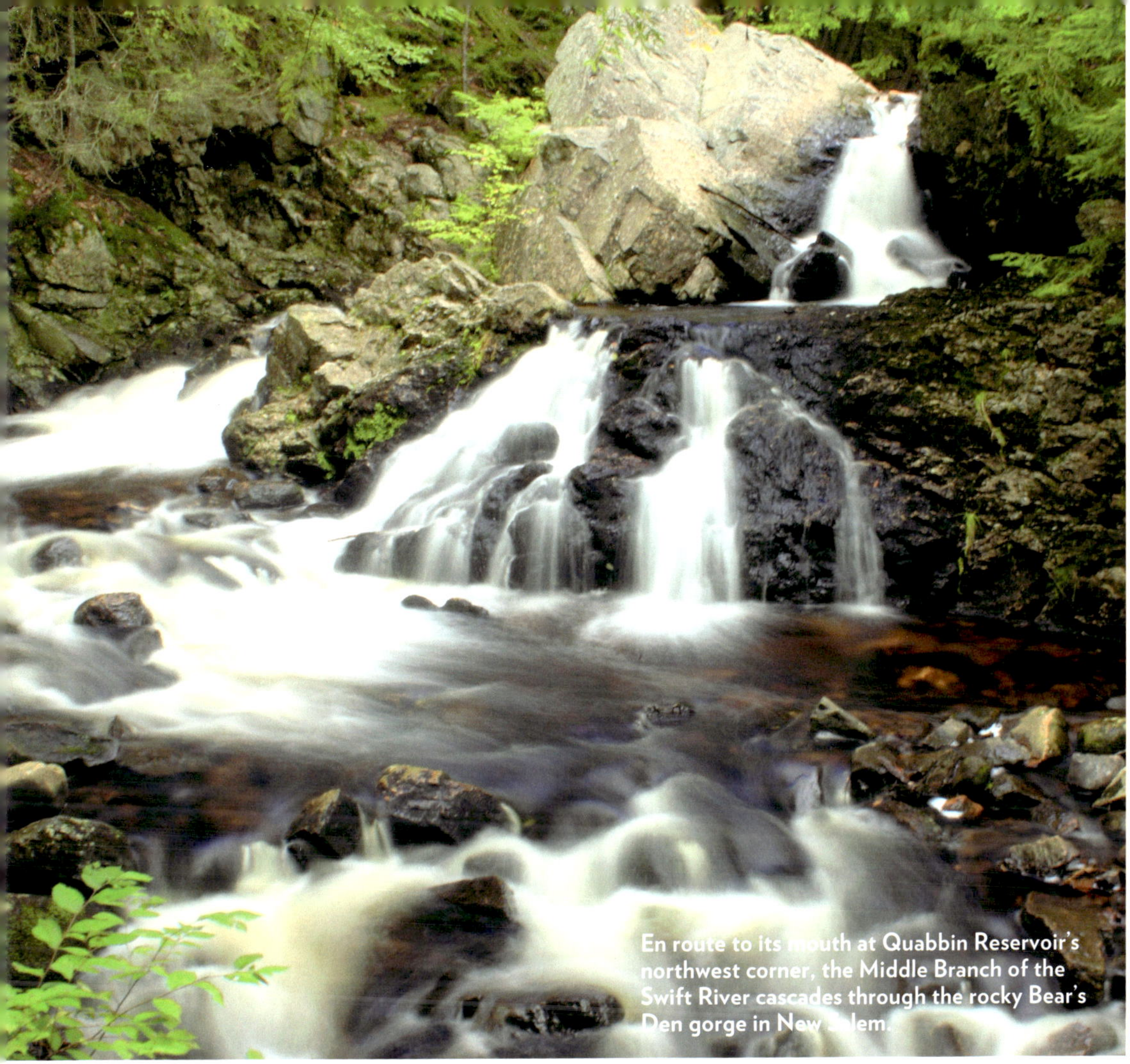

En route to its mouth at Quabbin Reservoir's northwest corner, the Middle Branch of the Swift River cascades through the rocky Bear's Den gorge in New Salem.

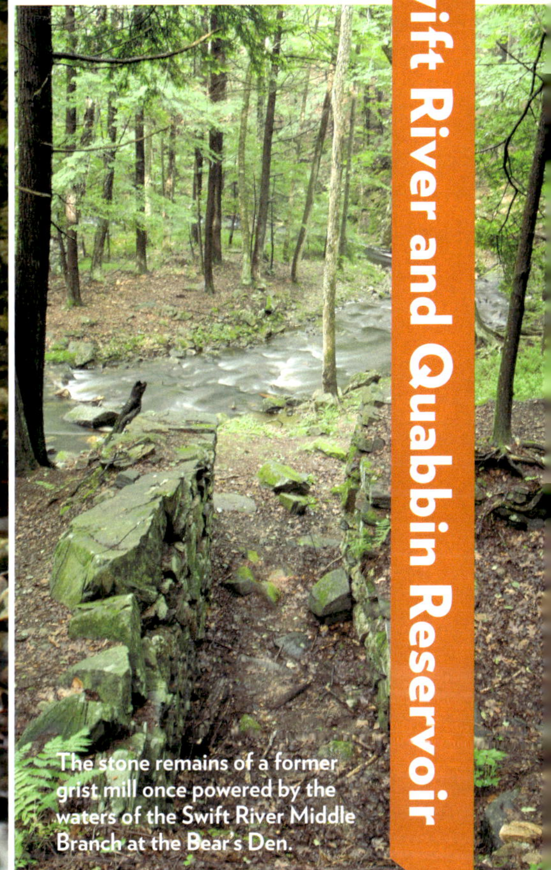

The stone remains of a former grist mill once powered by the waters of the Swift River Middle Branch at the Bear's Den.

En route to their confluence with Quabbin Reservoir, the Middle and West Branches of the Swift River wind through quiet woodlands and wetlands in New Salem and Wendell. As it nears the reservation boundary, the Middle Branch churns through the "Bear's Den," a small gorge where the river cascades around a large angular border and beneath 75-foot high granite cliffs. Legend has it that Metacomet (King Philip) used this secluded ravine as a meeting area during King Philip's War to plan attacks on colonial settlements in the Connecticut Valley in 1675. History is also evident a few hundred feet downstream from the falls, where the stone remains of an old grist mill lie nestled at the base of the ravine. Not to be confused with the conservation area of the same name in Athol, this Bear's Den is so named because an early settler reputedly tracked and killed a black bear at the gorge.

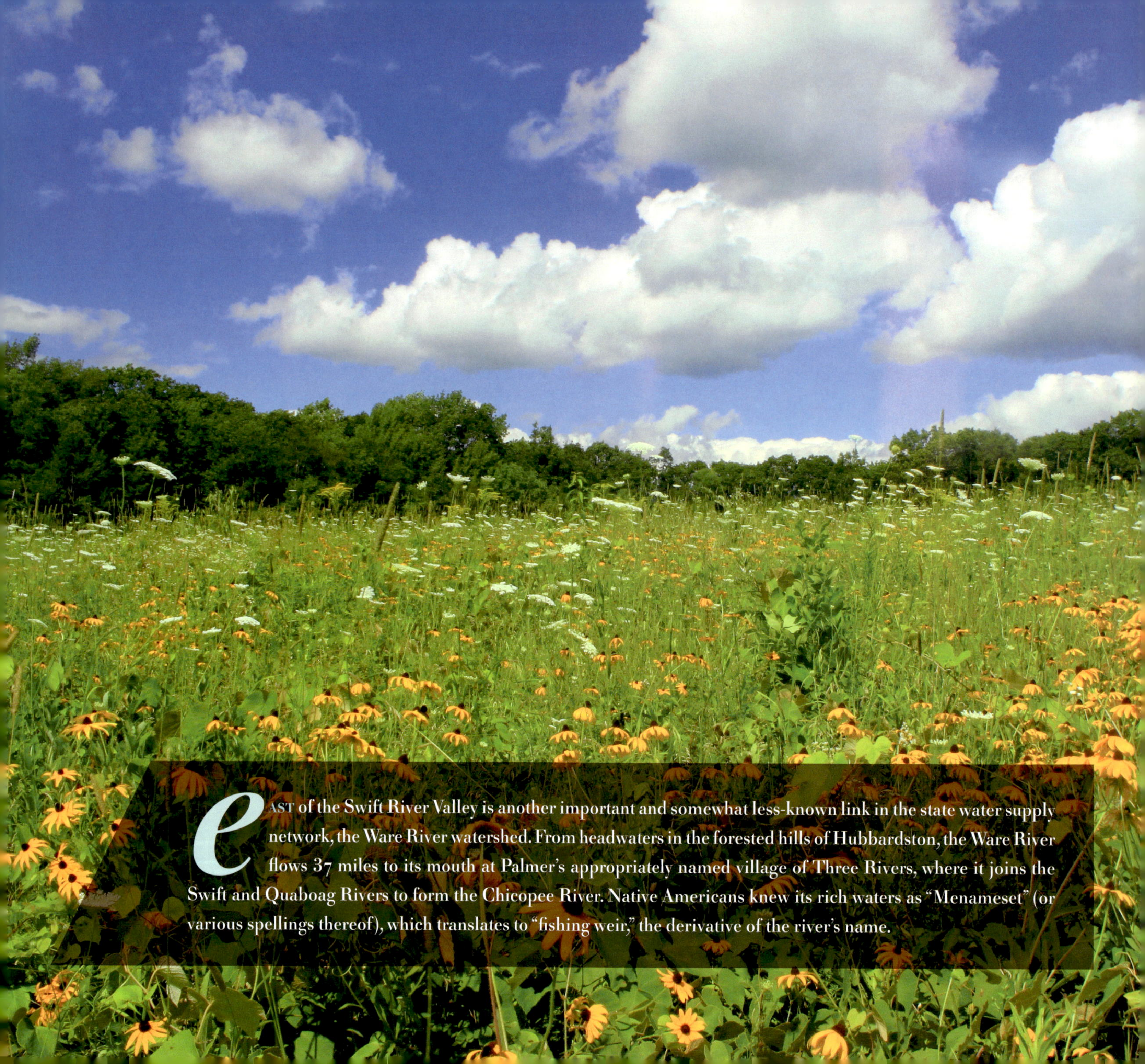

East of the Swift River Valley is another important and somewhat less-known link in the state water supply network, the Ware River watershed. From headwaters in the forested hills of Hubbardston, the Ware River flows 37 miles to its mouth at Palmer's appropriately named village of Three Rivers, where it joins the Swift and Quaboag Rivers to form the Chicopee River. Native Americans knew its rich waters as "Menameset" (or various spellings thereof), which translates to "fishing weir," the derivative of the river's name.

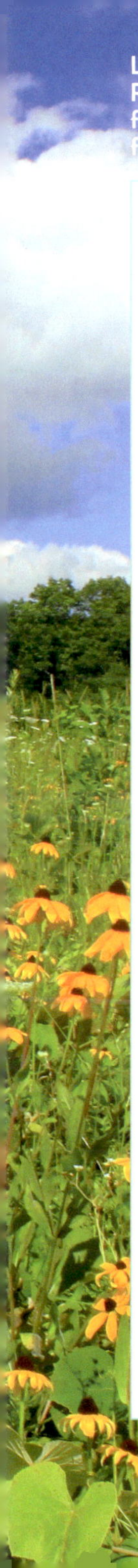

Large meadows at the Ware River Reservation offer diverse habitats for field wildflowers, butterflies, and other flora and fauna.

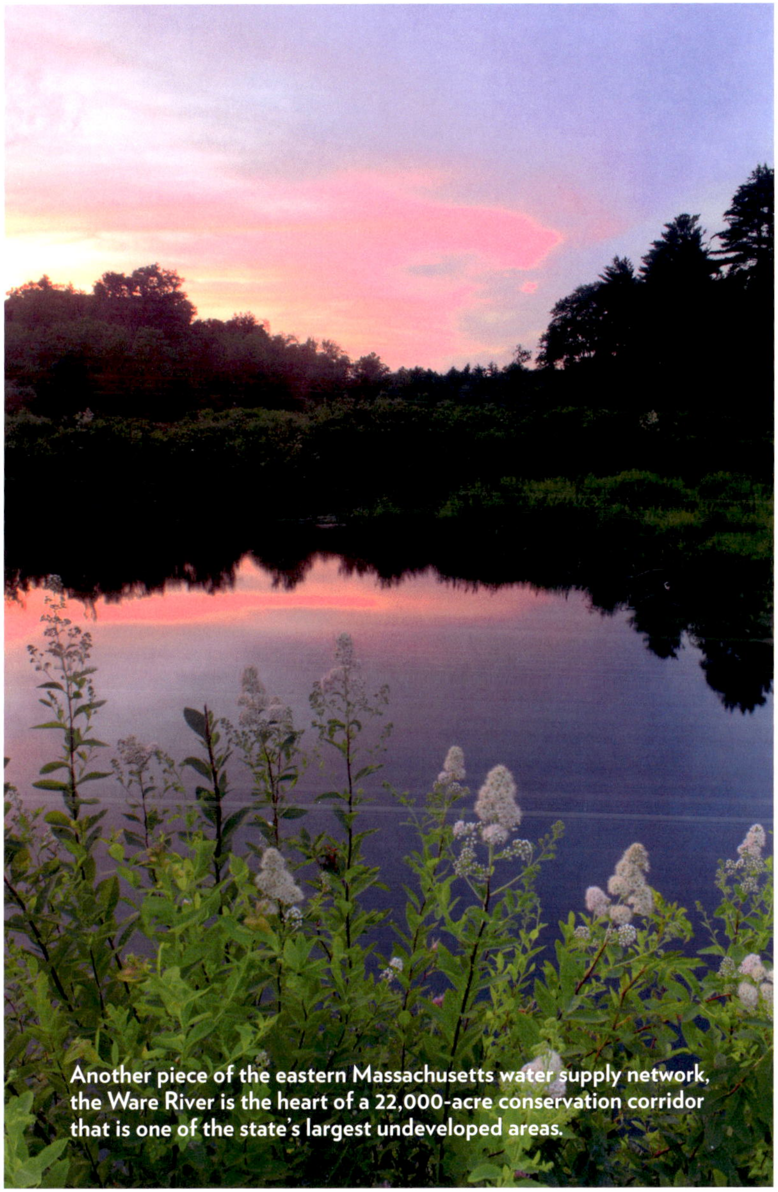

Another piece of the eastern Massachusetts water supply network, the Ware River is the heart of a 22,000-acre conservation corridor that is one of the state's largest undeveloped areas.

As part of the westward expansion of the eastern Massachusetts water supply system during the early 20th century, a 12-mile long aqueduct was built to connect the Ware River to the Wachusett Reservoir. The completion of the project in 1931 was rather timely, as a long drought had reduced Wachusett Reservoir to less than 20 percent of its capacity at that juncture. Two years later, another 25-mile tunnel running west from the river to Quabbin Reservoir was completed, allowing portions of the river flows to be diverted to Quabbin during high water periods from mid-October to mid-June.

At the junction of Route 122 and Coldbrook Road, near the Barre-Oakham town line, is a stone monument marking the former site of Coldbrook Springs, the largest of several villages, much less-known than the lost Quabbin and Wachusett Reservoir towns, that were abandoned when the state took over land in the watershed. It was once home to a large hotel, a general store, and thirty private homes. A large state prison camp, the remains of which are still visible, was located a few miles to the east near Rutland.

As was the case with Quabbin Reservoir, one benefit to the watershed protection of the Ware River was the establishment of one of the state's largest conservation areas, a wildlife-rich, 22,000-acre corridor of protected land that encompasses the Ware River Reservation, Barre Falls Dam, and Rutland State Park. One of the state's largest moose populations roams the beaver wetlands, swamps, and hills, while bluebirds, bobolinks, woodcock, butterflies, and dragonflies frequent the wildflower meadows and grassy fields that are maintained for habitat diversity amidst the extensive forests. Since its construction in 1958, the Barre Falls Dam, another piece of the central New England flood control network, has buffered flooding in the downstream communities in the Ware, Chicopee, and Connecticut River watersheds. Behind it is a "dry bed" reservoir that is only flooded when the dam's gates are closed during high water periods; the adjacent fields are part of another popular recreation area.

One of the Ware River's tributaries is Galloway Brook, which meanders past Barre's historic common to the quiet woodlands of the Massachusetts Audubon Society's Cook's Canyon Sanctuary. After flowing over an old mill pond dam, its character changes markedly as its waters cascade through a narrow, rocky gorge named in honor of George Cook, a town resident who devoted nearly forty years to improving the property. His efforts included nearly 100,000 planted trees on the grounds, access roads that are now sanctuary trails, and a footbridge over the crest of the falls (since removed).

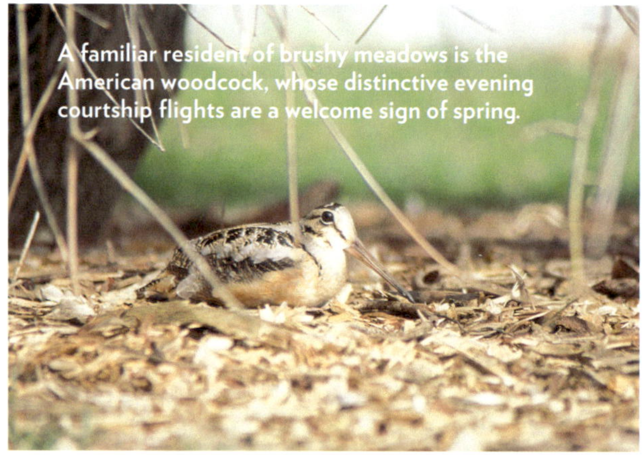

A familiar resident of brushy meadows is the American woodcock, whose distinctive evening courtship flights are a welcome sign of spring.

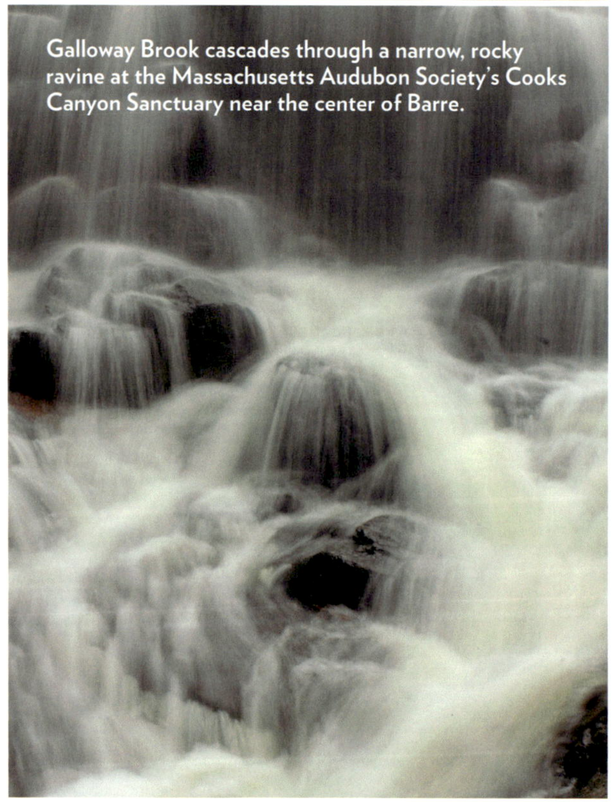

Galloway Brook cascades through a narrow, rocky ravine at the Massachusetts Audubon Society's Cooks Canyon Sanctuary near the center of Barre.

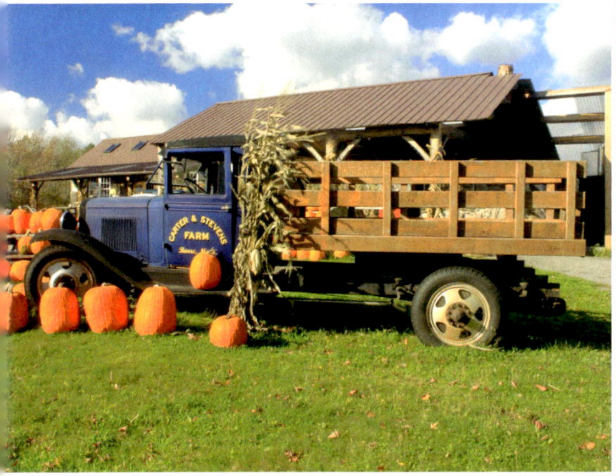

In addition to foliage, autumn brings harvest festivals and roadside displays, such as this antique truck at the Carter Stevens Farm in Barre.

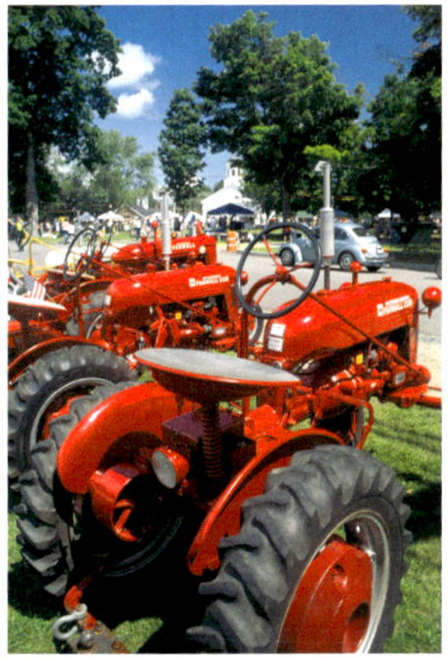

Hardwick's annual agricultural fair, which features live animals, arts and crafts, and farm equipment, has been a summer tradition since 1762.

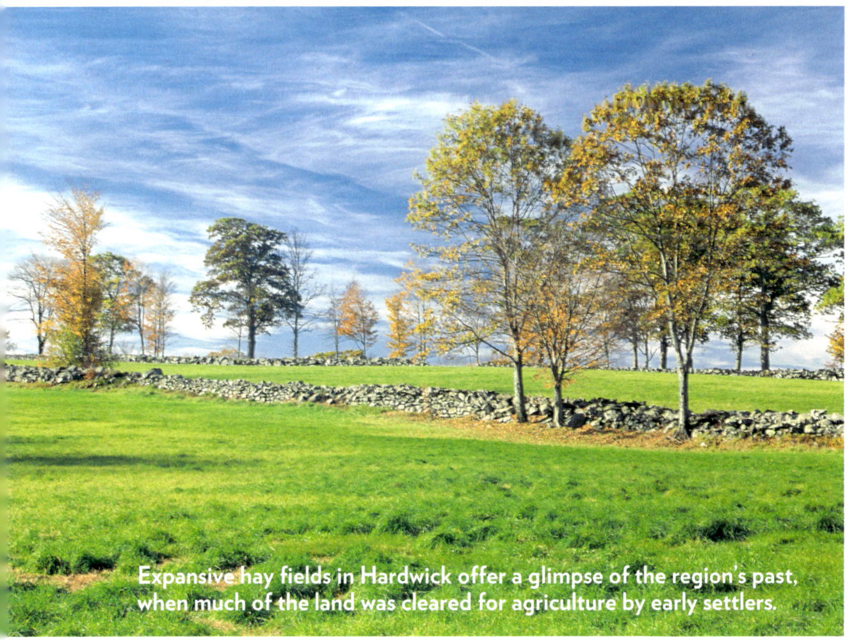

Expansive hay fields in Hardwick offer a glimpse of the region's past, when much of the land was cleared for agriculture by early settlers.

Cook died in 1936, shortly before the 1938 hurricane undid much of his efforts and heavily damaged the young forests. The sanctuary subsequently became the site of a popular Audubon day camp, and its resilient woodlands continue to recover from natural disturbances such as the 2008 ice storm and the Halloween blizzard of 2011.

Further downstream, the Ware River winds through the hills and fields of New Braintree and Hardwick, where a number of still-active farms offer more glimpses of the region's agricultural heritage. Since 1762, Hardwick has hosted a popular summer weekend agricultural fair on the town's historic common; 2012 marked the event's 250th anniversary. A short distance east of the town center is the East Quabbin Land Trust's Mandell Hill preserve, which functions as both a working farm with cow herds and a conservation area with woodland and meadow trails. Field wildflowers, grassland birds, and colorful butterflies, such as monarchs, black swallowtails, and American ladies, benefit from the expansive open fields, where visitors enjoy long views across the countryside to Wachusett Mountain and other nearby farms.

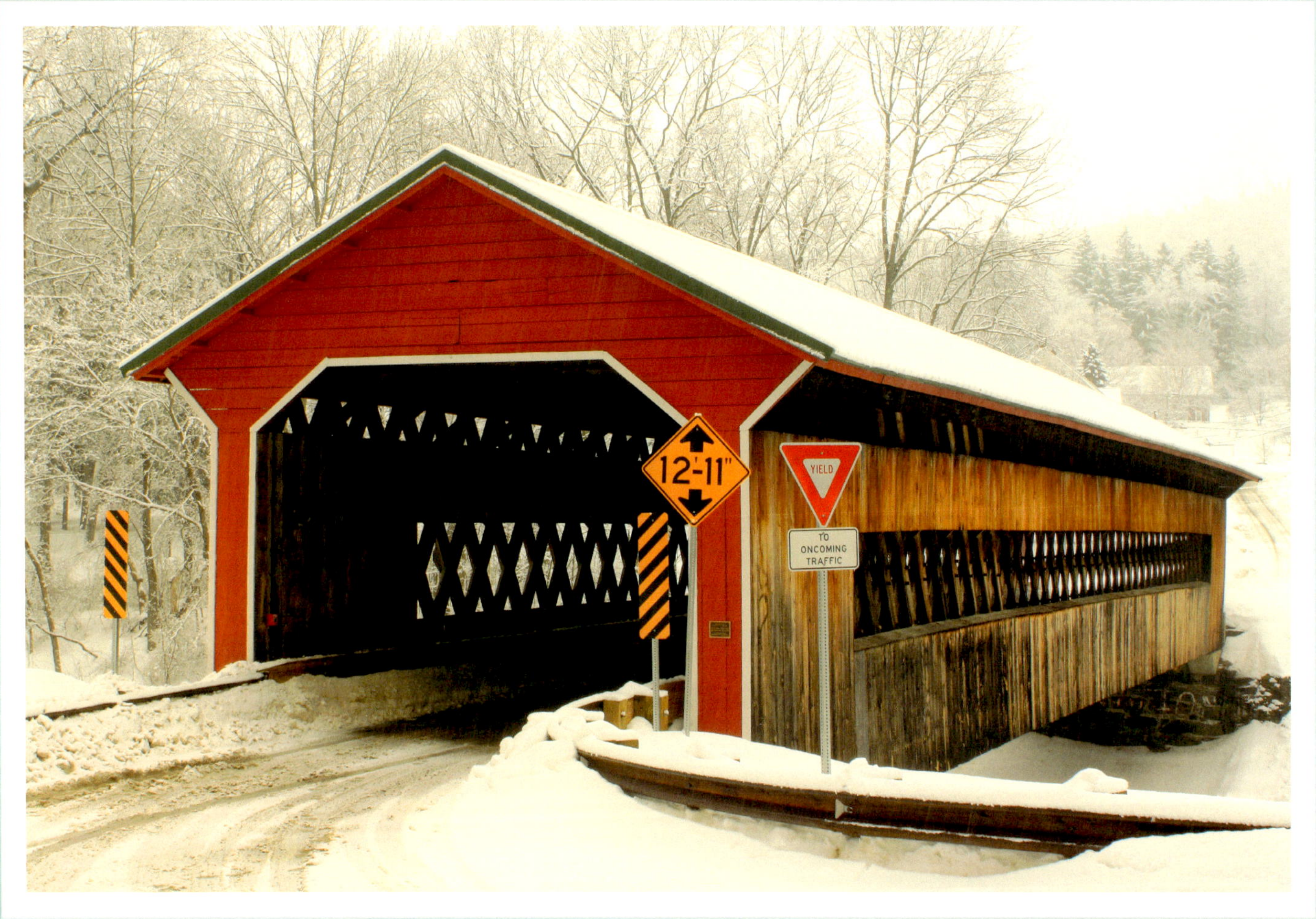

Built in 1886 and renovated in 2010, the historic Ware-Gilbertville Covered Bridge spans the Ware River near Hardwick's village of Gilbertville.

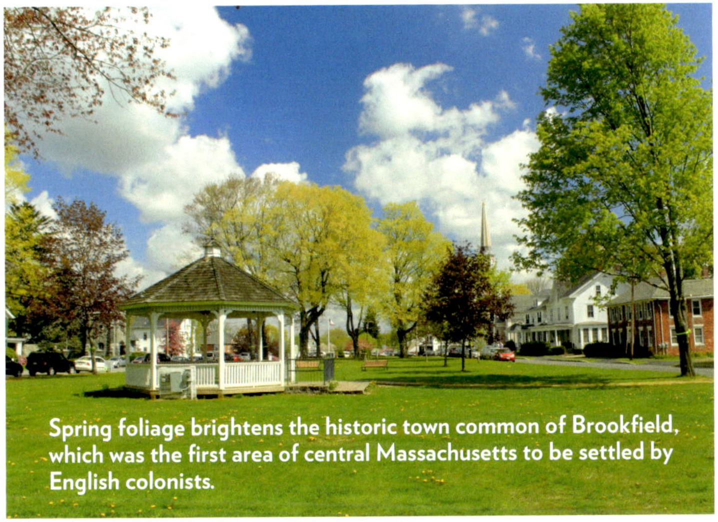

Spring foliage brightens the historic town common of Brookfield, which was the first area of central Massachusetts to be settled by English colonists.

Another legacy of the past is the covered bridge (c. 1886) that spans the Ware River at Hardwick's village of Gilbertville. It has the unusual distinction of being part of two separate counties, and in years past the different maintenance activities of Ware and Hardwick gave it a rather unusual appearance at times. It was built in 1886, a relatively late date for covered bridge construction that is likely one of the reasons for its longevity. The bridge was one of the few covered spans in Massachusetts that survived the storms of the 1930s, even though nearby mills in Gilbertville suffered extensive damage. After being damaged and closed to traffic in 2002, it was renovated in 2010 and is now one of the state's four covered bridges that are open to traffic.

Neighboring West Brookfield had the distinction of being the first colonial settlement in central Massachusetts, after settlers from Ipswich established "Quabaug Plantation" near Foster Hill in 1660. This small agricultural community was likely the state's most isolated outpost, as the nearest town of Springfield was a full day's journey through untamed wilderness to the west. Its vulnerability was all too evident in mid-1675, when it was the scene of a harrowing siege during the height of King Philip's War.

As succinctly summarized by author and historian Michael Tougias, this conflict "was America's first major war, and on a per capita basis there were more casualties than any other war in the country's history." The battles began in 1675 as a series of skirmishes between Wampanoag and Colonial soldiers in southeastern Massachusetts, and spread west after Wampanoag sachem Metacomet, also commonly known as King Philip, moved his people into the wilds of central Massachusetts. Hoping to establish a treaty with the Nipmuck tribe, colonial leaders attempted to meet and negotiate (primarily through a show of force) with their leader near Quabaug on July 31, 1675. However, the troops, operating in unfamiliar terrain, were ambushed and forced to retreat to the village, where they joined with the settlers in establishing a makeshift garrison in a tavern.

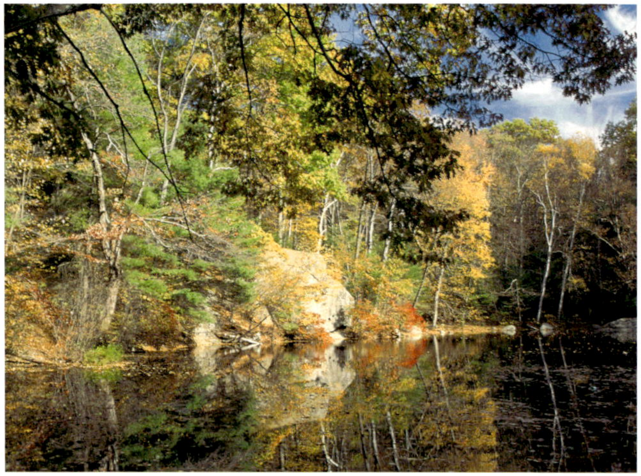

At the Rock House Reservation in West Brookfield, Carter Pond abuts rock caves at a former Native American winter camp site.

For three tense and bloody days, a standoff ensued as the Nipmuck surrounded the building, trading volleys of shot with the colonists while trying to burn it down. It seemed the colonists were doomed when a large cart of burning hay was pushed towards the building, but a heavy downpour miraculously—and fortuitously—snuffed out the fires. By this time, word of the siege had reached Colonial troops near Lancaster, who quickly rode forty miles to the scene and forced the Nipmuck to retreat. Not surprisingly, Quaboag was then abandoned as a settlement until after the wars drew to a close. Brookfield was eventually resettled and incorporated in 1718, then subsequently divided into four towns.

A favored Native American winter camp site here was the "Rock House," a jumble of giant boulders and caves west of the Quabaug settlement. It is named for a ledge that offered the dual benefits of open exposure to the sunny southeast and shelter from cold northerly winds and storms. An archaeological dig during the 1930s uncovered pottery shards and tools, along with the bones of large game animals such as wolves, deer, and bear. The shelter was near several well-travelled Native pathways, so it quite possibly was used throughout the year. The Rock House has been a popular tourist destination since the early 20th century, when visitors arrived by trolley and enjoyed picnics in the surrounding abandoned pastures. It is now the centerpiece of a 135-acre Trustees of Reservations preserve that includes a scenic small pond (named for and built by former property owner George Carter in the 1930s), nature center, and forest trails.

The primary waterway of the Brookfields is the Quaboag River, which was originally known to the Nipmuc as "Red River." Fed by the waters of Quaboag Pond on the Brookfield-East Brookfield town line, the river meanders on a northwesterly course past White's Landing and Route 148, passing a series of wildlife-rich marshes and a state wildlife area. One of its more secretive residents is the elusive American bittern, a brown and white wading bird that is nearly impossible to spot when it blends into wetland vegetation. It is more commonly distinguished by its unmistakable, deep-throated *"UNK-A-LUNK"* call. Much more visible are great blue herons, which stalk the

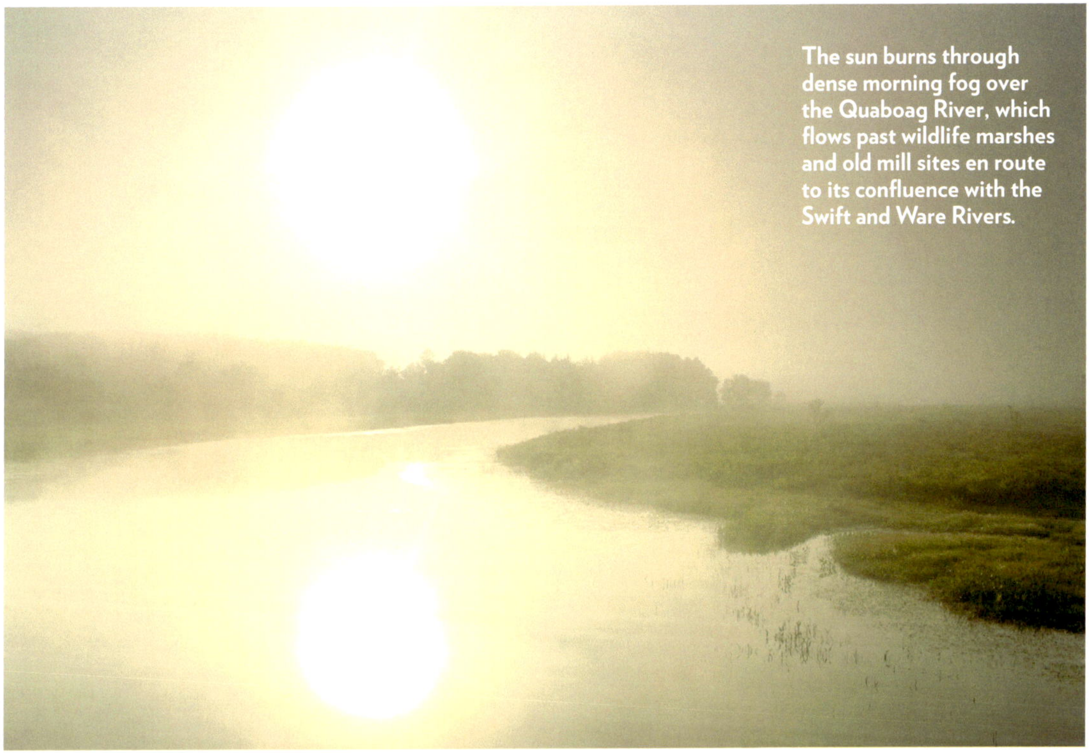

The sun burns through dense morning fog over the Quaboag River, which flows past wildlife marshes and old mill sites en route to its confluence with the Swift and Ware Rivers.

water's edge in search of fish and frogs. As common as they are today, it's hard to imagine that as recently as the 1930s, just a single known colony of great blues was known to reside in Massachusetts in tall pines bordering Harvard Pond in Petersham. In addition to protection from hunting, blue herons have benefitted from the marked increase in beavers and their associated wetlands, which create ideal nesting trees, in recent decades.

After passing Wickaboag Pond in West Brookfield, which is another of its main sources, the Quaboag bends to the south and begins a gradual 300-foot drop as it flows towards Warren. A number of mills and dams were built here to take advantage of the river's waterpower. Though most have been lost to floods, their remains are still visible on the riverbanks, and today the various rapids and small falls offer recreational opportunities for paddlers. After flowing twenty-six miles from its headwaters, the Quaboag ultimately joins with the Swift and Ware Rivers at Three Rivers in Palmer to form the Chicopee River.

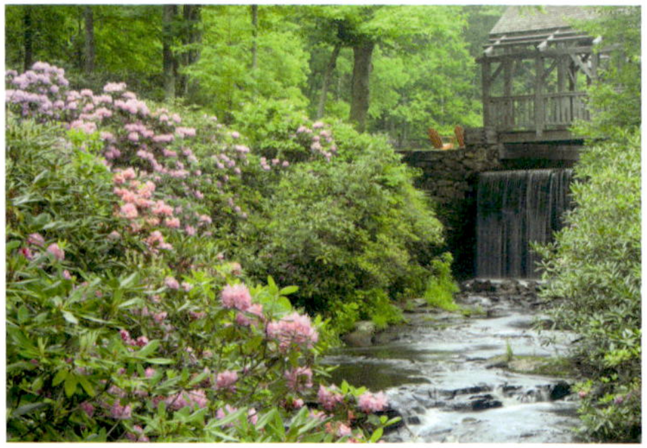

Another historic mill site is part of the many attractions at Moore State Park, a diverse natural and historical preserve set on the grounds of an old estate in Paxton. Fed by the outflow of Eames Pond, the 90-foot cascades of Turkey Hill Brook once powered a cluster of grist and saw mills before the grounds assumed an entirely different character as part of an elaborate 19th-century estate. Today the blooms of planted rhododendrons, irises, azaleas, laurel, and other flowers add waves of color to the walking paths and historic sites during the spring and summer, while naturalists enjoy trails that explore the adjacent forests, ponds, and wildflower meadows.

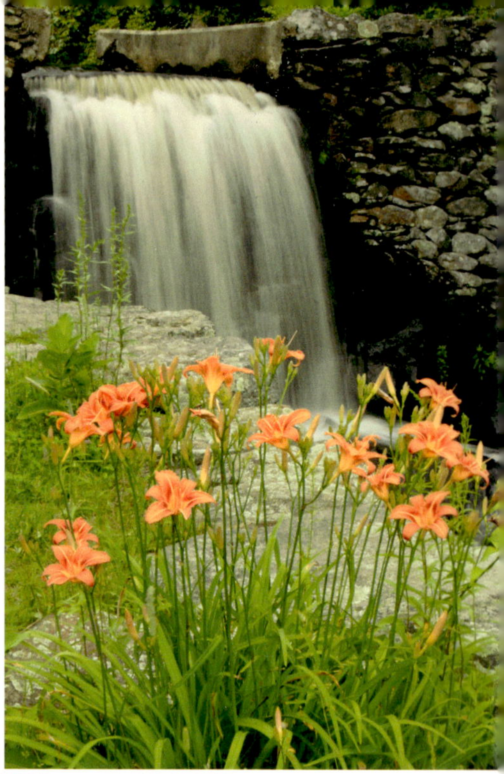

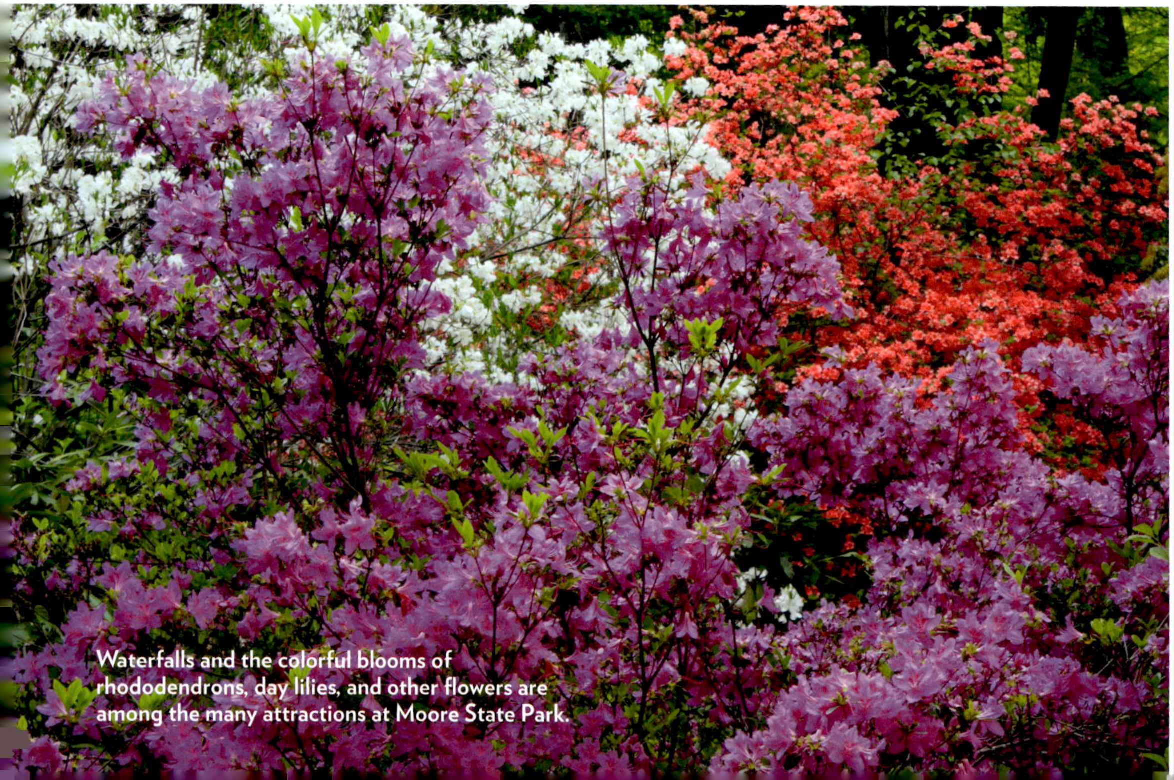

Waterfalls and the colorful blooms of rhododendrons, day lilies, and other flowers are among the many attractions at Moore State Park.

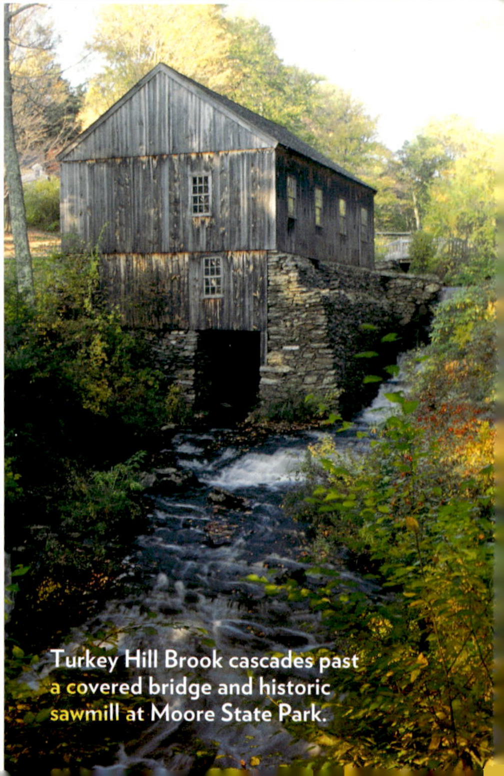

Turkey Hill Brook cascades past a covered bridge and historic sawmill at Moore State Park.

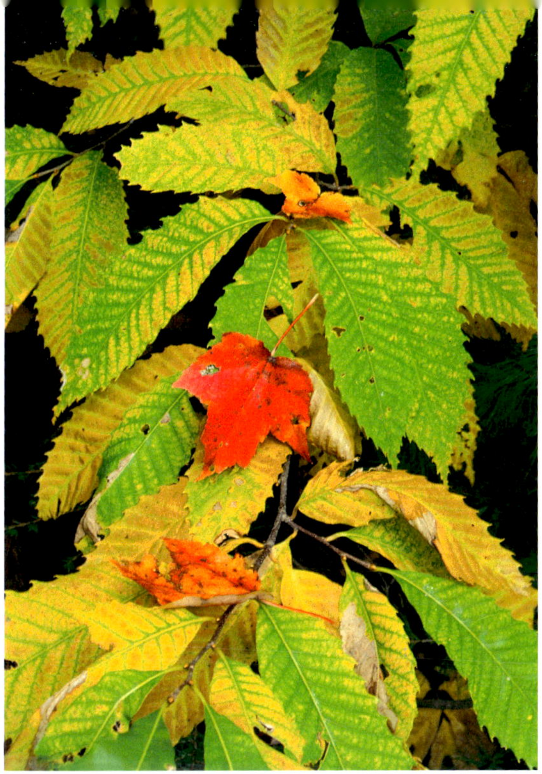

Though mature American chestnuts are gone from eastern forests, saplings from old stumps are fairly common.

Adjacent to Moore State Park's main entrance is a large plantation that is one of a handful of areas in the East where scientists are breeding blight-resistant chestnut trees. The American chestnut was once one of the Northeast's keystone forest species from both ecological and economic perspectives: it was a crucial food source for bears, deer, turkeys, passenger pigeons, and other wildlife, and its lumber was prized for a variety of uses. All of this changed after 1904, when a forester first noted several trees with a fatal fungal infestation in New York City. Within a matter of decades, the disease, known as chestnut blight, had essentially eliminated mature trees from eastern forests (the species is not wholly extinct, as saplings from dead stumps often grow to roughly 20 feet before dying). It's unlikely that chestnuts will ever reclaim their prominence in these woods—they are estimated to have comprised as much as 25 percent of the forests of the Appalachian Mountains—but scientists hope the resistant specimens will ultimately allow the species to reestablish to some degree.

As previously noted, when the Wachusett Reservoir was completed in 1905, it held the distinction of the world's largest water supply reservoir. Its source, the south branch of the Nashua River, is not naturally part of the Connecticut River's watershed, but instead ultimately discharges into the Merrimack River in southern New Hampshire, which in turn feeds into the Atlantic Ocean. However, since the construction of the Quabbin-Wachusett system, these waterways have been linked as part of the eastern Massachusetts water supply network.

The construction of Wachusett Reservoir set a rather ominous precedent for the Swift River project in that it obliged residents in the towns of West Boylston and Clinton to relocate, leaving behind their neighborhoods, mills, schools, and farms. Ironically, a few of the families moved west to the Swift River Valley, likely assuming that the new reservoir would suffice for Boston's long-term needs. In anticipation of future sources from the Swift and Ware River projects, engineers included intakes on Wachusett Reservoir's west shores.

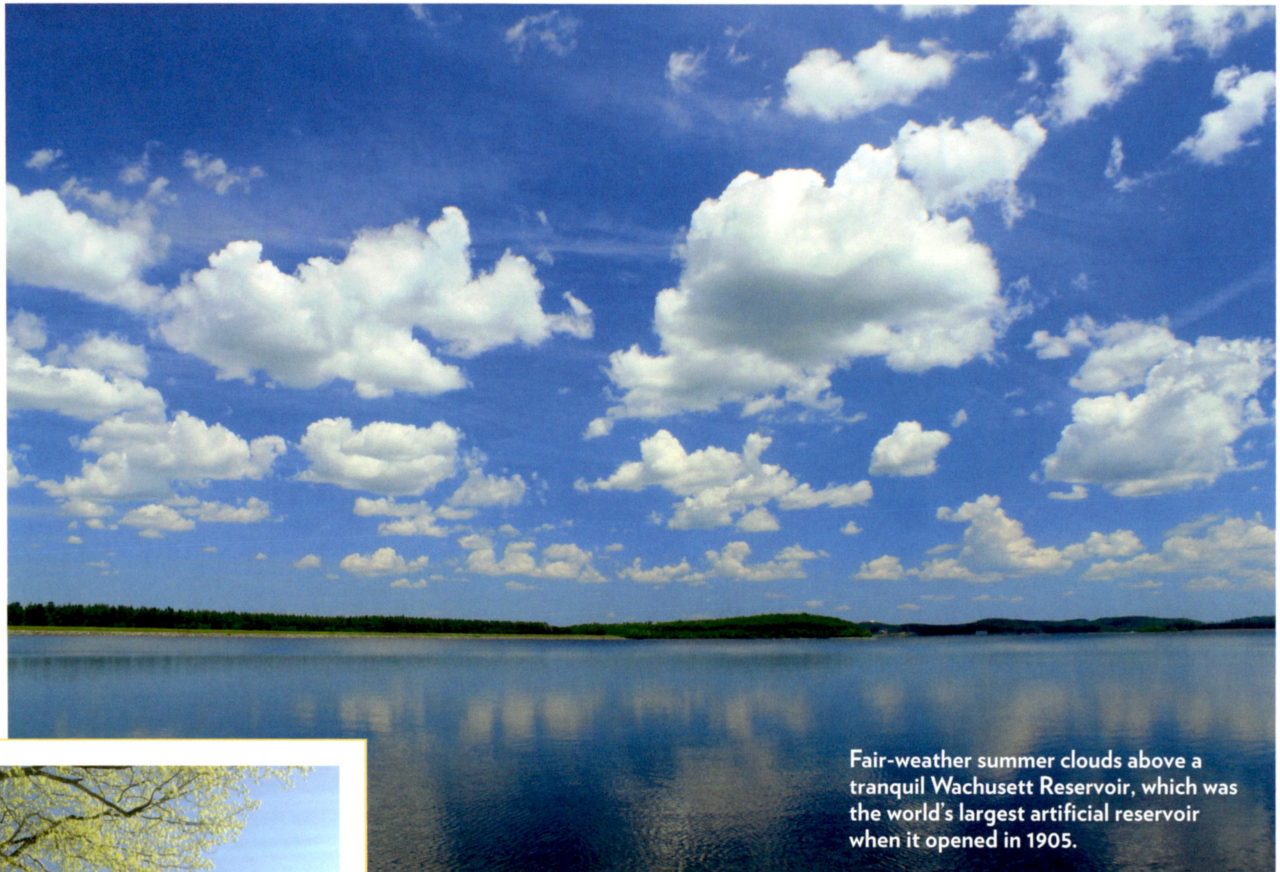

Fair-weather summer clouds above a tranquil Wachusett Reservoir, which was the world's largest artificial reservoir when it opened in 1905.

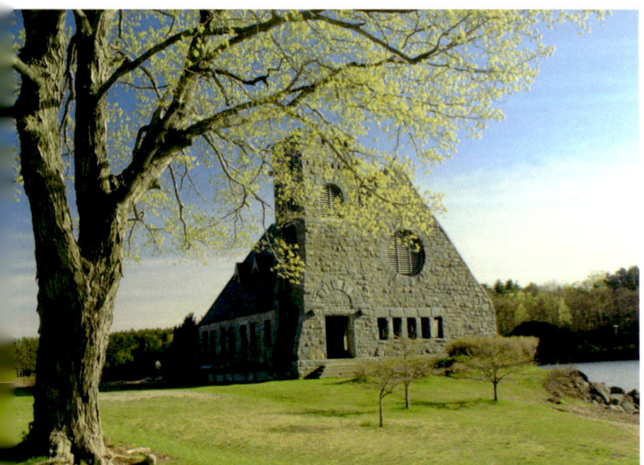

The lone remaining building from the lost Wachusett Reservoir communities is the Old Stone Church on the shores of the Thomas Basin, the reservoir's western finger. It was built in 1891 to replace the original Baptist church on this site, which was destroyed in a fire. Just six years later, the state paid the Baptist Society the sum of $22,500 as compensation for the taking of the property for the reservoir. Unlike other buildings in the Wachusett and Quabbin watersheds, it was left standing as a historic site and was designated as a National Historic Landmark in 1973.

Though it lacks the extensive forest buffer that surrounds Quabbin Reservoir—indeed, several state highways and an active railroad line follow or pass close by its shores—Wachusett Reservoir is nevertheless another of the region's significant conservation and wildlife areas. It is southern New England's second-largest freshwater lake, after Quabbin, and several breeding pairs of common loons call its waters home annually. The surrounding woods and outcroppings shelter migratory songbirds, coyotes, bobcat, and deer. It is a popular destination for shore fishermen, who enjoy fine stores of lake trout, landlocked Atlantic salmon, black bass, and white perch.

A short distance from Wachusett Reservoir's east shores are the beautifully landscaped grounds of the Tower Hill Botanic Garden in Boylston, which offer a unique combination of planted formal gardens and a surrounding natural landscape. Here eight distinct gardens showcase colorful flowering cherry trees, lilies, daffodils, violets, and vegetables, while a visitor center and two glass houses host popular plant shows and exhibits, along with tropical species less-suited to New England's year-round climate. Beyond the gardens, nature trails lead visitors to forest groves, a wildlife pond, and scenic vistas on Tower Hill.

Prominently visible from Tower Hill, the shores of Wachusett Reservoir, and countless other viewpoints across central New England is the distinctive profile of the region's most prominent natural landmark, Wachusett Mountain in Princeton. At just a shade over 2,000 feet, Wachusett Mountain's height pales in comparison to the higher summits of northern New England. Nevertheless, with its isolation and prominence from the surrounding landscape, it has the views and feel of a much larger eminence. Indeed, a 1677 survey by Massachusetts Bay Colony Governor John Winthrop estimated its height at 3,012 feet.

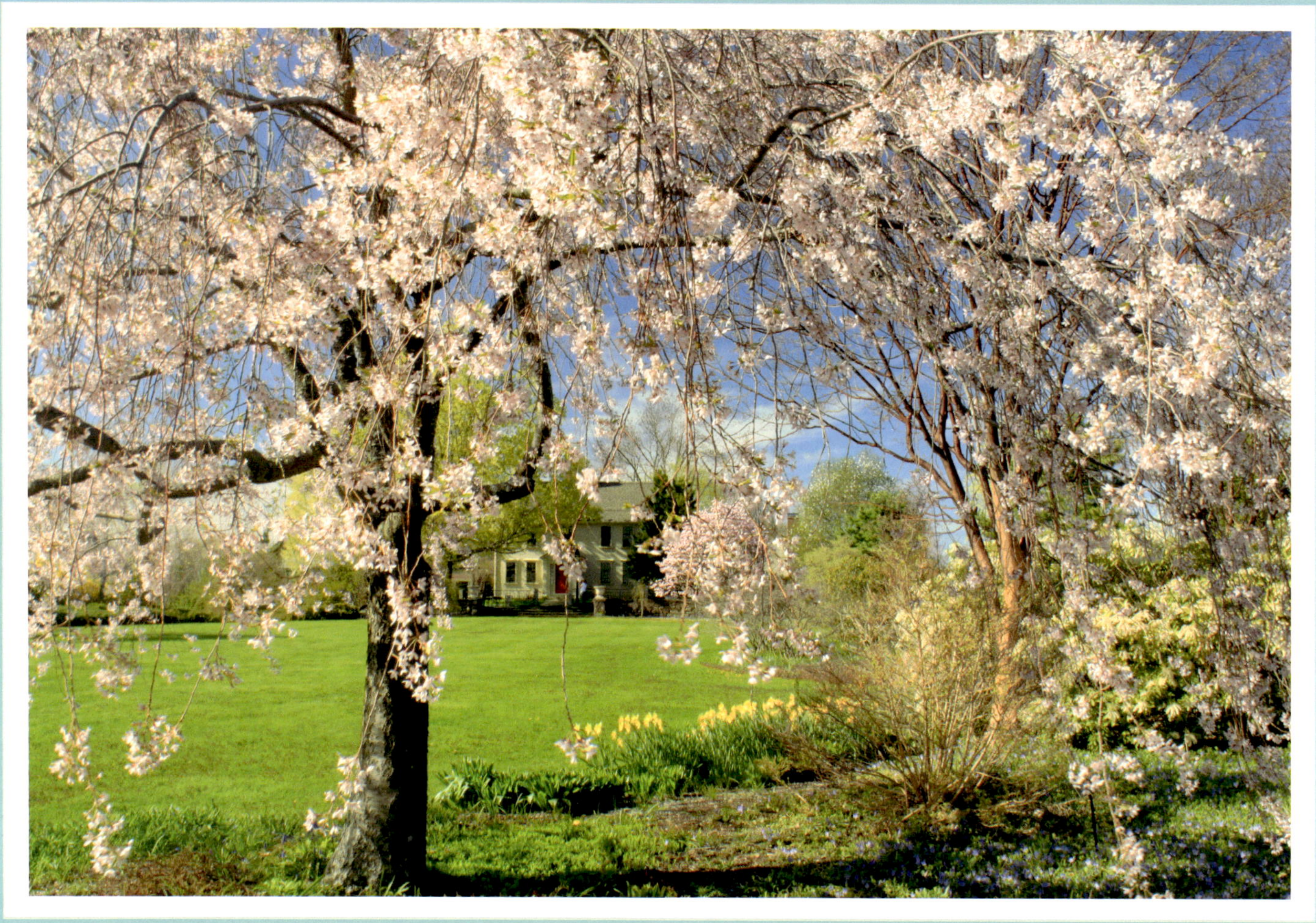

Flowering cherry trees mark the arrival of spring at the Tower Hill Botanic Gardens, which offer a unique combination of formal gardens and natural settings.

The familiar profile of Wachusett Mountain, the highest summit east of the Berkshires in Massachusetts, rises above the rock ledges of Crow Hill in the Leominster State Forest.

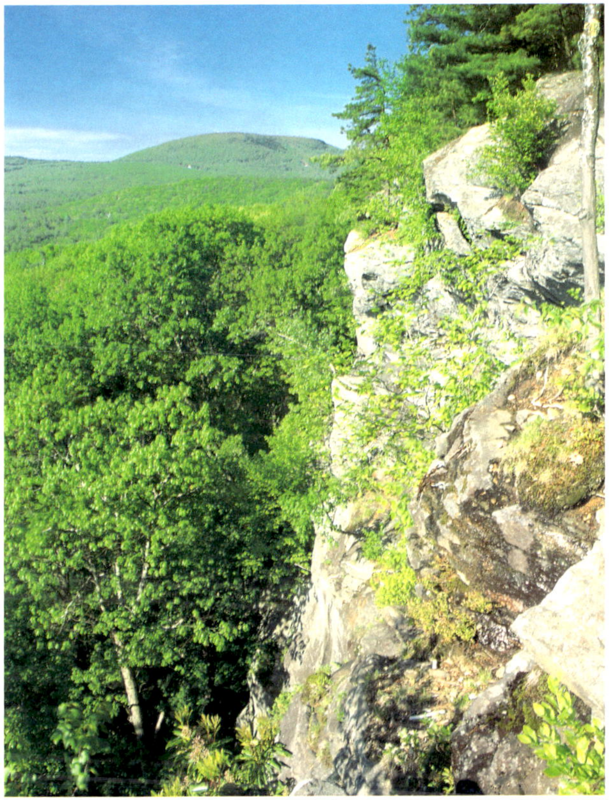

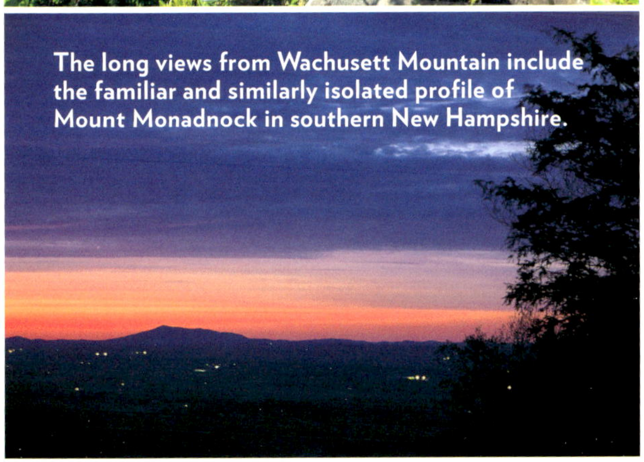

The long views from Wachusett Mountain include the familiar and similarly isolated profile of Mount Monadnock in southern New Hampshire.

In their reach, the summit views are, as related by Jeremiah Hanaford in his 1852 *History of Princeton*, "extensive and grand in the extreme....the whole state lies spread out like a map. On the one hand is seen the waters of Boston harbor, some fifty miles distant. On the North the renowned Monadnock of New Hampshire is visible, rearing its old bald, as well as broken summit, to the clouds. In other directions, the distant Hoosick and Green Mountains fade away in the distance, and mingle with the blue horizon."

Wachusett (an Algonquin word for "The Great Hill") has long been an important place for Native Americans, and its vantage points and rugged terrain made it an ideal encampment during King Philip's War. In February 1676, Wampanoag sachem Metacomet dispatched a raiding party of four hundred to the nearby colonial settlement of Lancaster. During the ensuing conflict, two dozen captives were taken by the Natives, including Mary Rowlandson, the wife of the town's minister (who, ironically, was away in Boston lobbying for help in fortifying the town). She spent the next eleven weeks travelling around central Massachusetts with her captors with colonial soldiers in pursuit; one 45-mile chase was finally abandoned on the banks of the Millers River in Athol. Ultimately, a settler who was friendly with the Natives was able to negotiate her release at a giant boulder, now known as "Redemption Rock," at the base of Wachusett Mountain. Today, the rock is a historic site on the Midstate Trail that makes for a fine starting point for a hike to Wachusett Mountain's summit or Crow Hill in the nearby Leominster State Forest.

Among the mountain's many 19th-century visitors was Henry David Thoreau, who could see the rounded summit across the then-open countryside of his Concord hometown. He ventured west to climb the mountain twice, including a moonlit evening in 1842 when he noted "a fire blazing on Monadnock which lighted up the whole western horizon, and, by making us aware of a community of mountains, made our position seem less solitary."

At the time of Thoreau's visit, the mountain's lower and middle slopes were nearly as barren as the surrounding countryside, after being mostly cleared for sheep pastures by settlers. Efforts to conserve the mountain began in earnest with the creation of the Wachusett Mountain State Reservation in 1899. A well-planned reforestation project was unfortunately wiped out by the 1938 hurricane, but over the past seventy-five years the woodlands have rebounded strongly.

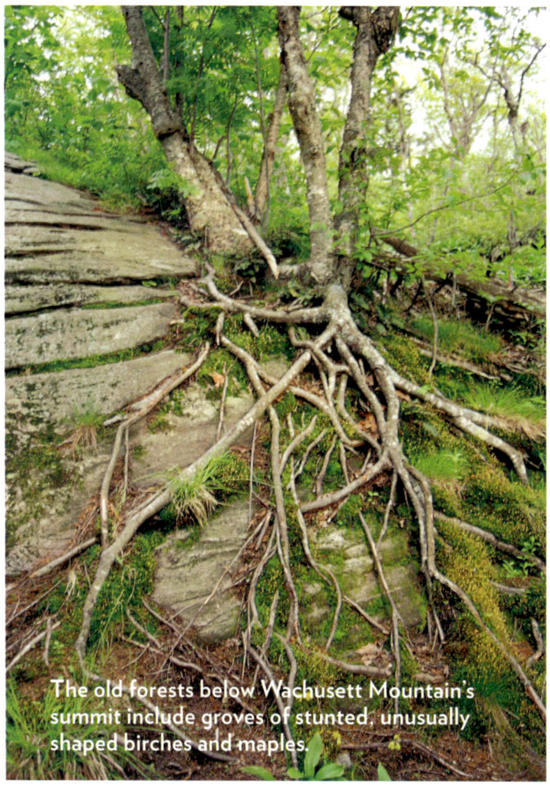
The old forests below Wachusett Mountain's summit include groves of stunted, unusually shaped birches and maples.

The steep, rocky upper slopes were one of the few areas that proved too rugged for the early settlers, and as a result they are home to a truly rare commodity: several groves of ancient trees that collectively form one of the largest old-growth forests in southern New England. The rather diminutive profile of many of the stunted, scrubby trees can be deceiving, as they don't fit the traditional image of giant old trees, such as the California redwoods or even the specimens in the Berkshires—indeed, it wasn't until the 1990s that they were confirmed as old-growth.

Yet within these woodlands grow the world's oldest red oaks and some of the oldest birches; the most venerable known individual is a yellow birch that is more than 370 years old; it was a small sapling when Colonial governor John Winthrop first noted the "very high hill due west." Much larger old hemlocks, which sadly are now vulnerable to infestation from the hemlock woolly adelgid, grow in a band on the upper southwest slopes. In the words of David Orwig, an old-growth forest ecologist who has conducted extensive research on the mountain and in other areas of the

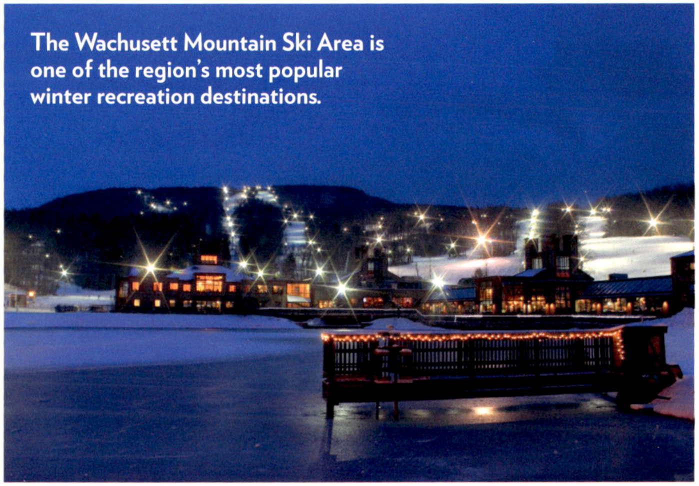

The Wachusett Mountain Ski Area is one of the region's most popular winter recreation destinations.

Northeast, "The old forests on Wachusett Mountain, including the extensive hardwood groves, are a truly remarkable natural feature given the mountain's heavy present and historic use and its proximity to eastern Massachusetts."

The mountain again felt the pressures of development during the mid-20th century, when, in an attempt to revive flagging tourism, the reservation administrators authorized the construction of a large ski area on the north slopes in the late 1950s. The operation was subsequently sold to private owners in 1968 and has become one of the state's most popular ski areas, thanks largely to its proximity and easy access from the greater Boston area.

On late summer and early autumn days, when there's a favorable wind from the north or northeast, visitors to Wachusett Mountain and several of the region's other low mountains and overlooks are treated to the striking spectacle of large flocks of hundreds to thousands of raptors passing over the mountain en route to wintering grounds in central America. Wachusett Mountain is part of a chain of hills and ridges that offer the migrants ideal thermal lift as they navigate across southern New England, and on some prime viewing days, more than 10,000 individual birds have been observed. Familiar species include broad-winged hawks, which are seen in great numbers during their mid-September flights, and lesser numbers of sharp-shinned and Cooper's hawks, bald eagles, osprey, and peregrine falcons.

Accompanying the birds in their southbound exodus are monarch butterflies, which skim over the top of hills, forests, and fields en route to wintering grounds in the mountains of Mexico. As summer draws towards a close and the days become shorter, one special, long-lived generation takes leave of the imminent cold weather and undertakes a journey of thousands of miles across the continent, navigating potential hazards such as wind, storms, predators, and topography. During the following summer, their offspring make their way back to their northern breeding grounds where milkweeds (their host plant) are present, and the cycle begins again.

A key breeding and resting area for monarchs and other butterflies in central Massachusetts is the Wachusett Meadows Wildlife Sanctuary near the base of Wachusett Mountain in Princeton. Insects, grassland birds, and mammals such as cottontail rabbits, deer, and foxes abound in the sanctuary's colorful wildflower meadows and old pastures, which are yet another legacy of the region's agricultural past. The other diverse habitats include mixed forests, vernal pools, glacial boulders, and a large beaver wetland that recently drained and now offers a fascinating glimpse of a habitat in transition as it reverts to a meadow. The low, rounded profile of Brown Hill rises out of the forests above the North Meadow and offers more fine views of Wachusett Mountain's summit and migrating hawks and monarchs.

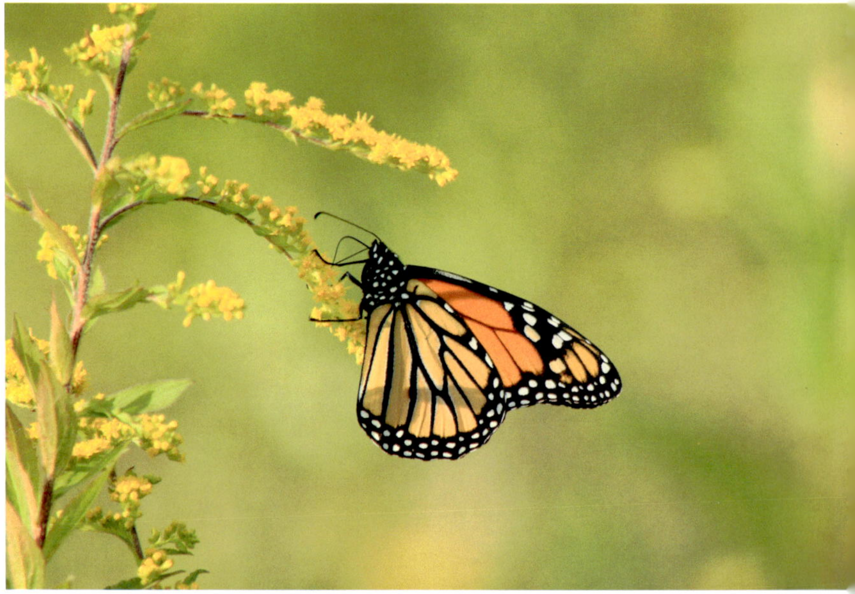

Wachusett Meadows Wildlife Sanctuary offers crucial habitat for monarch butterflies, which have declined in recent years.

Another prime raptor viewing area along this corridor is 1,832-foot Mount Watatic, which rises roughly 20 miles north of Wachusett on the New Hampshire state line. Mount Watatic marks the southern end of the Wapack Range, a 22-mile long ridge that extends into southern New Hampshire and offers some of New England's finest low-mountain trails and vistas. Panoramic views from Boston to the Berkshires await visitors to the rocky upper and lower summits, while the numerous lakes and ponds of Ashburnham and Ashby dot the valley below. Old stone walls and cart paths near the summit offer further evidence of the extent of past agriculture and forest clearing, even on these rugged high slopes. Adjacent to the summit is Nutting Hill, a shoulder of Mount Watatic with more views from its partially open, rocky crown.

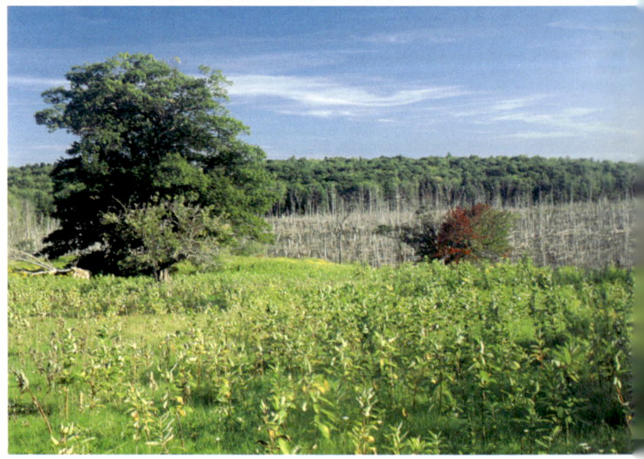

Old pastures and beaver wetlands are among the many diverse habitats of the Wachusett Meadows Wildlife Sanctuary in Princeton.

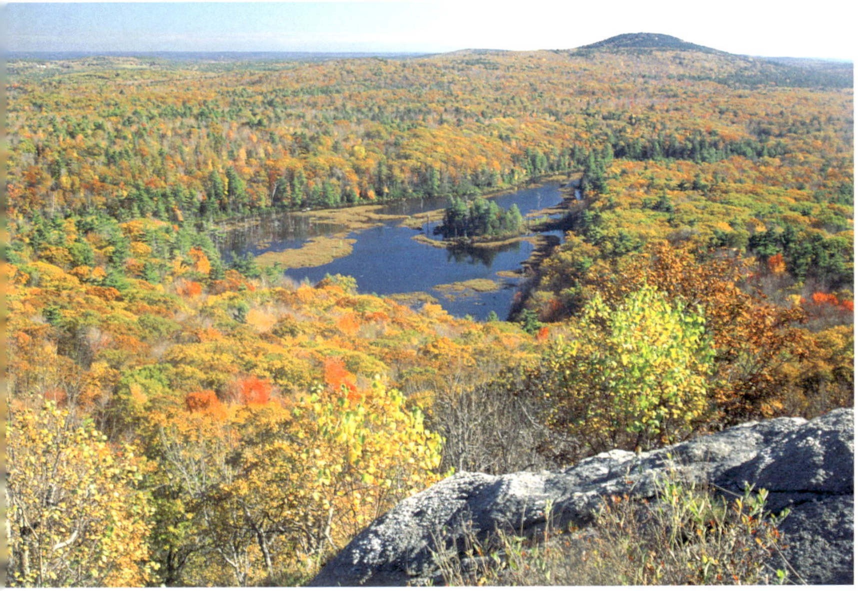

At the southern end of the Wapack Mountains, Mount Watatic rises in the distance over Binney Pond, as seen from an outlook on Pratt Mountain on an October afternoon.

Like many of the region's other mountains, Mount Watatic was once the site of a small ski area that opened in the mid-1960s and operated until 1984, and it was also a popular venue for concerts during the 1980s. The remains of concrete supports on the mostly open upper summit mark the site of an old fire tower that was removed in 1997. After being briefly owned by a communications company in 2000, the summit and a 280-acre tract of the mountain received permanent protection in 2002 from a collaborative of agencies including land trusts in the towns of Ashburnham and Ashby, the Massachusetts Department of Conservation and Recreation, and the Mount Grace Land Conservation Trust.

Mounts Wachusett and Watatic are the literal high points of the Midstate Trail, a 94-mile long footpath that crosses the heart of central Massachusetts. The route's origins date as far back as the 1920s, when a 22-mile path connected the summits of Wachusett and Watatic. After this trail fell into disrepair, a citizen's advisory committee oversaw the creation of the current, much longer route during the 1970s and 1980s. It was expanded to connect many of the region's natural and cultural features, including Crow Hill in Leominster State Forest, Redemption Rock, Wachusett Meadows Wildlife Sanctuary, the Ware River and Barre Falls Dam, a giant glacial boulder called "Sampson's Pebble" in Oakham, and the hilltop meadows of Moose Hill in Spencer.

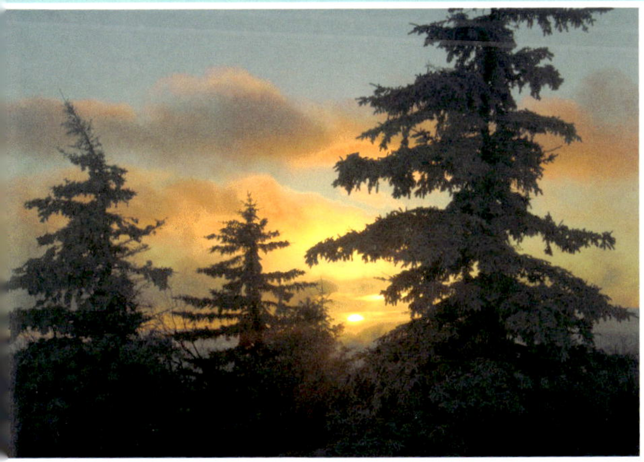

The setting sun drops behind groves of frozen high-elevation spruce trees on Mount Watatic's summit, which is the second-highest peak east of the Berkshires.

In addition to its recreational value, the trail serves as a vital conservation corridor on the margins of the developed greater Boston and Worcester

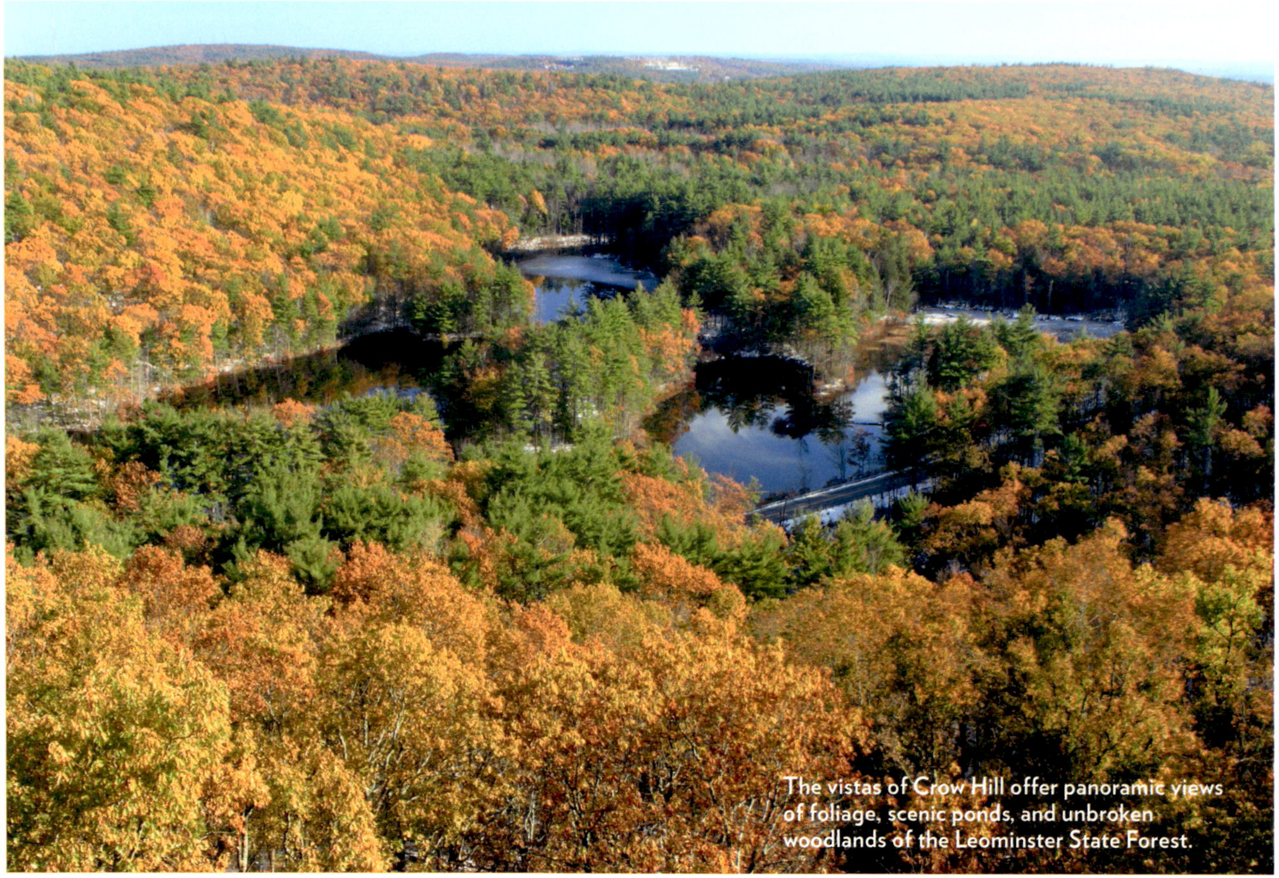

areas. It is part of a regional network that connects to the Wapack Trail, which begins at Mount Watatic and follows the ridge of the Wapack Mountains through southern New Hampshire, and the 78-mile Rhode Island North-South Trail. By combining these routes, a motivated hiker or animal can walk from the ocean beaches on Rhode Island's south coast through three states to the spruce-clad ridges and cliffs of Pack and North Pack Monadnock Mountain near Peterborough, New Hampshire.

Whether reached by a hike on the Midstate Trail or a more ambitious rock climb up its exposed face, Crow Hill is undeniably one of the most distinctive natural features in central Massachusetts. This 500-foot-long sheer cliff first became a popular venue for Appalachian Mountain Club rock climbers during the 1920s, then served

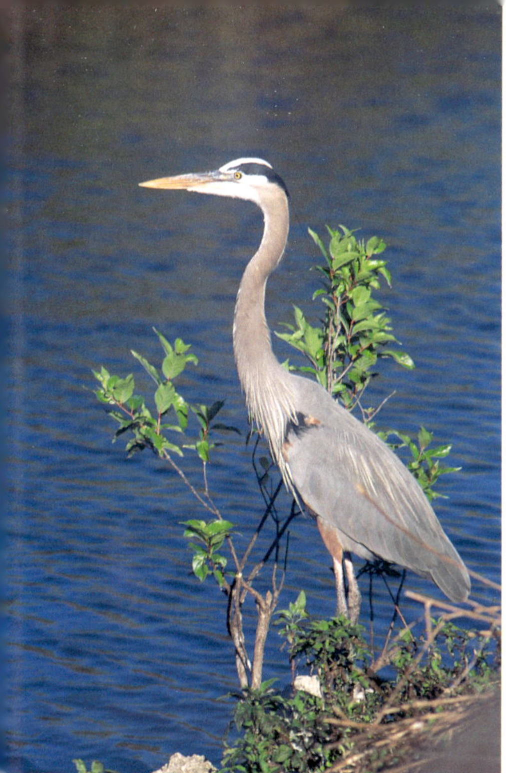

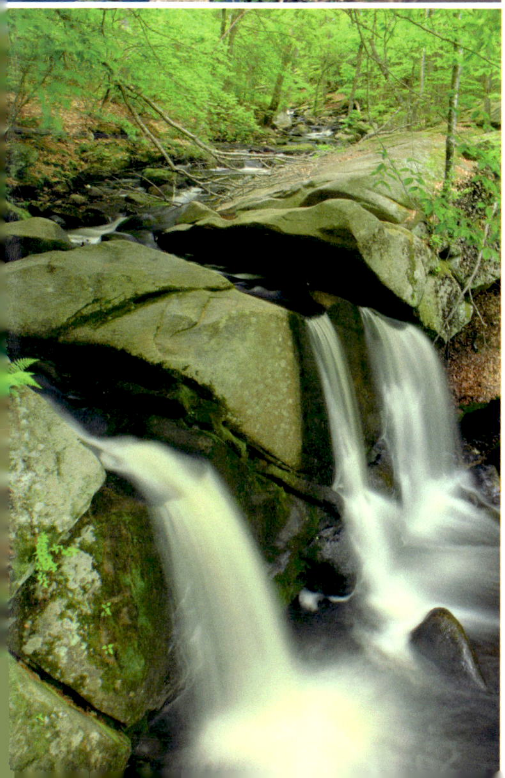

as a training area for Army troops during World War II. Today it is one of New England's best-known rock-climbing destinations, with a variety of routes suited to all skill levels.

Regardless of how one arrives at the crest of the ledges, the rewards are excellent views across the ponds and woodlands of the Leominster State Forest to the north slopes of nearby Wachusett Mountain and the distant tall buildings of Boston. Mountain laurel flowers are in abundance on the forested hillsides in June, and scenic Paradise Pond has hosted breeding pairs of common loons. The nearby Mohoosnoc Hills, home to more scenic views and a nine-mile hiking trail, rise above the development of Fitchburg and Leominster.

East of Wachusett Mountain, the landscape begins its transition from the rural uplands of central Massachusetts to the suburbs of the greater Boston area. In spite of their proximity to the Interstate 495 corridor, the towns of Harvard and Bolton have maintained a rural character with abundant apple orchards and pastoral country views. Here the Nashua River meanders north through a corridor of protected floodplain in the Oxbow National Wildlife Refuge and Bolton Flats Wildlife Area.

Oxbow is the westernmost of a series of refuges in the Eastern Massachusetts National Wildlife Complex, a diverse group of preserves that offer crucial habitat for wildlife in the heart of a developed region. It is named for the many bends, ponds, and wetlands that have formed as the river has shifted its course through the floodplain over thousands of years. Once cultivated for agriculture, the land became part of the Army's Fort Devens installation in 1917. The wildlife refuge was originally established in 1974, and the old tank road now is part of a loop trail that offers a variety of wetland views and excellent wildlife viewing opportunities.

Top: Once nearly eliminated from Massachusetts, great blue herons have strongly rebounded and are thriving in wetlands such as the Oxbow National Wildlife Refuge on the Nashua River.

Bottom: The distinctive triple cascades of Trap Falls are a popular attraction of the Willard Brook State Forest in Ashby.

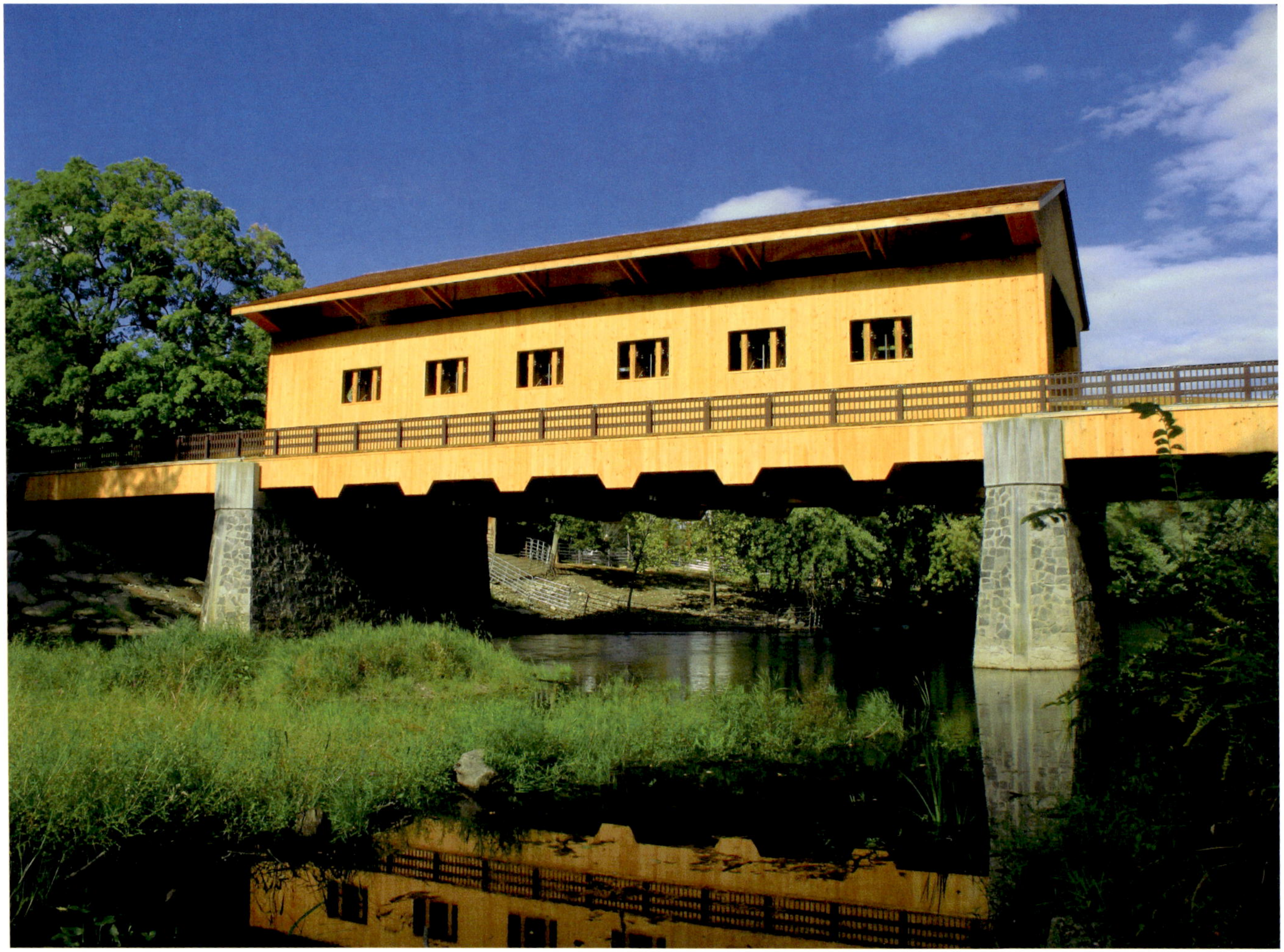

Dedicated in September 2010, the rebuilt Pepperell Covered Bridge once again spans the Nashua River.

With its gurgling streams and 3,000 acres of unbroken woodlands in the towns of Ashby and Townsend, the Willard Brook State Forest has a feel more characteristic of western Massachusetts than the outer Boston suburbs. One of its popular attractions is Trap Falls, where a forest brook spreads into a distinctive triple cascade as it plunges through a rock-strewn ravine. A recently opened 4-mile-long trail now connects nearby Damon Pond to the adjacent Pearl Hill State Park, which protects an additional 1,000 acres and includes campsites below tall pines. Willard Brook discharges into the Squannacook River, which is one of the Nashua's largest and most pristine tributaries. It was the subject of many writings by famed conservationist Benton MacKaye, founder of the Appalachian Trail who lived in Shirley.

As the Nashua meanders towards the New Hampshire border, it passes beneath another artifact of history, the easternmost of the state's remaining covered bridges in Pepperell. The present structure, which was dedicated during an elaborate ceremony attended by Governor Deval Patrick and other dignitaries in 2010, is the third covered bridge that has been built on this site since 1848. The first was a long, white structure with a distinctive checkerboard frame. It was replaced during the 1960s with a more elaborate structure that had a relatively short lifespan before falling into disrepair. The new structure is one of the three covered bridges in Massachusetts, along with the aforementioned Bissell Bridge in Charlemont and the Ware-Gilbertville Bridge, that are open to traffic.

After flowing 46 miles across the heart of central Massachusetts, the Nashua exits the Commonwealth and continues a short distance to its confluence with the Merrimack River in southern New Hampshire. It is yet another of the region's rivers that is recovering from industrial abuse, as evidenced by dark-humor bets that watershed residents once made on its daily color and a popular saying "too thick to pour, too thin to plow." Fortunately, following the establishment of the Nashua River Watershed Association in 1969, treatment plants and conservation efforts have removed the bulk of the pollutants, a cleanup effort that has received international recognition for its success. The revitalized river and the watershed's protected lands are especially significant given their proximity to the heavily developed coastal region. Along with the aforementioned conservation lands to the west, they are part of the mosaic of protected land that benefit forests, wildlife, and human recreational users alike in the heart of one of the country's most densely populated regions.

Bickford, Walter E. and Ute Janick Dymon (eds.). *An Atlas of Massachusetts River Systems: Environmental Designs for the Future.*

Burk, John S. *Massachusetts Covered Bridges: Images of America.* Charleston, SC: Arcadia Publishing, 2010.

——. *New England's Natural Wonders: An Explorer's Guide.* Atglen, PA: Schiffer Publishing, 2012.

Conuel, Thomas. *Quabbin: The Accidental Wilderness.* Amherst, MA: University of Massachusetts, 1990.

Foster, D.R. and John O'Keefe. *New England Forests Through Time: Insights from the Harvard Forest Dioramas.*

Greene, J.R. *Historic Quabbin Hikes.* Athol, MA: Highland Press, 1994.

Howe, Donald. *Quabbin: The Lost Valley.* Worcester, MA: The Davis Press, 1951.

Kershner, Bruce and Robert Leverett. *The Sierra Club Guide to the Ancient Forests of the Northeast.* San Francisco: Sierra Club Books, 2004.

Little, Richard. *Dinosaurs, Dunes, and Drifting Continents: A Geologic History of the Connecticut Valley.*

Pioneer Valley Planning Commission. *The Westfield River Open Space and Recreation Plan.* Pioneer Valley Planning Commission, 2003.

Scofield, Bruce. *Hiking the Pioneer Valley.* Amherst, MA: New England Cartographics, 1995.

Sinton, John, Elizabeth Farnsworth, and Wendy Sinton. *The Connecticut River Boating Guide: Source to Sea.* Guilford, CT: Falcon and Connecticut River Watershed Council, 2007.

Stekly, William and Evan Hill. *The Connecticut River.* Middletown, CT: Wesleyan, 1972.

Till, Michael J. *Along Massachusetts' Historic Route 20: Postcard History Series.* Charlestown, SC: Arcadia Publishing, 2012

Tougias, Michael. *Quabbin: A History and Explorer's Guide.* Yarmouth Port, MA: On Cape Productions, 2002.

Tougias, Michael, and Rene Laubach. *Nature Walks in Central and Western Massachusetts* (2nd Edition). Boston, MA: Appalachian Mountain Club, 2000.

Young, Allen. *North of Quabbin Revisited.* Athol, MA: Haley's, 2003.

——. *The Man who Got Lost: North Quabbin Stories.* Athol, MA: Haley's, 2012.